LetterPerfect® Made Easy

LETTERPERFECT® MADE EASY

Steve Dyson

Osborne McGraw-Hill
Berkeley New York St. Louis San Francisco
Auckland Bogotá Hamburg London Madrid
Mexico City Milan Montreal New Delhi Panama City
Paris São Paulo Singapore Sydney
Tokyo Toronto

Osborne **McGraw-Hill**
2600 Tenth Street
Berkeley, California 94710
U.S.A.

Osborne **McGraw-Hill** offers software for sale. For information on software, translations, or book distributors outside of the U.S.A., please write to Osborne **McGraw-Hill** at the above address.

This book is printed on recycled paper.

LetterPerfect® Made Easy

Copyright © 1991 by McGraw-Hill, Inc. All rights reserved. Printed in the United States of America. Except as permitted under the Copyright Act of 1976, no part of this publication may be reproduced or distributed in any form or by any means, or stored in a database or retrieval system, without the prior written permission of the publisher, with the exception that the program listings may be entered, stored, and executed in a computer system, but they may not be reproduced for publication.

1234567890 DOC 9987654321

ISBN 0-07-881696-3

Information has been obtained by Osborne McGraw-Hill from sources believed to be reliable. However, because of the possibility of human or mechanical error by our sources, Osborne McGraw-Hill, or others, Osborne McGraw-Hill does not guarantee the accuracy, adequacy, or completeness of any information and is not responsible for any errors or omissions or the results obtained from use of such information.

To my parents, Glenn and Carol Dyson, who are responsible for my addiction to computers, but not responsible for any ill that comes of it. (They made me write that last part.)

CONTENTS AT A GLANCE

Introduction xxi
Why This Book Is for You 1

PART I BASIC FEATURES 3

1   Getting Started with LetterPerfect 5
2   Creating a Document Layout 35
3   Special Features for Text 67
4   Editing a Document 83
5   Using the Speller and Thesaurus 115
6   Using the Graphics Features 127
7   Printing Your Documents 147
8   Managing Your Document Files 163

PART II PRACTICAL APPLICATIONS 181

9   Creating Memos and Outlines 183

10	**Letters and Envelopes** 201
11	**Merging Letters and Mailing Labels** 215
≡	PART III APPENDIXES 239
A	**Installing the LetterPerfect Program** 241
B	**Using the Shell Program** 257
C	**Information for WordPerfect Users** 261
D	**LetterPerfect Macros** 267
	Index 277

CONTENTS

Introduction xxi
Why This Book Is for You 1

PART I   BASIC FEATURES 3

1   **Getting Started with LetterPerfect** 5

    STARTING THE LETTERPERFECT PROGRAM   6
        Starting from a Single Floppy Drive   6
        Starting from Two Floppy Drives   7
        Starting from a Hard Disk   8
        Starting with the Shell Program   9
    A TOUR OF THE LETTERPERFECT SCREEN   9
    YOUR KEYBOARD AND LETTERPERFECT   10
        The Function Keys   11
        ESC   12
        DEL and BACKSPACE   12
        CAPS LOCK   12
        NUM LOCK   14
        INS   14
        ENTER   14
    TYPING TEXT AND MOVING THE CURSOR   14
        Typing with Word Wrap   15
        Moving the Cursor with the Arrow Keys   15

   Extended Cursor Movement 16
   Scrolling Through the Text 18
  USING THE LETTERPERFECT MENUS 18
   Using the Function Keys 19
   Using the Pull-Down Menus 19
   LetterPerfect Fast Keys 21
   Hiding the Menu Bar 21
  USING A MOUSE WITH LETTERPERFECT 21
   Moving the Cursor with the Mouse 22
   Selecting Menu Items 22
   Canceling with the Mouse 23
  EXERCISE: CREATING THE PARTY SHACK FLYER 23
  SAVING YOUR DOCUMENT 24
  PREVIEWING THE DISPLAYED DOCUMENT 25
  PRINTING YOUR DOCUMENT 27
  CLEARING THE SCREEN 27
  RETRIEVING A DOCUMENT 28
  GETTING HELP 29
   Using the On-Line Help Feature 29
   Context-Sensitive Help 32
   Contacting WordPerfect Customer Support 32
  EXITING THE PROGRAM 33

2 Creating a Document Layout 35

  FORMATTING WITH CODES 36
  CHANGING YOUR MARGINS 37
   Defining Top and Bottom Margins 38
   Defining Left and Right Margins 40
   Centimeters, Points, and WordPerfect Units 40
  SELECTING A PAPER SIZE 41

    Selecting a New Paper Size   41
    Paper Size and Page Orientation   44
    Creating Your Own Paper Size   44
CENTERING TEXT ON THE PAGE   47
JUSTIFICATION AND LINE SPACING   47
    Changing the Text Justification   47
    Changing the Line Spacing   49
PARAGRAPH INDENTS AND TAB SETTINGS   49
    Indenting with the TAB Key   50
    Indenting Paragraph Margins   51
    Creating a Hanging Indent   51
    Defining Tab Settings   52
    Editing the Tab Settings   54
    Setting Absolute Tabs   55
ADDING PAGE NUMBERS   56
ADDING PAGE HEADERS AND FOOTERS   56
    Creating a Header or Footer   57
    Page Numbering with Headers or Footers   58
    Turning Off a Header or Footer   59
DOCUMENT PAGINATION   59
    Soft Page Breaks   60
    Hard Page Breaks   60
EXERCISE: CREATING A RÉSUMÉ   60

3 Special Features for Text 67

SELECTING FONTS AND TEXT ATTRIBUTES   68
    Fonts, Text Attributes, and Your Printer   68
    Selecting a New Font   68
    Selecting Text Attributes   70

ALIGNING TEXT   71
    Centering Text Between Margins   71
    Aligning Text at the Right Margin   72
USING THE DATE FEATURES   72
    Inserting Today's Date into Your Text   72
    Inserting a Date Code   73
    Changing the Date Format   73
PLACING ENDNOTES INTO YOUR DOCUMENT   76
    Creating a New Endnote   76
    Editing Endnotes   76
HYPHENATION   77
    Manual Hyphenation   77
    Automatic Hyphenation   79
INSERTING SPECIAL CHARACTERS   79
    Composing Accented Characters   80
    Using the WordPerfect Character Sets   80

4 Editing a Document 83

USING THE BLOCK FEATURE   83
    Defining a Block with the Keyboard   84
    Defining a Block with the Mouse   85
    Applying Attributes to a Block   86
    Tips and Tricks for the Block Feature   87
DELETING AND RESTORING TEXT   87
    Using the Delete Keys   88
    Deleting a Block of Text   89
    Using the Move Key to Delete Text   90
    Restoring Deleted Text   91
MOVING AND COPYING TEXT   92
    Moving a Block of Text   93

Copying a Block of Text   94
Using the Fast Keys to Move and Copy   95
SEARCHING AND REPLACING TEXT   96
Searching for Text and Codes   96
Replacing Text and Codes   97
EDITING DOCUMENT CODES   98
Editing with Reveal Codes   98
LetterPerfect Codes   101
WordPerfect Codes   101
INITIAL CODES FOR DOCUMENTS   105
Creating a Format at the Initial Codes Screen   106
Copying Document Codes to the Initial Codes Screen   109
EXERCISE: EDITING THE PARTY SHACK FLYER   109
Editing the Document Layout   109
Editing the Text   111
Creating a Table   112

5   Using the Speller and Thesaurus 115

USING THE SPELLER   116
Correcting Spelling Errors   116
Spell-Checking a Page or Block   119
SPELLER DICTIONARIES   119
Creating Your Own Dictionaries   120
Foreign-Language Dictionaries   121
USING THE THESAURUS   122
Finding the Right Word   122
Navigating Through the Thesaurus Menus   123

6   Using the Graphics Features 127

INSERTING A GRAPHIC IMAGE   128

        Creating a Figure Box   129

        Sizing the Figure Box   133

        Shortcuts for Inserting Graphics   133

        Figure Box Numbering   134

EDITING A GRAPHIC IMAGE   134

        Editing the Figure Box Settings   134

        Adjusting for the Edited Graphic Image   135

        Why Does the Graphic Image Jump to the Next Page?   136

EXERCISE: ADDING GRAPHICS TO THE PARTY SHACK FLYER   136

DRAWING LINES AND BOXES   140

7   Printing Your Documents 147

YOUR PRINTER AND LETTERPERFECT   147

        Installing Your Printer   148

        Selecting a Printer   150

        Editing Printer Settings   152

        Using WordPerfect's Printer Drivers   155

PREVIEWING A DOCUMENT   156

PRINTING YOUR DOCUMENT   157

        Printing the Entire Document   157

        Printing Multiple or Single Pages   158

        What to Do When the Printer Doesn't Print   159

OPTIONS FOR PRINTING   159

        Adding Space for Binding   159

        Printing Several Copies   161

        Selecting the Print Quality   161

8   Managing Your Document Files 163

SAVING AND RETRIEVING FILES   163

        File Names   164

Saving a File   164
Retrieving a File   165
Directories and Path Names   166
Creating a Document Directory   166

SAVING AND RETRIEVING OTHER FILE FORMATS   168
WordPerfect Files   168
DOS Text Files   169
Generic Files   169

DOCUMENT PASSWORDS   170
Adding a Document Password   170
Removing a Document Password   171
Additional Information   172

AUTOMATIC FILE BACKUP   172

MANAGING YOUR DOCUMENTS WITH LIST FILES   173
The List Files Screen   174
Viewing a Document in the List   175
Searching for a File Name   176
Marking Document Files   177
Copying and Deleting Files   178
Moving and Renaming Files   178
Changing the File Directory   179
Creating a New Directory   180

PART II   PRACTICAL APPLICATIONS 181

9   Creating Memos and Outlines 183

CREATING A BUSINESS MEMO   184
Creating the Memo Format   184
Creating the Heading   186
Typing the Message and Printing the Memo   187

AUTOMATED MEMOS 188
    Creating the Memo Format 189
    Creating the Heading with Merge Commands 189
    Saving the Document and Clearing the Screen 191
    Using Merge to Create the Memo 192
CREATING AN OUTLINE 193
    Starting an Outline 194
    Reorganizing Your Outline 197

10 Letters and Envelopes 201

CREATING A PERSONAL LETTER 201
CREATING A BUSINESS LETTER 204
FORMATTING FOR ENVELOPES 206
    Creating the Standard Envelope Layout 207
    Including Your Company Logo on the Envelope 210
    Printing the Envelope 210
    Troubleshooting Tips for Printing on Envelopes 210

11 Merging Letters And Mailing Labels 215

CREATING AN ADDRESS LIST 217
    Assigning Names to the Fields 217
    Creating the Records 220
CREATING A PRIMARY FILE FOR LETTERS 223
MERGING THE FILES 226
CREATING MAILING LABELS 227
    Creating Continuous Labels 228
    Creating Sheet Labels 232
CREATING A PRIMARY FILE FOR LABELS 235

PART III APPENDIXES 239

A   Installing the LetterPerfect Program 241

HARDWARE REQUIREMENTS   242
INSTALLATION WITH A HARD DISK SYSTEM   242
INSTALLATION WITH A FLOPPY-DRIVE SYSTEM   246
YOUR REGISTRATION NUMBER   250
INSTALLING AN UPDATED VERSION OF LETTERPERFECT   250
DEFINING PROGRAM OPTIONS   251
   Define Screen Colors   251
   Automatic File Backup   253
   Selecting the Unit of Measurement   253
   Location of Document Program Files   253
   Defining Initial Codes   254
   Menu Options and the F1 Key   254
   Automatic Document Formatting   254

B   Using the Shell Program 257

STARTING THE SHELL PROGRAM   257
USING THE SHELL PROGRAM   259
   Starting Programs from the Shell Menu   259
   Using the Shell Hot-Keys   259
USING THE CLIPBOARD   260
ADDITIONAL INFORMATION   260

C   Information for WordPerfect Users 261

SHARING FILES WITH LETTERPERFECT   261
WORDPERFECT CODES IN LETTERPERFECT DOCUMENTS   262
USING THE SPELLER   262
SHARING WORDPERFECT'S HYPHENATION MODULE   263

PRINTER DRIVERS   264
WORDPERFECT CHARACTERS   264

D LetterPerfect Macros 267

CREATING AND USING A MACRO   268
MACRO NAMES   269
MACRO OPTIONS: PAUSE AND DISPLAY   270
   Pause   271
   Display   271
MACRO APPLICATIONS   271
   Typing the Closing for a Letter   272
   Changing the Document Format   273
   Changing the Unit of Measure   274
ADDITIONAL INFORMATION   275

Index 277

ACKNOWLEDGMENTS

Several people helped me with this project, and I appreciate their contributions. I'm grateful to Roger Stewart for keeping me on track and taking care of the details. Laurie Beaulieu was the perfect editor, as always. Many thanks to Julie Denver for her thorough technical editing. I also appreciate the efforts of Madhu Prasher, the project editor, Ann Krueger Spivack, the copy editor, Erica Spaberg, the proofreading coordinator, and Judy Wohlfrom, the art director. Finally, thanks go to Sybil Ihrig of VersaTech Associates for her typesetting services.

INTRODUCTION

In a market known for its fierce competition, there are over 70 word processing programs that are available for the IBM PC. Everyone needs to use a word processing program, but no single package meets the needs of all users. Some word processing programs are tailored for the office environment, while others produce legal documents or complex scientific papers. The leading word processing packages—WordPerfect, Microsoft Word, and DisplayWrite—are designed to perform a wide variety of word processing tasks, and each includes enough features to satisfy most users. If you already own one of these programs, it's likely that you aren't using it to its full potential, and with good reason. You probably don't need to create 600-page documents with tables of contents, cross references, and mathematical equations—and even if you do, you probably do not need to create them everyday.

Thus, a new breed of word processing program is becoming increasingly popular. *Executive* word processing programs are scaled-down versions of their powerhouse cousins, designed with the assumption that most people are content with writing memos, letters, and other brief documents. LetterPerfect is the latest entry in this category of sleek, powerful, and friendly software packages. It includes the standard word processing features, plus the superb printing capabilities found in WordPerfect. Also included are graphics, merge, and file management features to help you enhance and manage your document files. It requires only 330K of computer memory, and fits comfortably on any PC computer or network station.

Of course, LetterPerfect doesn't do it all. If you're familiar with WordPerfect, you'll miss the Tables feature, footnotes, indexing, and probably several other features as well. But LetterPerfect isn't supposed to do everything—in fact, herein lies the beauty of this program. It includes the powerful features you need to produce a professional document, without requiring you to memorize the commands of a 500-page reference manual. All the basic word processing features are here, with just enough polish and pizazz to make it all interesting. Many word processing programs can help you type a letter or structure an outline, but few perform with the finesse of LetterPerfect.

ABOUT THIS BOOK

This book assumes that you know how to use your computer equipment, and that you are familiar with common DOS commands.

The exercises in this book are designed to help you learn the features of Letter-Perfect through practical examples and exercises. Step-by-step instructions guide you through each exercise, whether you're new to word processing software or a seasoned pro. If you are a WordPerfect user, several LetterPerfect features and procedures may be familiar to you. When you are finished reviewing the chapters, you will be able to create many documents for business and personal use.

HOW THIS BOOK IS ORGANIZED

LetterPerfect Made Easy was designed to help you learn LetterPerfect as quickly as possible. This book will help you get started with the program, and will prepare you for more advanced applications.

Part I of this book consists of Chapters 1 through 8. Step-by-step instructions present the basic typing, page layout, and document editing skills. Chapter 1 is your introduction to the LetterPerfect program. Chapter 2 explains how to create a document layout, including margin changes, tab definitions, text justification and indents, and page numbering. Chapter 3 shows you how to enhance your text with font and attribute changes; also included in this chapter is information about text hyphenation, endnotes, and special text characters. In Chapter 4, you'll learn more about document editing, and will select features for deleting and restoring text, copying and moving, searching for specific phrases, and editing document codes. In Chapter 5, you'll learn how to check your spelling and find alternate words with the built-in Speller and Thesaurus. Chapter 6 explains how to incorporate graphic images into your text with LetterPerfect's Graphics feature. Chapters 7 and 8 will show you how to print and manage your document files.

Part II includes Chapters 9 through 11. These chapters present practical applications for common business documents. Chapter 9 shows you how to create business memos and outlines. In Chapter 10, you'll learn how to create the document layouts for letters and envelopes. Chapter 11 explains how to use LetterPerfect's Merge features to create form letters. Also included in this chapter are instructions for creating mailing labels.

Part III is comprised of four appendixes with specific information about installing the program files and using the Shell program, using LetterPerfect with Word-Perfect, and the LetterPerfect Macro features. Appendix A explains how to install the LetterPerfect program. In Appendix B, you'll learn how to use the Shell program included with LetterPerfect. Appendix C presents information that will be helpful to WordPerfect users. Appendix D explains the macro features of LetterPerfect, and includes a few useful applications.

CONVENTIONS USED IN THIS BOOK

This book includes special commands that are shown in a different format than the regular text. These indicate when you need to type something or press a particular keystroke.

Bold text indicates text that you should type. For example, if a step says "Type **party.doc** as the file name," this means to type the bolded text.

Keystrokes are listed as small capital letters in the text. For example, keys such as ENTER, PGUP, and HOME, LEFT ARROW appear as shown in this paragraph. Function keys are referred to by the feature name assigned to the key, and are followed by the actual keystroke in parentheses. For example, function key features—such as Save (F10), List Files (F5), and Print (SHIFT-F7)—appear as shown.

When two or more keys should be pressed together, a hyphen joins the keys. For example, the reference for LetterPerfect's Retrieve feature appears in the text as Retrieve (SHIFT-F10). To access this feature, hold down the SHIFT key and press the F10 key—then release both keys.

Boldfaced letters are added to the menu commands to indicate mnemonic selections. For example, the File pull-down menu option is listed as **F**ile in the text. The boldfaced **F** means that you can type this letter to select the File feature.

WHY THIS BOOK IS FOR YOU

Perhaps the most difficult moment in any software program occurs when you start the program for the first time. There are so many new things to learn—new terms, commands, and even procedures that determine how the software will work for you. The only thing that isn't new is the frustration you may feel when trying to make the program do what you want.

If you're like most people, you probably don't care about the names and keystrokes for all the features in your software; you just want to get your work done. You've got specific things that you want to do, and you need to know how to do them, period.

LetterPerfect Made Easy is a no-nonsense tutorial that approaches the Letter-Perfect program as you would yourself—through practical applications. You won't need to hunt through the reference manual to find what you need; step-by-step instructions show you how to produce actual documents that you can use, including business letters, office memos, mailing labels, and printed envelopes.

LetterPerfect is a wonderful program, with many surprises. You'll learn how to insert graphic images into your documents, create memos that automatically prompt you for information, and create mailing labels that are always formatted correctly. You'll also learn several tips to help LetterPerfect perform well for you—these include file-sharing with WordPerfect, LetterPerfect macros, and a trick that enables LetterPerfect to hyphenate your text—even though there is no such feature on its menus.

Even newcomers to word processing software will feel comfortable with the clear and simple instructions. You won't have to memorize everything about the program before you begin; you'll learn about the features as you need them. Important information is organized according to the task at hand. So if you want to learn LetterPerfect quickly and effectively, *LetterPerfect Made Easy* is the perfect companion for you.

part I

BASIC FEATURES

Getting Started with LetterPerfect
Creating a Document Layout
Special Features for Text
Editing a Document
Using the Speller and Thesaurus
Using the Graphics Features
Printing Your Documents
Managing Your Document Files

If you are a new computer user, or if you have never used LetterPerfect or WordPerfect, this section will help you get started. In Chapter 1, you will create and print a simple document, using many of the basic LetterPerfect features. Chapter 2 shows how to create a new document layout, and Chapter 3 explains the font features and other text enhancements. You will learn about the LetterPerfect editing features in Chapter 4. In Chapter 5, you will learn how to check the spelling of your documents, and will use the LetterPerfect Thesaurus to find alternate words for text. Chapter 6 shows how to incorporate graphic images into your documents, Chapter 7 covers the printing features in detail, and Chapter 8 explains document file management. Each chapter presents step-by-step instructions that will help you learn the program quickly; before you know it, you'll be able to create a wide variety of business and personal documents.

chapter 1

GETTING STARTED WITH LETTERPERFECT

Starting the LetterPerfect Program
A Tour of the LetterPerfect Screen
Your Keyboard and LetterPerfect
Typing Text and Moving the Cursor
Using the LetterPerfect Menus
Using a Mouse with LetterPerfect
Exercise: Creating the Party Shack Flyer
Saving Your Document
Previewing the Displayed Document
Printing Your Document
Clearing the Screen
Retrieving a Document
Getting Help
Exiting the Program
Summary

This chapter will help you begin using LetterPerfect. You'll learn how to start the program and use the LetterPerfect menus to create a simple document, save the document to a file, and then print it. You will also learn how to get help when you need more information about the LetterPerfect features.

If you are already using WordPerfect, or other software programs from WordPerfect Corporation, many LetterPerfect commands and features will be familiar to you. However, there are several differences between LetterPerfect and WordPerfect, which are noted in the following chapters. You'll soon discover that LetterPerfect is faster and more efficient than other word processors you may have used.

STARTING THE LETTERPERFECT PROGRAM

LetterPerfect will run on virtually any PC with 330K of free computer memory and one high-density floppy disk drive or two floppy disk drives. Of course, you can also run LetterPerfect from a computer with a hard disk. LetterPerfect works best when you run it from two floppy drives or from a hard disk.

Before you can start LetterPerfect, you must install the program files as described in Appendix A, "Installing the LetterPerfect Program."

Starting From a Single Floppy Drive

If you are running LetterPerfect on a laptop computer—such as the Toshiba T1000—use the following instructions to start and run LetterPerfect from a single 720K floppy drive.

1. Place your DOS boot disk in drive A and turn on your computer. After the computer is booted, you should see the DOS prompt A> on your screen.

2. Remove the boot disk from the A drive and replace it with the LetterPerfect 1 diskette. This is one of two program diskettes that you created during the installation process. (If necessary, refer to Appendix A.)

3. From the A> prompt, type **lp** and press ENTER. The LetterPerfect title screen appears with copyright information. A message instructs you to insert the LetterPerfect 2 diskette.

4. Remove the LetterPerfect 1 diskette from the A drive, and replace it with the LetterPerfect 2 program diskette.

5. Press ENTER to continue, and the main LetterPerfect screen appears.

At this point, you're ready to use the program, but there are a few things you need to know about running LetterPerfect from a single floppy system. First, the LetterPerfect 2 diskette must remain in the A drive while you are using the program. Two exceptions are when you use the Thesaurus and Help features; in each case you will be prompted to insert the Utilities/Images diskette into the A drive. This is the only time you may remove the LetterPerfect 2 diskette from the drive. After you use the Thesaurus or Help feature, return the LetterPerfect 2 diskette to the A drive.

Second, any document files must be saved on the LetterPerfect 2 diskette while you are using the program. Then, after you exit LetterPerfect, you can use the DOS COPY command to transfer the files to another disk. Refer to your DOS manual for information about the COPY command.

Also, when you are running LetterPerfect on a single floppy system, the List Files feature can only display the files on the LetterPerfect 2 diskette. If you want to look at files on another diskette, you will need to exit LetterPerfect and view a directory list from the DOS prompt. Refer to your DOS manual for more information about the DIR command.

note If this is the first time you have started LetterPerfect, you will be prompted to enter your registration number. This is a unique number assigned to your copy of LetterPerfect, and is printed on the registration card included in the Letter-Perfect package. Type the number and press ENTER to continue the program. After you enter the registration number, it will appear at the top of your screen when you use the LetterPerfect Help features.

Starting from Two Floppy Drives

The following instructions show you how to start the LetterPerfect program using two floppy disk drives. You will need the working program diskettes that you created while installing LetterPerfect, as described in Appendix A.

1. Place your DOS boot disk in drive A, and turn on your computer. After the computer is booted, you should see the DOS prompt A> on your screen.

2. Remove the boot disk from the A drive and replace it with the LetterPerfect 1 diskette. This is one of two program diskettes that you created while installing the LetterPerfect program.

3. Insert a formatted diskette into drive B. This disk, sometimes called the *data diskette,* will contain the document files that you will create in LetterPerfect.

8 ≡ **LetterPerfect Made Easy**

4. Now, change to the B drive. This is done by typing **b:** at the DOS prompt and pressing ENTER. Your DOS prompt should change (i.e., B>) to indicate that the active drive is now drive B.

5. At the DOS prompt, type **a:lp** and press ENTER. You will be prompted to insert the LetterPerfect 2 program diskette into drive A.

6. Remove the LetterPerfect 1 diskette from drive A, and replace it with the LetterPerfect 2 diskette. Press ENTER to continue.

A title screen appears briefly with copyright information. Then, the main LetterPerfect screen appears and you are ready to begin a new document. While you are using the program, you must keep the LetterPerfect 2 diskette in drive A. It is assumed that your data diskette, which contains your document files, is in the B drive. When you want to use the Thesaurus feature, or access files on other diskettes, you will need to replace the diskette in drive B with the appropriate diskette.

Starting from a Hard Disk

The following instructions explain how to start LetterPerfect from the C> DOS prompt, with the program files installed on a hard disk. If you have not yet installed LetterPerfect, refer to Appendix A. It is assumed that your computer is already turned on and ready to work.

1. With the system booted, change to the directory on your hard disk where LetterPerfect is located. To do so, type **cd** at the DOS prompt, followed by the name of the LetterPerfect directory, and press ENTER. For example, if you accepted the standard directory when you installed LetterPerfect, you would type **cd\ lp10** and press ENTER.

2. Type **lp** and then press ENTER to start the LetterPerfect program.

A title screen appears briefly with copyright information. Then, the main LetterPerfect screen appears and you are ready to begin a new document.

≡*note*≡ If this is the first time you have started LetterPerfect, you will be prompted to enter your registration number. This is a unique number assigned to your copy of LetterPerfect, and is printed on the registration card included in the LetterPerfect package. Type the number and press ENTER to continue the program.

After you enter the registration number, it will appear at the top of your screen when you use the Help features of LetterPerfect.

Starting with the Shell Program

You've just learned how to start the program from the DOS prompt, but you can also start LetterPerfect with the Shell program included with your LetterPerfect diskettes. The Shell is a memory-management program that allows you to start your programs from an on-screen menu. The Shell is not necessary—you can run LetterPerfect without it—but it does enhance the capabilities of the LetterPerfect program. You can install the Shell only if you have a hard disk. For more information about installing and using the Shell with LetterPerfect, see Appendix B, "Using the Shell Program."

A TOUR OF THE LETTERPERFECT SCREEN

Figure 1-1 shows the main LetterPerfect screen. At the top of the screen, you will see the *pull-down menu bar*. You can use the menu bar to select formatting and editing features, or you can press keys on your keyboard to access the features.

The *status line* appears at the bottom of the screen, and shows where the text cursor is located in your document. When you first start LetterPerfect, the status line will appear as: Pg 1 Ln 1" Pos 1". The Pg label tells you the number of the page displayed on the screen; the Ln and Pos labels display horizontal and vertical measurements respectively. The Ln label shows how far the cursor is located from the top of the page; the Pos label shows the cursor position from the left edge of the page. As you create your documents, you will notice that the numbers change to show the current cursor position.

In addition, Pos will tell you whether certain keyboard modes are active. For example, when the NUM LOCK key is pressed, the Pos label blinks to let you know that the numeric keypad is active; when the CAPS LOCK key is pressed, the Pos label appears as "POS," in uppercase letters.

The status line also displays messages that tell you what is happening in the program, and when necessary, prompts you to perform an action. Once you have saved a document, its file name appears in the lower-left corner of the screen.

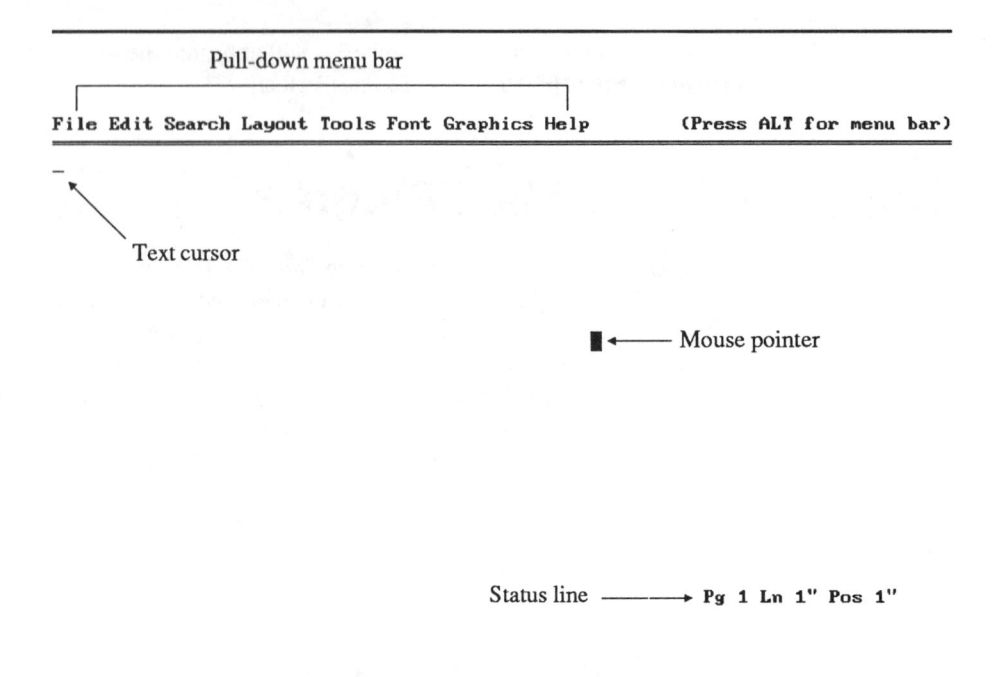

```
                    Pull-down menu bar
         ┌─────────────────────────────────┐
File Edit Search Layout Tools Font Graphics Help    (Press ALT for menu bar)
─
 ↖
   Text cursor


                                            ■ ◄─── Mouse pointer




                                    Status line ────► Pg 1 Ln 1" Pos 1"
```

FIGURE 1-1.   The main LetterPerfect screen

note — The LetterPerfect Setup menu provides options that let you customize the appearance of your screen. For more information on these options, refer to Appendix A, under "Defining Program Options."

The blinking dash at the top-left corner of the screen is the *text cursor*; this is where you can type or edit text. If you have a mouse input device attached to your computer, you may also see the *mouse pointer*, which appears as a small rectangle on the screen. You can use the mouse pointer to choose menu options and move the text cursor to another location. For more information, see "Using a Mouse with LetterPerfect," in this chapter.

YOUR KEYBOARD AND LETTERPERFECT

Figure 1-2 shows the two types of keyboards that are available for IBM PCs and compatible computers. There may be a few differences between your keyboard and those shown in the illustration, but the functions are basically the same.

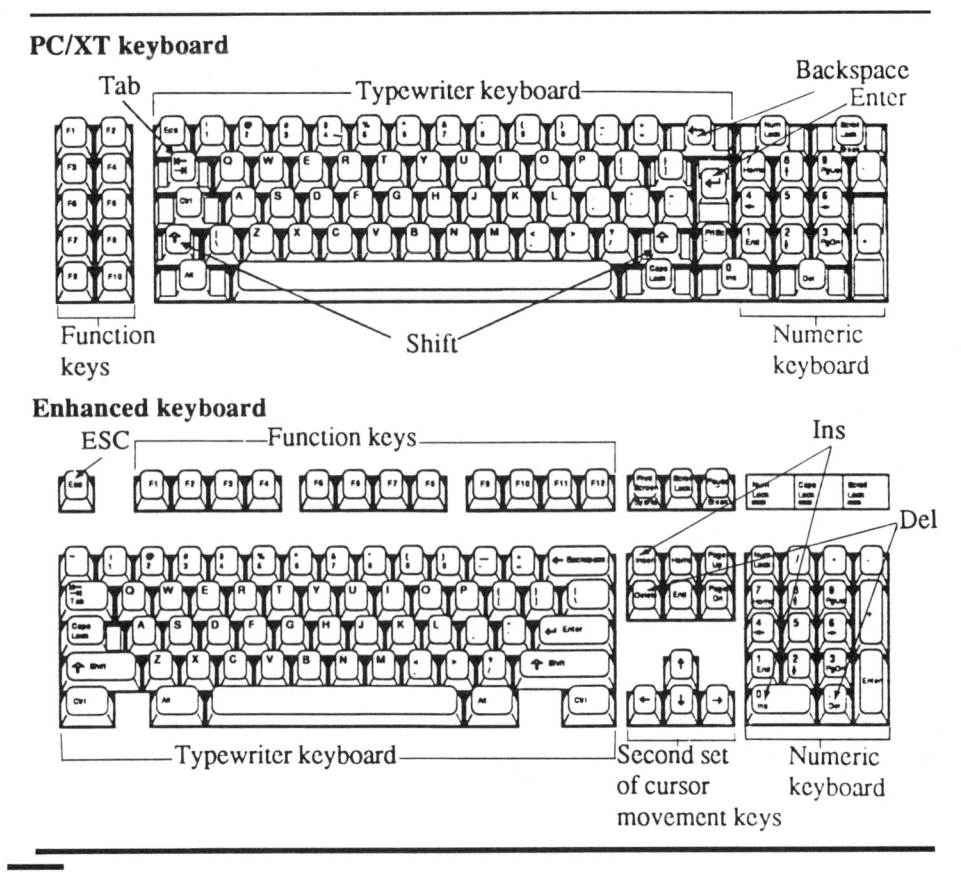

Chapter 1　　　　　　　　　　　　　　　Getting Started with LetterPerfect　　11

FIGURE 1-2. The IBM PC/XT and Enhanced keyboards

Before you can type text or select program features, you need to know how LetterPerfect works with your keyboard. You can select most commands from the menu bar at the top of your screen; however, there are several keys that perform special functions in LetterPerfect.

The Function Keys

Your keyboard has at least ten function keys, numbered F1 through F10, which perform different functions depending on the software program you are using. If you own an enhanced keyboard, you will also have two additional function keys:

F11 and F12. The CTRL, SHIFT, and ALT keys are often used with the function keys, allowing each key to have up to four feature assignments. Table 1-1 lists the function key combinations and the features they perform in LetterPerfect.

The LetterPerfect features are also accessible from the pull-down menus. However, if you currently work with WordPerfect, most of the function key assignments may already be familiar to you. As you read through the following sections, you will have the opportunity to select features with the function keys, or if you prefer, you can use the pull-down menus instead.

ESC

The ESC key cancels a program command or a menu selection. For example, if a pull-down menu is displayed, ESC will remove it from the screen. When no menus or messages are displayed, ESC activates the Undelete feature, which allows you to restore text that you have deleted from your document. (In Chapter 4, you'll read more about the Undelete feature.)

DEL and BACKSPACE

DEL and BACKSPACE can delete single characters from your text. If you press DEL, the character at the text cursor is deleted; if you press BACKSPACE, the character to the left of the text cursor is deleted. If you hold down either of these keys, you will delete several characters; BACKSPACE deletes to the left, and DEL deletes to the right. These keys can also be used, when the Block feature is active, to remove a block of text from your document.

CAPS LOCK

The CAPS LOCK key is useful when you need to type uppercase text. When CAPS LOCK is pressed, the Pos label on the status line appears as "POS," and any text you type will appear in uppercase letters. Press CAPS LOCK again to return to the normal typing mode.

Keystroke	Action
F1	Cancel or Help
CTRL-F1	Shell
SHIFT-F1	Setup Program Options
ALT-F1	Thesaurus
F2	Search Forward
CTRL-F2	Spell
SHIFT-F2	Search Backward
ALT-F2	Replace Text
F3	Help
CTRL-F3	Line Draw
ALT-F3	Reveal Codes
F4	Left Margin Indent
CTRL-F4	Move
SHIFT-F4	Left/Right Margin Indent
ALT-F4	Block Text
F5	List Files
CTRL-F5	Text Out (ASCII file conversion)
SHIFT-F5	Date/Outline
F6	Bold Text
CTRL-F6	Tab Align (decimal-aligned tab)
SHIFT-F6	Center Text
ALT-F6	Flush Right (right justify)
F7	Exit
CTRL-F7	Create/Edit Endnote
SHIFT-F7	Print
F8	Underlined Text
CTRL-F8	Fonts
SHIFT-F8	Format (create layout)
ALT-F8	Select Language
F9	End Field (insert Merge code)
CTRL-F9	Merge Documents
SHIFT-F9	Select Merge Codes
ALT-F9	Graphics
F10	Save Document
SHIFT-F10	Retrieve Document
F11	Reveal Codes
F12	Block Text

TABLE 1-1. Function Key Assignments

NUM LOCK

The NUM LOCK key enables the numeric keypad, which allows you to type numbers without using the keys along the top of your keyboard. The numeric keypad is the group of keys at the right edge of your keyboard. When NUM LOCK is pressed, the Pos label on the status line blinks to remind you that the numeric keypad is active; it will continue to blink until you press another key. Press NUM LOCK again to turn off the numeric keypad.

INS

LetterPerfect provides two methods for typing text into your documents. The first method, called the *Insert mode,* is already selected when you start LetterPerfect. When the Insert mode is active, everything you type is inserted into your text at the cursor position.

The second method, called the *Typeover mode,* types the new text over the existing text. This mode is particularly useful during editing, when you want to rewrite an entire sentence or paragraph without first deleting it. Press INS to select this mode and a "Typeover" message appears on the status line. Now, any text you type will be written over the existing text, beginning at the cursor position. Press INS again to turn off the Typeover mode.

ENTER

The ENTER key performs two different functions in LetterPerfect. When you are typing text, ENTER indicates that you want to end the current line and move to the next line; it accomplishes this by inserting an invisible *hard return* ([HRt]) code into your text. You'll read more about formatting codes in the following chapters. You also press ENTER to accept something that you've typed, such as a file name, in response to a menu prompt.

TYPING TEXT AND MOVING THE CURSOR

As soon as you start the LetterPerfect program, you're ready to create a new document. You don't need to open or reserve a file name before you start typing. In fact, you can create a document, make corrections, and print it without even saving to a file on disk. This gives you complete freedom to create documents as you wish, allowing you to print quick notes or memos that don't need to be saved as disk files.

LetterPerfect has predefined margins, tab settings, and line spacing, so you can begin typing immediately. In Chapter 2, you'll learn how to change these and other format settings, and define your own format specifications.

Typing with Word Wrap

If this is the first time you've used a word processor, remember that you don't need to press ENTER at the end of each line, as you would with a typewriter. LetterPerfect includes a feature called *word wrap*, that automatically arranges the text to fit the current margin settings. To test this feature, type the following text at the main LetterPerfect screen, without pressing the ENTER key:

The Party Shack offers complete catering services for all your entertainment needs. Our creative directors have the perfect ideas for every occasion: birthday parties, weddings, holidays—we can even bring Spunky the Magic Clown and twelve trained dachshunds to add some excitement to a boring dinner party!

If you make a mistake while typing, press BACKSPACE to delete any unwanted characters. When you are finished typing the text, press ENTER twice to end the paragraph. Your screen should look similar to Figure 1-3. Notice that when text extends beyond the right margin, LetterPerfect wraps it to the next line, to format it for the paragraph. This allows you to concentrate on the writing, without worrying about whether there's room to fit your text on the current line. Remember, you should press ENTER only when you want to end a paragraph or text heading. Keep this paragraph on the screen; you'll need it for an exercise, later in this chapter.

Moving the Cursor with the Arrow Keys

Now that you have some text on the screen, you can use the arrow keys to move the text cursor through your document. If you have an IBM PC/XT-style keyboard, you can use the four arrow keys on the numeric keypad to move the cursor. Remember to turn NUM LOCK off if you plan to use these arrow keys. Press UP ARROW to move the text cursor to the line above, or DOWN ARROW to move the cursor down to the

```
File Edit Search Layout Tools Font Graphics Help        (Press ALT= for menu bar)
The Party Shack offers complete catering services for all your
entertainment needs.  Our creative directors have the perfect
ideas for every occasion:  birthday parties, weddings, holidays--
we can even bring Spunky the Magic Clown and twelve trained
dachshunds to add some excitement to a boring dinner party!

_




                                                         Pg 1 Ln 2" Pos 1"
```

FIGURE 1-3.   Typing a paragraph with word wrap

next line. Press LEFT ARROW to move the cursor to the previous text character or RIGHT ARROW to move to the next character.

If you have an IBM Enhanced keyboard, you have an extra set of arrow keys that appears between the numeric keypad and the main typing keys (see Figure 1-2). Experiment with the arrow keys and move the text cursor through the text on your screen.

Extended Cursor Movement

Moving the cursor with only the arrow keys can be quite tedious. Fortunately, LetterPerfect supports other keystroke combinations that enhance and magnify the power of the arrow keys. Also, there are several keys that let you move quickly between the pages of your document. Table 1-2 shows a complete list of cursor movement keystrokes you can use in LetterPerfect. As you read through the following text, press the appropriate keys to test the cursor movement features.

Press the HOME key before pressing an arrow key to magnify the distance that the cursor will move. For example, press HOME, UP ARROW to move the text cursor to the top of the screen; HOME, DOWN ARROW moves the cursor to the bottom of the screen or to the last text line on the screen. HOME, RIGHT ARROW and HOME, LEFT ARROW move the cursor to the right or left end of the current line. Pressing END also moves the cursor to the right end of the current line, just like HOME, RIGHT ARROW does. Press HOME, HOME, UP ARROW to move to the beginning of the document; HOME, HOME, DOWN ARROW moves the cursor to the end of the document.

Sometimes, you need to move quickly through a line of text, but you don't want to move to either end of the line. In this case, you can hold down the CTRL key while pressing an arrow key to move to an adjacent word. CTRL-RIGHT ARROW moves the cursor to the next word on the line; CTRL-LEFT ARROW moves the cursor to the previous word on the line.

When you have a document with several pages, there are other keystrokes that help you move through the text. Press PGUP to move the text cursor to the previous page; if the cursor is on the first page of the document, PGUP moves the cursor to the

Keystroke	Action
LEFT ARROW	Move one character to the left
RIGHT ARROW	Move one character to the right
UP ARROW	Move up one line
DOWN ARROW	Move down one line
CTRL-LEFT ARROW	Move to the previous word
CTRL-RIGHT ARROW	Move to the next word
END	Move to the right end of the line
HOME, LEFT ARROW	Move the the left end of the line
HOME, RIGHT ARROW	Move to right end of the line
HOME, UP ARROW	Move to the top of the screen
HOME, DOWN ARROW	Move to the bottom of the screen
HOME, HOME, UP ARROW	Move to beginning of document
HOME, HOME, DOWN ARROW	Move to end of document
PGUP	Move to the previous page
PGDN	Move to the next page
– (minus on keypad)	Move one-half page up
+ (plus on keypad)	Move one-half page down
CTRL-HOME	Move to a specific page

TABLE 1-2. Cursor Movement Keystrokes

beginning of the text. Press PGDN to move to the next page in the document; likewise, if the cursor is on the last page, PGDN moves it to the end of the text. You can also press Go To (CTRL-HOME), type a page number, and press ENTER, to jump directly to a specific page.

Sometimes you'll want to move the cursor only half a page, which is approximately equal to one screen of text. Press the − key on the numeric keypad to move up one-half page; press the + key on the keypad to move down a half page.

Scrolling Through the Text

It's important to note that LetterPerfect will not let you move the text cursor to a place where you haven't typed text characters or spaces. When you use the UP ARROW or DOWN ARROW key to move the cursor through the text, LetterPerfect will try to keep the text cursor at the original horizontal position.

To see how this works, move the text cursor to the first line of the paragraph on your screen. Then, press END to move the text cursor to the end of the first line. Now, press the DOWN ARROW key to move the cursor through the paragraph. Notice that the text cursor jumps to meet the next available character on each line.

At first, this may seem a bit confusing because the cursor jumps to the left when you move down to a shorter line; then it jumps back to the original horizontal position when you move up or down to a longer line. This is because the cursor cannot move to a place where text or spaces do not exist. Instead, the cursor moves to the next occupied space on the line as you scroll through the document.

This feature is important because it keeps the text cursor aligned correctly when you scroll through tables and tabular columns. However, when you are working with paragraph text, you probably won't see a radical change in cursor movement.

USING THE LETTERPERFECT MENUS

LetterPerfect provides several ways to access the program features. It doesn't matter which method you choose; you can select features from the pull-down menu bar, press function keys to display appropriate menus, or use Fast Keys (explained later in this chapter) to select a specific feature. If you are already familiar with WordPerfect, you will most likely feel comfortable with the function keys. If this is the first time you've used WordPerfect software, you may prefer the pull-down menus and the Fast Keys.

Using the Function Keys

As described earlier, the function keys allow you to display menus and select program features. Refer back to Table 1-1 for a complete list of features assigned to these keys. Included with your LetterPerfect package is a paper template that fits over the function keys on your keyboard. This template will remind you which keys to press to access specific program features.

You will notice that the feature names are printed on the template in different colors. If a feature is printed in black, this means you can press the corresponding function key alone to access the feature. If a feature appears in red, you need to hold down the CTRL key and press the function key to access the feature. For feature names printed in green, hold down the SHIFT key before pressing the function key. If a feature is printed in blue, hold down the ALT key and press the appropriate function key.

Many of the function keys display menus with feature options. For example, when you press Font (CTRL-F8), this menu appears at the bottom of the screen:

    1 Bold; 2 Underline; 3 Normal; 4 Base Font; 5 Italc; 6 Suprscpt; 7 Subscpt: 0

You can select one of the menu options by typing the number that precedes the feature name, or by selecting the highlighted *mnemonic* letter. Suppose you wanted to choose the Italc (Italics text) option; you could type either **5** or **i** to select the feature. Usually, the first letter of the feature name is also the mnemonic letter, but there are several menus where two or more features begin with the same letter and alternate letters must be used as the mnemonics.

If you select a feature, but then decide not to continue the action, press ESC or Cancel (F1) to cancel it. The ESC or Cancel (F1) key can stop a program command or remove a menu that is displayed on the screen.

note: It is possible to redefine the F1 key so that it accesses the LetterPerfect Help features. If, during the program installation or from the Setup menu, you have redefined the F1 key, it will not cancel a program command. In this case, you must use the ESC key instead.

Using the Pull-Down Menus

The pull-down menu bar provides an alternate way of selecting features in Letter-Perfect. The labels at the top of the screen represent the feature categories for the pull-down menus. As the name implies, a *pull-down menu* opens a panel that pulls down, much like a window shade. The panel lists all the selections for one feature category, and allows you to choose a feature from the list. The following steps will show you how to use the pull-down menus. Before you continue, press HOME, HOME, UP ARROW to move the cursor to the beginning of the text on your screen.

note: The following steps explain how to use the pull-down menus with the keyboard. If you are using a mouse with LetterPerfect, see the upcoming section, "Using a Mouse with LetterPerfect."

1. Press ALT or ALT-= (hold down the ALT key and type an equal sign). The first option on the menu bar, File, is highlighted to indicate that the pull-down menu bar is active.

2. Press RIGHT ARROW four times to highlight the **T**ools option. Press the DOWN ARROW key to display the pull-down menu.

3. Assume you want to see the features of the other pull-down menus. You can press RIGHT ARROW or LEFT ARROW to display the adjacent pull-down menus.

4. Finally, use the arrow keys to display the **L**ayout pull-down menu. Press DOWN ARROW four times to move to the → Indent option.

5. Press ENTER to select the feature, and the left margin of your text is indented. Once you select a feature, the pull-down menu is removed from the screen.

6. You don't really want the text indented, so press BACKSPACE to remove the indent.

Remember that when a label on the menu bar is highlighted, the pull-down menu bar is active and you cannot type text. You may have noticed that each menu option has a highlighted mnemonic letter. If the pull-down menu bar is active you can type the mnemonic letter to select a feature, instead of using the arrow keys to move through the menus.

You can press Cancel (ESC or F1) to remove a pull-down menu from the screen, but you'll have to press it twice—once to remove the pull-down menu, and again to deactivate the pull-down menu bar.

As you follow the exercises in this book, you will be instructed to select features from the pull-down menus. If you are using the mouse, you can simply click on the menu options to select them (this is explained later in this chapter). If you are using the keyboard, you must press ALT or ALT-= to activate the pull-down menu bar before you can choose an option from the menu.

LetterPerfect Fast Keys

You may have also noticed that keystroke equivalents are listed next to each feature that appears on the pull-down menus. You can press these *Fast Keys* to select the features, rather than selecting from the pull-down menu bar. Most of the keystrokes are intuitive, such as CTRL-B to create **B**old text and CTRL-R to show or hide the **R**eveal Codes window. If you feel comfortable with the keyboard, and don't mind memorizing a few commands, these keystrokes are the fastest way to select features in LetterPerfect.

To see a complete list of LetterPerfect Fast Keys, press Help (F3 or F1) twice to display a diagram of function keys. Then, type **2** to display the Fast Key list. Press Exit to exit the Help screen and return to your document.

Hiding the Menu Bar

When you first install LetterPerfect, the pull-down menu bar is automatically shown on the screen; however, you can use the Setup feature (SHIFT-F1, option **7,** "Menu Bar Remains Visible") to hide the pull-down menu bar until you are ready to select features from it. After you select this option, press Exit (F7) to return to the document screen. When the menu bar is hidden, you can display it by pressing ALT or ALT-=, or by clicking the right mouse button.

USING A MOUSE WITH LETTERPERFECT

If you have a mouse input device connected to your computer, you can use it to move the cursor, block text, and select items from the program menus. You do not need a mouse input device to use LetterPerfect but it can make several tasks, such as blocking text, easier to perform. You'll learn how to block text in Chapter 4.

If a mouse is available, LetterPerfect automatically makes use of it, providing that you are running the *mouse driver* that was included with your mouse. Generally, the mouse driver is a program file, called MOUSE.COM on your disk, that helps your computer communicate with the mouse. If you do not have this program installed and running, your mouse may not work properly with LetterPerfect. Consult the manual that came with the mouse, for more information about the mouse drivers for your equipment.

Moving the Cursor with the Mouse

When you are using a mouse with LetterPerfect, you will see two cursors on the screen. One is the text cursor, described earlier, that lets you enter text and perform editing tasks. You might recall that the second cursor, which appears as a small rectangle on the screen, is called the mouse pointer.

To move the mouse pointer, simply move the mouse across the top of your desk or table. Notice that the movement of the mouse directs the movement of the mouse pointer on the screen. When the mouse pointer is located within the text of your document, you can use it to reposition the text cursor. Simply move the mouse pointer to the place where you want to move the text cursor, and quickly press and release the left mouse button. This "press and release" action is called a *click*. When you click on a specific place in your document, the text cursor is moved to that position, or to the closest available text character.

Selecting Menu Items

When the mouse pointer is located on the menu bar or over a menu item, you can use it to select a feature. Suppose you want to view a list of the files on your disk; this feature is located on the File pull-down menu, and you can use the mouse to select it. First, move the mouse pointer to the File option on the menu bar. Then, click (quickly press and release) the left mouse button. The File pull-down menu is displayed. Move the mouse pointer to the List Files option and click the left mouse button to select the feature. For this feature, a directory prompt appears on the screen; press ESC to cancel the directory listing.

You can click on any pull-down menu or menu item to select one of the features. You can also use the mouse to click on any Yes or No prompts that appear on the status line.

Sometimes you will want to use the mouse to browse through the pull-down menus until you find the feature you're looking for. To do this, click on the File option to display the corresponding pull-down menu. With the mouse pointer still on the File option, press and hold down the left mouse button; do not release it. Now, move the mouse to the right, to highlight the other labels on the menu bar. Notice that as each option is highlighted by the mouse, its pull-down menu is displayed. Make sure the mouse pointer is on one of the menu bar labels; then, release the left mouse button.

This action of moving the mouse, while holding down the left mouse button, is called *dragging* the mouse pointer. You can also drag the mouse pointer into a pull-down menu to highlight any menu items. If you release the left mouse button while a feature on the menu is highlighted, that feature will be selected.

In some situations, you can quickly click the mouse twice, or *double-click*, to select certain features. For example, when the List Files screen is displayed, you can move the mouse pointer to a file name, and then double-click the mouse to retrieve the file. In other cases, you can press the right mouse button to mimic the ENTER and Exit (F7) keys. For example, you can press the right mouse button, rather than ENTER, to accept a file name while saving a document file. When a menu is displayed, you can click the right mouse button to return to the document screen.

Canceling with the Mouse

The mouse can also act as the Cancel (ESC or F1) key, to remove a menu from the screen or cancel a program command. If you have a two-button mouse, click both buttons at once to cancel a menu or action. If you have a three-button mouse, click the center button to cancel.

You can test this by moving the mouse pointer to one of the labels on the pull-down menu bar and clicking the left mouse button to display the menu. Then press the center mouse button, or press both mouse buttons simultaneously, to cancel the menu. You will need to first cancel the displayed menu, and then the pull-down menu bar, to return to the document editing mode.

EXERCISE: CREATING THE PARTY SHACK FLYER

Now that you know some of the basics of LetterPerfect, you're ready to create a complete document. You will add to the text that already appears on your screen, and create a flyer for a catering company called "The Party Shack." Don't worry about remembering all the keystrokes and features in the following steps; this exercise is meant to let you practice moving the cursor and typing text.

1. First, you need to make room for a headline at the top of the flyer. Press HOME, HOME, UP ARROW, or move the mouse pointer to the first character of your paragraph and click the left mouse button. This will move the text cursor to the beginning of the text on your screen. Press ENTER three times to add a few line spaces above the paragraph.

2. Press HOME, HOME, UP ARROW, or move the mouse pointer and click the left mouse button, to move the text cursor to the top of the document. Press Center (SHIFT-F6), or choose **Layout/Center** from the pull-down menu to center the text cursor between the margins. Press CAPS LOCK and type **greetings from the party shack!**. Then, press CAPS LOCK again.

3 Press HOME, HOME, DOWN ARROW, or use the mouse pointer, to move the cursor to the end of the text—presumably to the end of paragraph that you typed earlier.

4. Type the following text to create a second paragraph for your document:

   Why cook? Our chefs can do it for you! Certified with the renowned Crockett Institute of Fine Party Cuisine, we can create the most exotic and creative dishes, suitable for any backyard barbecue or corporate Christmas party.

5. Press ENTER twice to add space for a third paragraph, and type the following text:

   And now is the best time to get acquainted with our services. If you plan a party before July 31st, we'll give you a 10% discount on all party favors! So drop by the Party Shack, where there's always a party going on!

Press ENTER twice to end the last paragraph. You're now finished with the text for the flyer. Figure 1-4 shows how your screen should look. In the next section, you will save this document to a file on disk. In Chapter 4, you'll edit this document and add some new text. Later, you will also add graphic images to the flyer, to make it more visually interesting.

SAVING YOUR DOCUMENT

As you work with LetterPerfect, document information is stored in your computer's memory. If you turn off your computer or if a power failure occurs, your document may be lost. For obvious reasons, it's important that you save your document to a file on disk so that it may be retrieved at a later date. The following steps describe the basic procedure for saving the document on your screen.

1. Press Save (F10), or select File from the pull-down menu bar and choose the Save option.

2. LetterPerfect prompts you with "Document to be saved: ". You can type a file name with eight or fewer characters and an extension of three characters or less. For this exercise, type **party.doc** and press ENTER.

```
File Edit Search Layout Tools Font Graphics Help          (Press ALT for menu bar)
                        GREETINGS FROM THE PARTY SHACK!

The Party Shack offers complete catering services for all your
entertainment needs.  Our creative directors have the perfect
ideas for every occasion:  birthday parties, weddings, holidays--
we can even bring Spunky the Magic Clown and twelve trained
dachshunds to add some excitement to a boring dinner party!

Why cook? Our chefs can do it for you!  Certified with the
renowned Crockett Institute of Fine Party Cuisine, we can create
the most exotic and creative dishes, suitable for any backyard
barbecue or corporate Christmas party.

And now is the best time to get acquainted with our services.  If
you plan a party before July 31st, we'll give you a 10% discount
on all party favors!  So drop by the Party Shack, where there's
always a party going on!

-

                                                    Pg 1 Ln 4.17" Pos 1"
```

FIGURE 1-4. The finished document

LetterPerfect saves the current document under the PARTY.DOC file name, and stores it in the default directory. After you save the file, its name is displayed in the lower-left corner of the screen. For complete information about the Save and Retrieve features, see Chapter 8, "Managing Your Document Files."

PREVIEWING THE DISPLAYED DOCUMENT

LetterPerfect uses a *character-based* display, meaning that the standard IBM character set is used to display your documents on the screen. Unfortunately, this display type does not show your text as it will appear when printed. For this reason, LetterPerfect includes a special preview screen that can show the printed document—including font changes and graphics—before you actually send the document to the printer. The following steps show how to preview the on-screen document with LetterPerfect's View Document feature.

1. Press Print (SHIFT-F7), or select **File** from the pull-down menu bar and choose **Print**. The Print screen is displayed.

2. Choose option **3**, View Document, and a graphics screen appears that shows how your document will look when printed. Figure 1-5 shows how your screen might look.

note: You can also press the equivalent Fast Key, CTRL-P, from the main document screen to preview your document.

3. At this graphics screen, you can use most of the cursor movement keys to move around your document. For example, you can press PGUP and PGDN to move to the different pages.

A menu at the bottom of the View Document screen presents options for viewing your document. Choose option **1** to view the document at 100 percent, or roughly the actual printing size; choose option **2** to display a magnified view (200 percent). Option **3** lets you see the entire page on one screen, while option **4** lets you see facing pages, almost as if you were turning the pages of a book. Option **5**, **Invert**, allows you to reverse the colors of the View Document display, creating an inverse image of the current screen. When you are finished viewing your document, press Exit (F7) to return to the normal editing screen.

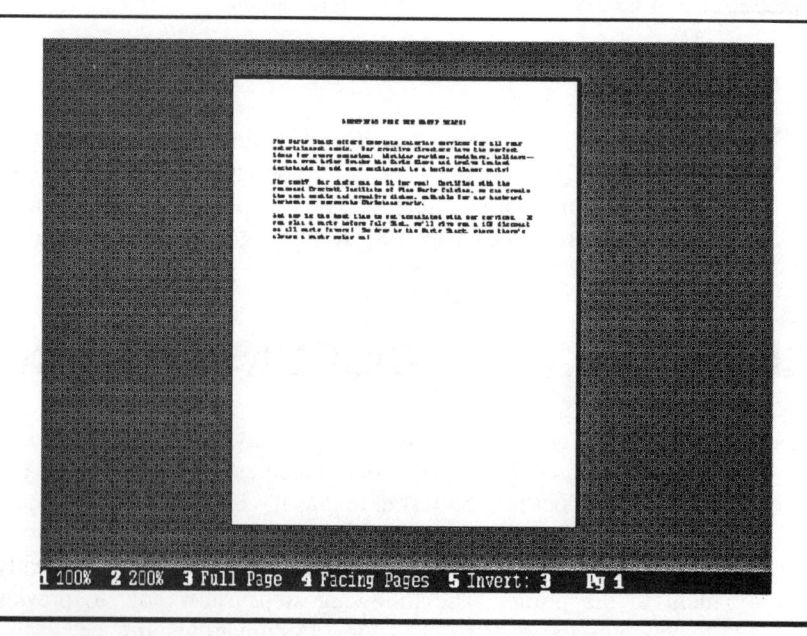

FIGURE 1-5. The View Document screen

PRINTING YOUR DOCUMENT

This section explains how to print the document that is currently displayed on the screen. Before you attempt to print your document, make sure that the printer is turned on and ready to print. If you have not yet installed and selected a printer, refer to Chapter 7.

1. Press Print (SHIFT-F7), or select File/Print from the pull-down menu. The LetterPerfect Print menu is displayed, as shown in Figure 1-6.

2. Type **1** to print the Full Document that is currently on your screen. If you are using a mouse, simply move the mouse cursor to the Full Document option and click the left mouse button.

LetterPerfect sends a copy of your document to the printer. Once the document is sent, the LetterPerfect Printer Control screen is displayed, with information about the status of the printing process. After your document is printed, press Exit (F7) to return to the main LetterPerfect screen.

This is the basic procedure for printing a document; for more detailed information about printing and print options, read Chapter 7, "Printing Your Documents."

CLEARING THE SCREEN

You should always clear the screen before you create a new document or retrieve a different document file. This is an important feature, and you will use it often as you create and edit documents. If you want to keep the current document, make sure you save it to a file on disk before you clear the screen. You will use LetterPerfect's Exit feature to exit the current document and clear the screen.

1. Press Exit (F7), or select Exit from the File pull-down menu.

2. LetterPerfect prompts you with "Save document? Yes (No)". In this case, assume you have already saved your document and type **N** for No. If you type **Y** in response to this prompt, you will have the opportunity to enter a document name and save the file.

3. Next, LetterPerfect prompts you with "Exit LP? No (Yes)". Type **N** for No to indicate that you do not want to exit LetterPerfect, but you do want to clear the

```
Print

    1 - Full Document
    2 - Multiple Pages
    3 - View Document
    4 - Initialize Printer

Options

    5 - Select Printer          HP LaserJet IIP
    6 - Binding Offset          0"
    7 - Number of Copies        1
    8 - Graphics Quality        Medium
    9 - Text Quality            High




Selection: 0
```

FIGURE 1-6. The LetterPerfect Print menu

screen. When you type **Y** in response to this prompt, you will exit LetterPerfect and return to DOS or to the Shell program.

The screen is cleared, and you can create or retrieve a new document. As you work through the exercises in this book, follow this procedure when instructed to clear the screen. Also, make sure you save important documents before clearing the screen; once a document has been cleared, the only way to get it back is to retrieve it from a file on disk.

RETRIEVING A DOCUMENT

The Retrieve feature lets you display a document file on the screen, allowing you to edit and print the file. The following steps outline the basic procedure for retrieving document files.

1. Press Retrieve (SHIFT-F10), or select **Retrieve** from the File pull-down menu.

2. LetterPerfect prompts you with "Document to be retrieved: ". You can enter the name of a file on disk to retrieve the file. For this exercise, type **party.doc** and press ENTER to retrieve the document that you created earlier.

A copy of your "party" document is retrieved and displayed on the screen. Note that what you see is only a copy of the information in the disk file. Any changes you make to the displayed document will not be in the disk file until you save the document again under the same file name. For complete information about the Save and Retrieve features, see Chapter 8, "Managing Your Document Files."

If you retrieve a file while another document is already displayed on the screen, LetterPerfect inserts it into your document, at the current cursor position. Sometimes you will want to do this, to append one file to another, but be careful. If you accidentally retrieve a document into another document, you cannot "undo" the action; you'll need to delete the unwanted text, or clear the screen and start again.

GETTING HELP

LetterPerfect includes a superb on-line help utility that provides information about the program features, and, unlike earlier versions of WordPerfect, displays context-sensitive help for any feature that is currently active. You can also activate a feature directly from the Help system. If you need information or help that is not available in on-line help or in the LetterPerfect manual, you can contact the WordPerfect Customer Support group for further assistance.

Using the On-Line Help Feature

There are several ways to find the information you need with the LetterPerfect Help feature. You can always select **Help** from the pull-down menu, but the function key you use to select help depends on how your copy of LetterPerfect is set up. The Help key can be either F1 or F3; you decide which key you want from the Setup feature (SHIFT-F1, option 8).

Once you access the main Help screen, you can get help through an alphabetical index of LetterPerfect features, you can press a key to display information about the use of the key, or you can display a template of the function key assignments. You can also display a list of the LetterPerfect Fast Keys and the functions they perform.

To access the Help feature, press Help (F1 or F3) or select **Help/Help** from the pull-down menu bar. Assuming that no other features are active, this will display the main Help screen shown in Figure 1-7. The right side of the screen explains general information about the Help system. The left side of the screen is the feature index, through which you can look for more information and even select a feature for the current document. A menu at the bottom of the screen lists different options that are available while the Help system is active.

FEATURE INDEX HELP From the main Help screen, you can move the cursor and scroll through the alphabetical feature index. The Name Search option allows you to quickly move to an entry in the index, when you know what the feature is called. For example, select Name Search from the menu and type a feature name. The highlighted cursor moves directly to the name that you type. Notice that when Name Search is active, the Help menu is not displayed. You must press ENTER to restore it.

Once a feature name is highlighted, you can select **1** **H**elp for Function, or simply press ENTER, to display a Help screen about the feature. Choose option **2**, **P**erform Function, to perform the highlighted feature and exit the Help system.

For example, assume that you want to know how to create underlined text. Choose the **N**ame Search option from the Help menu and type **underline**. The highlighted cursor moves to the entry for "Underline Text." Press ENTER once to

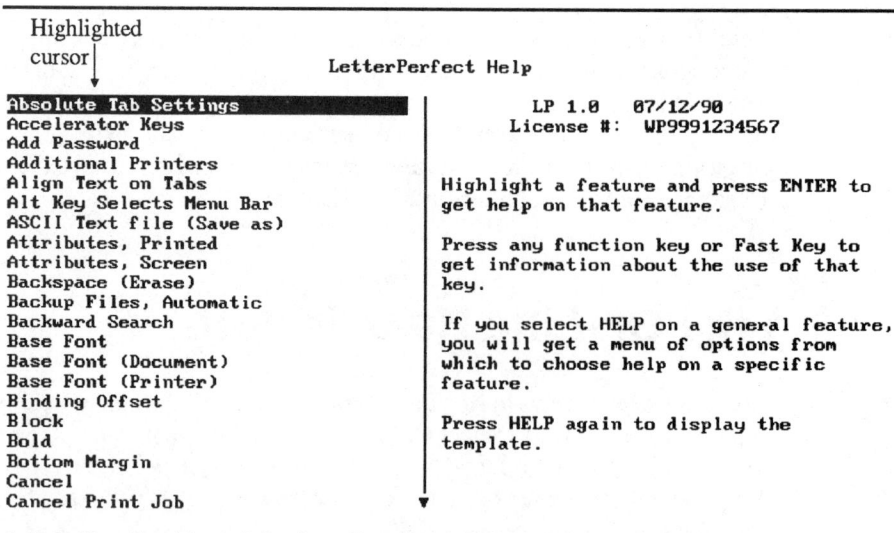

```
Highlighted
cursor
                                    LetterPerfect Help

Absolute Tab Settings              LP 1.0    07/12/90
Accelerator Keys                   License #:  WP9991234567
Add Password
Additional Printers
Align Text on Tabs                 Highlight a feature and press ENTER to
Alt Key Selects Menu Bar           get help on that feature.
ASCII Text file (Save as)
Attributes, Printed                Press any function key or Fast Key to
Attributes, Screen                 get information about the use of that
Backspace (Erase)                  key.
Backup Files, Automatic
Backward Search                    If you select HELP on a general feature,
Base Font                          you will get a menu of options from
Base Font (Document)               which to choose help on a specific
Base Font (Printer)                feature.
Binding Offset
Block                              Press HELP again to display the
Bold                               template.
Bottom Margin
Cancel
Cancel Print Job

1 Help for Function; 2 Perform Function; 3 Exit Help; N Name Search: 1
```

FIGURE 1-7. The main Help screen

restore the Help menu. Press ENTER again, or choose option **1, Help for Function,** to display a Help screen about the feature. Information is included on the screen that tells you how to access the feature with the function keys or from the pull-down menus. The screen will also list the Fast Key for the feature, if one is available.

At this point you can press ENTER to return to the main Help screen, and, if you wish, choose option **2, Perform Function,** to select the highlighted feature. Press Exit (F7) or the SPACEBAR to exit the Help system and return to the document editing screen.

TEMPLATE AND FAST KEY HELP While the Help feature is active, you can press Help (F1 or F3) again to display a keyboard template that lists the function key assignments. This screen is shown in Figure 1-8. Initially, the template for Enhanced-style keyboards is displayed, but you can type **1** to view the XT-style keyboard template. If you want to display a list of the Fast Keys, type **2** instead.

FUNCTION KEY HELP If you are already familiar with the keys and their feature assignments, you can bypass the feature index, and display full-screen help information. From the main Help screen, press a function key or a Fast Key to display information about the use of the key. For example, assume you want to know more

```
LetterPerfect 1.0 Template (Enhanced Layout)
   ┌──F1──────┬──F2──────┬──F3──────────┬──F4──────┐    Legend:
   │ Shell    │ Spell    │ Line Draw    │ Move     │    Ctrl + Function Key
   │ SETUP    │ ←SEARCH  │              │ →INDENT← │    SHIFT + FUNCTION KEY
   │ Thesaurus│ Replace  │ Reveal Codes │ Block    │    Alt + Function Key
   │Cancel/Help│ →Search │ Help         │ →Indent  │    Function Key alone
   └──────────┴──────────┴──────────────┴──────────┘

              ┌──F5──────┬──F6──────────┬──F7──────┬──F8──────┐
              │ Text Out │ Tab Align    │ Endnote  │ Font     │
              │DATE/OUTLINE│ CENTER     │ PRINT    │ FORMAT   │
              │          │ Flush Right  │          │ Language │
              │List Files│ Bold         │ Exit     │ Underline│
              └──────────┴──────────────┴──────────┴──────────┘

                        ┌──F9──────┬──F10─────┬──F11────────┬──F12─────┐
                        │ Merge    │          │             │          │
                        │MERGE CODES│ RETRIEVE │             │          │
                        │ Graphics │          │             │          │
                        │End Field │ Save     │Reveal Codes │ Block    │
                        └──────────┴──────────┴─────────────┴──────────┘

  Press 1 to view the PC/XT keyboard template          Press 2 for Fast Key list
  Press F7 to exit Help.   Press ENTER for Help List.
```

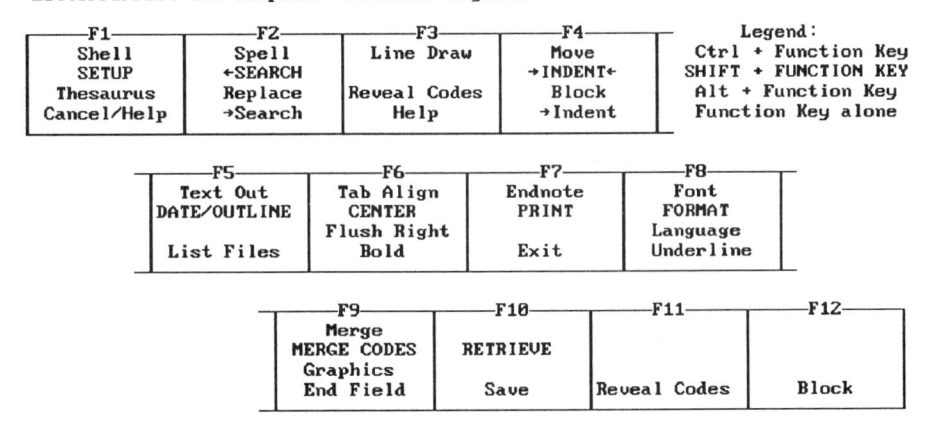

FIGURE 1-8. The Help template

about the F10 key; press Help (F1 or F3) from the main document screen. Now press Save (F10), and a full-screen help message appears and explains how to use the Save feature. This will work for most keys on the keyboard, including the cursor movement keys. Press Exit (F7) or the SPACEBAR to exit the Help system and return to the document editing screen.

Context-Sensitive Help

LetterPerfect provides *context-sensitive help* for most features. This means that if you are performing an action in the program, and you want to know more information about the features, you can press Help (F1 or F3) to get immediate help. When you are finished reading the help information, press Exit (F7) or SPACEBAR to return to the feature that you were using before you selected Help.

For example, assume you are at the main document screen. You can display the Search pull-down menu, highlight the Go To option, and then press Help (F1 or F3), to display a Help screen about the highlighted feature. This also works for any other displayed menu; press the Help key, and LetterPerfect will display a Help screen about the current menu or feature.

Contacting WordPerfect Customer Support

As you use LetterPerfect, you may encounter a problem that you cannot solve. Perhaps your printer is not working correctly or the cursor is not responding to the movement of your mouse. The WordPerfect Customer Support Group can help you find the answers you need. Toll-free telephone support is available to all registered users of LetterPerfect. Simply call the telephone number listed in your LetterPerfect manual; for best results, call from a touchtone phone.

The support operator may ask you for the registration number from your LetterPerfect package, so keep it nearby. If you entered your registration number when you first installed and started LetterPerfect, you can press Help (F1 or F3) and it will appear at the top of your screen with the release date for your copy of LetterPerfect.

Before you call, make sure you've done everything you can to solve the problem on your own. If you still can't find a solution, make sure you have enough information about your computer equipment and software; this will enable the support operator to find a solution to the problem.

EXITING THE PROGRAM

LetterPerfect's Exit feature can perform two tasks: it can save the displayed document and clear the screen, and it can exit LetterPerfect. Both features are important for managing the program. Here are the steps for exiting LetterPerfect:

1. Press Exit (F7), or select **File** from the pull-down menu bar and choose Exit.

2. LetterPerfect prompts you with "Save Document? Yes (No)". In this case, type **N** or click on "No" to exit without saving.

3. LetterPerfect now prompts you with "Exit LP? No (Yes)". Type **Y**, or click on "Yes," to exit the program. If you had selected No instead of Yes, LetterPerfect would have cleared the screen and reset the program options to the standard settings.

note If you select Yes instead of No when prompted about saving the document, LetterPerfect gives you the opportunity to save your document before you exit. If you have not made any changes since the last time the document was saved, the message "Text was not modified" appears on the status line. This tells you that the document, in its current form, is already saved on your disk.

It is very important that you exit LetterPerfect when you are finished using the program. Each time you start LetterPerfect, the program opens *overflow files* that help the program manage information. LetterPerfect closes and deletes these files when you exit the program properly.

If you do not exit correctly, the overflow files remain open and waste space on your disk. Also, when you start LetterPerfect again, you may see the message "Are other copies of LetterPerfect currently running? (Y/N)". This message appears because LetterPerfect finds the open overflow files on your disk and assumes that another copy of LetterPerfect is already running. When this occurs, simply type **N** for No and continue the steps for starting the program.

SUMMARY

This chapter is your introduction to LetterPerfect. You've learned how to start the LetterPerfect program and use the keyboard to type text and move the cursor. You also know how to use the mouse to select menu items. You have created and printed a simple document, and you learned how to save and retrieve document files. These basic tasks form the foundation for the next chapter, "Creating a Document Layout."

chapter 2

CREATING A DOCUMENT LAYOUT

Formatting with Codes
Changing Your Margins
Selecting a Paper Size
Centering Text on the Page
Justification and Line Spacing
Paragraph Indents and Tab Settings
Adding Page Numbers
Adding Page Headers and Footers
Document Pagination
Exercise: Creating a Résumé
Summary

LetterPerfect's unique text formatting system allows you complete control over the layout of your documents. But, like many things that give you full control, this system can be overwhelming until you understand a few basic concepts. If you've never used LetterPerfect or WordPerfect, this chapter will help you become familiar with the concepts of document formatting. You will also learn how to indent your paragraphs, add page numbers, and construct page headers and footers.

FORMATTING WITH CODES

When you first install the LetterPerfect program, *default* or standard program settings determine what the margins, paper size, line spacing, and tabular settings will be for the printed page. This is good because it saves you the trouble of setting up a new layout each time you want to create a document. The default layout includes one-inch margins on each side of the page, single line spacing, and text that is aligned at the left margin, with the document printed on 8.5" x 11" paper. You don't need to worry about these format settings, unless you want something other than the standard layout.

When you do want to select a different setting for your document layout—different line spacing, for instance—the change must be made at the place in the text where the new format should occur. You do this by moving the text cursor to the location where the new margins, line spacing, or tab settings should begin, and then selecting the desired feature from the LetterPerfect menus. Format changes are inserted into your text as *invisible codes* that can be displayed and edited from a special window on the screen. Press Reveal Codes (CTRL-R or ALT-F3) to display the window that shows the codes in your document. Only the text that falls after a code is affected by the format change. Press Reveal Codes again to return to the normal document display.

When you select the format settings, you need to consider what the change should affect. The position of your cursor is very important when selecting certain features. If, for example, you change your top margin when your cursor is in the middle of a page, that format won't go into effect until the beginning of the next page. Format settings such as top/bottom margins, paper sizes, page headers/footers, and page numbering must be selected while you are at the top of the page. Left/right margins, tab settings, line spacing, justification, font changes, paragraph indents, text attributes, and text alignment must be selected immediately before the text they should affect.

For example, suppose your document should be single-spaced, with the exception of one paragraph, which should be double-spaced. Since the standard layout already includes the single line spacing, you need to change the spacing for only one paragraph. To do this, you must move the text cursor to the beginning of that paragraph and use the Format menu to select double line spacing. When you do so, an invisible code is inserted into the text that tells LetterPerfect to double-space everything that lies beneath the current cursor position.

If you want the double spacing to affect only the one paragraph, you must move the text cursor to the end of that paragraph and select single line spacing. This inserts another invisible code that directs LetterPerfect to resume with single-spaced text. Figure 2-1 shows how this example would appear on your screen.

This method of formatting is not difficult, but it does require a bit of practice. Generally, it's best to begin your document layout by defining the margins and the

Chapter 2   Creating a Document Layout   37

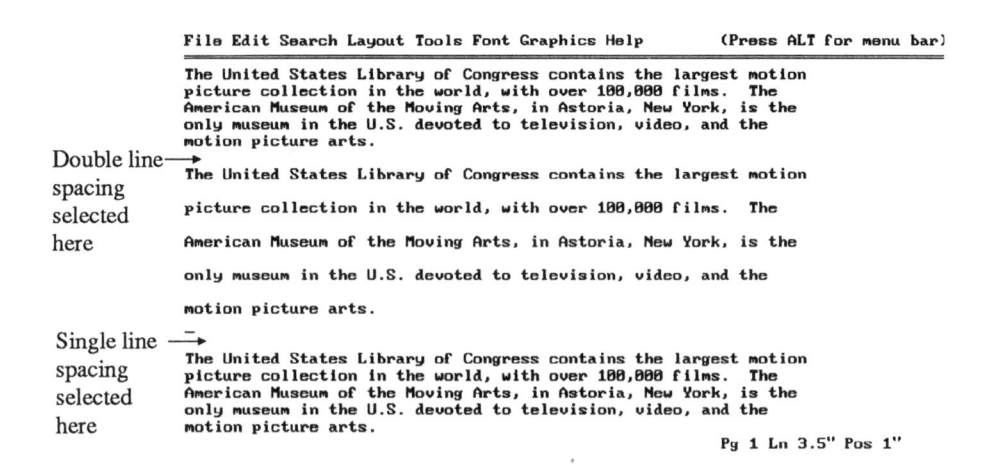

```
 File Edit Search Layout Tools Font Graphics Help     (Press ALT for menu bar)
```
                    The United States Library of Congress contains the largest motion
                    picture collection in the world, with over 100,000 films. The
                    American Museum of the Moving Arts, in Astoria, New York, is the
                    only museum in the U.S. devoted to television, video, and the
                    motion picture arts.
Double line ──▶
spacing   The United States Library of Congress contains the largest motion
selected
here   picture collection in the world, with over 100,000 films. The

                    American Museum of the Moving Arts, in Astoria, New York, is the

                    only museum in the U.S. devoted to television, video, and the

                    motion picture arts.

Single line ──▶
spacing   The United States Library of Congress contains the largest motion
selected   picture collection in the world, with over 100,000 films. The
here   American Museum of the Moving Arts, in Astoria, New York, is the
                    only museum in the U.S. devoted to television, video, and the
                    motion picture arts.
                                                              Pg 1 Ln 3.5" Pos 1"

FIGURE 2-1.   Inserting codes to change the line spacing

paper size that you want. Then, select the line spacing and tab settings. You do not always need to define each format setting; select only those features that will differ from the standard settings. If the format you want is already included in the standard layout, you do not need to redefine it.

In the following sections, you will create new margin settings, select a paper size, add page numbers, and adjust other format settings. After you choose each format command, you can press Reveal Codes (CTRL-R or ALT-F3) at the document screen to see the code in your text; press Reveal Codes again to return to the normal display.

Before you begin, you should clear the screen by pressing Exit (F7) and typing **n** twice to indicate that you want to exit the current document, but remain in Letter-Perfect. Once the screen is clear, you're ready to create a new document layout.

CHANGING YOUR MARGINS

The margin settings determine how much space is allowed between the edges of the paper and the text in your document, as shown in Figure 2-2. The standard settings are one-inch margins on each side of the page, but you can change them by following the instructions in this section.

Defining Top and Bottom Margins

Top and bottom margins can be changed as often as you like, but when you select this feature, the text cursor must be at the top of the page where the change should begin. Follow these steps to change the top and bottom margins:

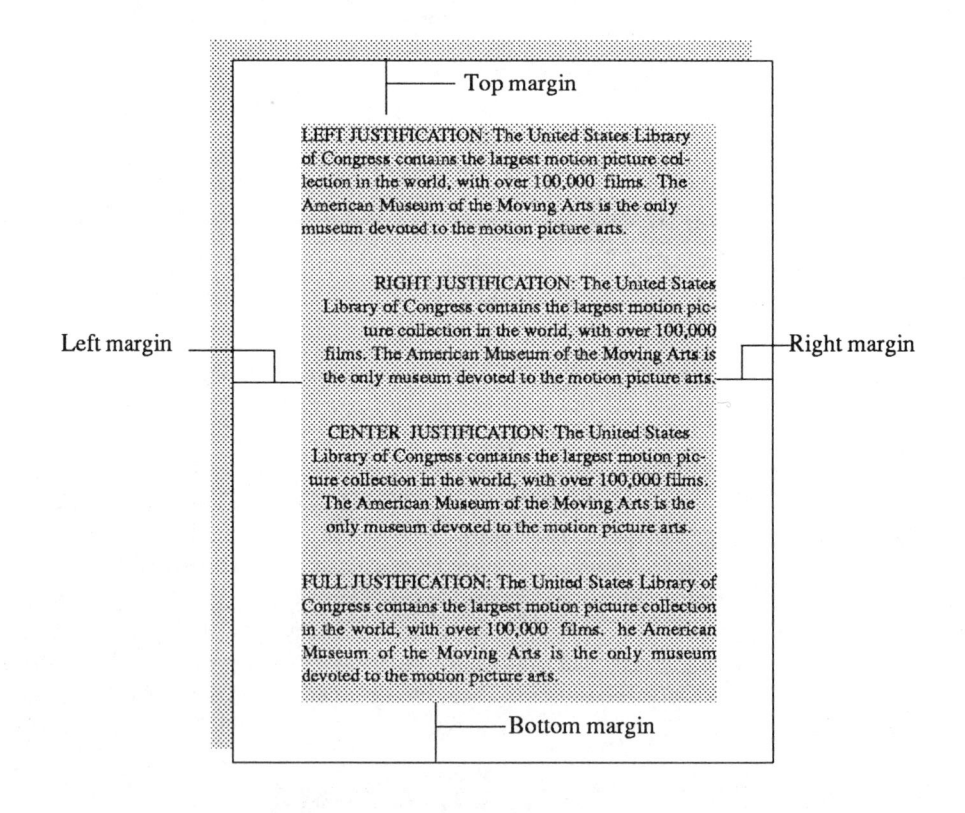

FIGURE 2-2. Margins create space at the top, bottom, and sides

Chapter 2 — Creating a Document Layout

1. Move the text cursor to the beginning of your document, or to the beginning of the page where the new top and bottom margins should begin.

2. Press Format (SHIFT-F8), or choose Format from the Layout pull-down menu. This displays the Format menu, as shown in Figure 2-3.

3. Select option **3**, Top/Bottom Margins, and the cursor moves to the entry for the top margin.

4. Type a measurement for the top margin and press ENTER. The cursor moves to the entry for the bottom margin. Type the measurement for the bottom margin and press ENTER. For example, if you wanted to change the margins to 0.75", you would enter **0.75** for both margins.

5. Press Exit (F7), or click the right mouse button, to return to the main document editing screen.

Notice that the new top margin is displayed after the Ln label on the status line. The top and bottom margins will remain in effect from the current cursor position until you change them again.

```
Format

        1 - Justification                      Left

        2 - Line Spacing                       1

        3 - Top/Bottom Margins                 1"        1"

        4 - Left/Right Margins                 1"        1"

        5 - Tabs                               Rel; -1", every 0.5"

        6 - Header/Footer

        7 - Page Numbering                     No page numbering

        8 - Paper Size                         8.5" x 11"
                Type                           Standard

        9 - Center Page (top to bottom)        No

        I - Document Initial Codes/Base Font   Courier 10cpi

Selection: 0
```

FIGURE 2-3. The LetterPerfect Format menu

Defining Left and Right Margins

You can change the left and right margins as often as you wish, but the text cursor must be at the left margin before you select the command. If you change left and right margins when the cursor is in the middle of a line or paragraph, LetterPerfect will automatically add a hard return and wrap the text cursor to the next line. So, before you try to change margins, make sure the cursor is at the beginning of a new line. Follow these steps to change the left and right margins:

1. Move the text cursor to the beginning of the line where the new left and right margins should begin.

2. Press Format (SHIFT-F8), or choose Format from the Layout pull-down menu. This displays the Format menu.

3. Select option 4, Left/Right Margins, and the cursor moves next to the entry for the left margin.

4. Type the measurement for the left margin and press ENTER. The cursor moves to the right margin option. Type the measurement for the right margin and press ENTER. Remember, higher numbers create more space between the edges of the paper and your text; lower numbers decrease the amount of space.

5. Press Exit (F7), or click the right mouse button, to return to the main document editing screen.

Notice that the new left margin is displayed after the Pos label on the status line. Now, all the text that lies below the cursor will be formatted with the new left and right margins. These margin settings will affect the text that is after the current cursor location.

Centimeters, Points, and WordPerfect Units

When you change the margins, or other format settings, it is assumed that you are entering the measurement in inches. However, you can specify a different unit of measurement by adding one of four letters to the end of the number you type. These letters are: **c** for centimeters, **p** for typesetting points, **u** for WordPerfect 4.2 units, and **w** for "WordPerfect Units"—roughly the equivalent of 1200ths of an inch.

Simply type one of these letters at the end of the number, and LetterPerfect converts it to the equivalent inch measurement.

For example, assume you want to define a margin of three centimeters. You would select the appropriate margin feature, type **3c**, and press ENTER to accept the measurement. The letter *c* tells LetterPerfect that you want the inch equivalent of three centimeters. LetterPerfect converts the centimeter measurement into inches and displays the result as the margin.

> *note:* You can use the Choose Units of Measure feature from the LetterPerfect Setup menu to permanently change the measurement type for all LetterPerfect menus. See Appendix A for more information about defining this program option.

SELECTING A PAPER SIZE

Several predefined *forms*, or paper sizes, are available for your documents. The paper size determines the dimensions of the page, and makes it possible for Letter-Perfect to format and print your document for a specific size of paper.

Figure 2-4 shows a few examples of the supported paper types. The standard paper size is 8.5" x 11"—the size of a business letter. However, you can select new sizes to create layouts for envelopes, labels, and legal-sized documents. There are over 14 paper sizes that LetterPerfect directly supports; however, the number of paper sizes that you can select depends on the types of forms that your printer can handle. For some printers, you can create your own paper sizes for the less-common form types.

> *note:* LetterPerfect stores its paper size definitions in a forms resource file called {LP}SPC.FRM, while WordPerfect stores forms information in its printer drivers (files with a .PRS extension). If you copied printer drivers from Word-Perfect 5.1 to the LetterPerfect program directory or diskette, the information in the forms resource file is ignored. Instead, you will have the paper sizes that were defined for the WordPerfect 5.1 printers.

Selecting a New Paper Size

The Paper Size feature is found on the LetterPerfect Format menu. Before you select a new paper size, you should move the text cursor to the top of the document or to the top of the page that should be printed on the new paper size. You can select

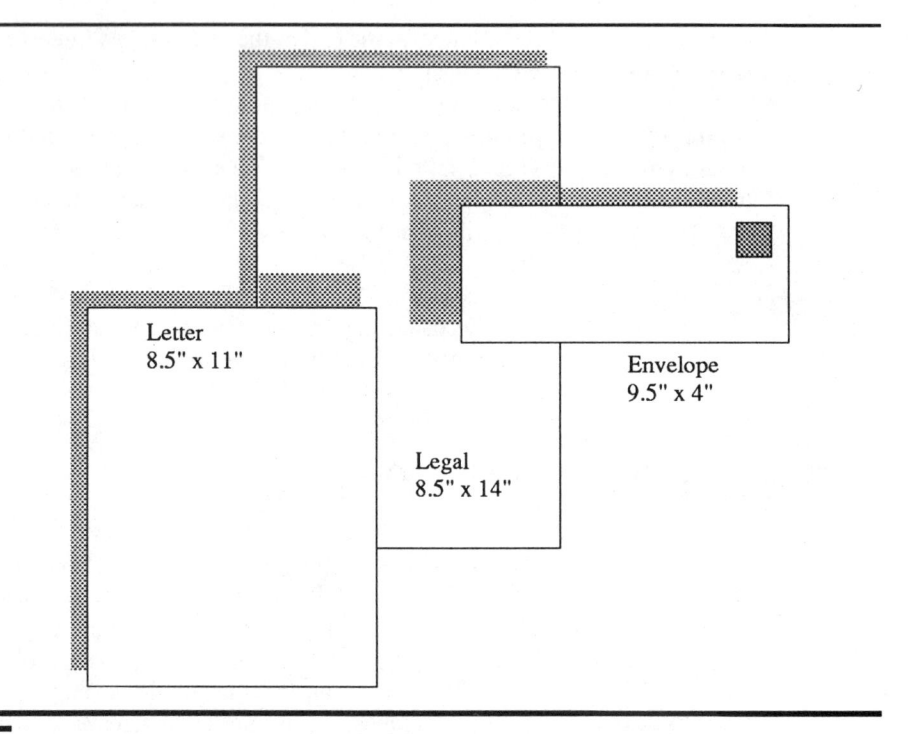

[Figure: Letter 8.5" x 11", Legal 8.5" x 14", Envelope 9.5" x 4"]

FIGURE 2-4. Paper types supported by LetterPerfect

as many paper sizes as you wish, but remember to insert each one at the beginning of the page it should affect. The following steps show how to select a new paper size for your document:

1. Move the text cursor to the beginning of your document, or to the beginning of the page that should be formatted with the new paper size.

2. Press Format (SHIFT-F8) or choose Format from the Layout pull-down menu.

3. Select option **8**, Paper Size/Type. The Paper Size/Type screen appears and lists the paper sizes that are currently available for your printer. Figure 2-5 shows how your screen may appear.

4. Use the cursor arrow keys to move the reversed bar down to the paper size you want, and choose option **1**, Select, from the menu at the bottom of the screen. Or, if you are using a mouse, move the mouse pointer to the paper size you want and double-click the left mouse button.

Chapter 2   Creating a Document Layout   43

5. The Format menu is redisplayed. Press Exit (F7) to return to the document editing screen. You may not notice the new size, but you can view the entire page with the View Document feature.

6. To view the new paper size, press Print (SHIFT-F7), or select File and then choose Print from the pull-down menu. The Print menu is displayed. Select option 3, View Document.

note: You can also press the Preview Fast Key, CTRL-P, from the main document screen, to display the View Document screen.

The current page is displayed with the dimensions of the new paper size. Any existing text is reformatted to fit the new measurements. For example, if you select a legal-sized paper, 14" x 8.5", as the new paper size, your document might look like Figure 2-6. When you are finished viewing the page, press Exit (F7) or click the right mouse button, to return to the main editing screen.

Format: Paper Size/Type

Reversed bar

Paper type and Orientation	Paper Size	Location	Font Type	Labels
3 X 10 Labels	8.5" x 11"	Continuous	Portrait	3 x 10
4 X 1 Labels - Wide	4" x 1"	Continuous	Portrait	1 x 1
A4 Envelopes - Wide	8.58" x 4.33"	Manual	Landscape	
A4 Labels	8.27" x 11.69"	Continuous	Portrait	2 x 7
A4 Standard	8.27" x 11.69"	Continuous	Portrait	
A4 Standard - Wide	11.69" x 8.27"	Continuous	Landscape	
Envelope - Wide	9.5" x 4"	Manual	Landscape	
Half Sheet	5.5" x 8.5"	Continuous	Portrait	
Half Sheet - Wide	8.5" x 5.5"	Manual	Landscape	
Standard	8.22" x 12"	Continuous	Portrait	
Standard	8.5" x 11"	Continuous	Portrait	
Standard	8.5" x 14"	Continuous	Portrait	
Standard - Wide	11" x 8.5"	Continuous	Landscape	
Standard - Wide	14" x 8.5"	Continuous	Landscape	
[ALL OTHERS]	Width ≤ 8.5"	Manual		

1 Select; 2 Edit; N Name Search: 1

FIGURE 2-5.   Forms are listed on the Paper Size/Type screen

FIGURE 2-6. Viewing the legal landscape paper type

Paper Size and Page Orientation

The paper size also determines the *orientation* of the page. If "Wide" appears after the paper size name (that is, "Envelope – Wide"), then the text will be printed sideways by the printer. This is called printing with *landscape* orientation. Normal printing is referred to as *portrait* orientation. Figure 2-7 shows examples of portrait and landscape printing.

Not all printers can print with landscape orientation. For example, you may select a "Wide" paper size, and discover that your dot-matrix printer still prints with portrait orientation. In this case, try feeding your paper sideways into the printer. This may help you get the desired results when your printer does not support landscape printing.

Creating Your Own Paper Size

If you need to print on paper that has a width or length of less than 8.5 inches, you will need to create your own paper size. This is done from the Paper Size/Type

Chapter 2   Creating a Document Layout   45

screen. Assume that you need to print on 3" x 5" index cards. Clear the screen, and then follow these steps to create your own paper size:

> **note** If you create a paper size as described in the following steps, the form information is stored with your document, and not with the forms resource file ({LP}SPC.FRM) or the printer file (.PRS).

1. Press Format (SHIFT-F8) or choose **Format** from the Layout pull-down menu. The Format menu is displayed.

2. Select option **8**, Paper Size/Type, to display the Paper Size/Type screen.

3. Use the cursor arrow keys to move the reversed bar to the "[ALL OTHERS]" paper size definition. If you are using a mouse, simply move the mouse pointer to the "[ALL OTHERS]" definition, and double-click the left mouse button.

4. A message appears at the bottom of the screen that prompts you to enter a width measurement for the new paper size. Figure 2-8 shows the message. Type **5** and press ENTER to indicate a width of five inches. Then, you are prompted to enter the height. Type **3.5** and press ENTER.

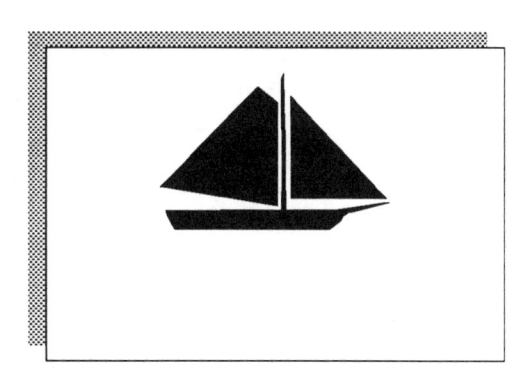

Portrait

Landscape

FIGURE 2-7.   Portrait and landscape orientation

46 LetterPerfect Made Easy

5. Next, you are prompted with "Other form type: ". This asks you to type a name to identify the paper size. Type **Index Card** and press ENTER.

6. The Format menu reappears, and the paper size that you created is listed next to the menu entry. Press Exit (F7) to return to the main document editing screen.

7. To view the new paper size, press Print (SHIFT-F7), or select **File** and then choose **Print** from the pull-down menus. The Print menu is displayed. Select option **3**, **View Document**.

The page is displayed with the new paper size. When you are finished viewing the page, press Exit (F7) to return to the document editing screen. Now, you can enter the text for the index card. When you print the document, LetterPerfect will pause at the Printer Control screen, and prompt you to insert the correct paper into your printer. Then, you can press G for **Go** to continue printing.

PAPER SIZE RESTRICTIONS When you enter sizes for the width and height of the new paper size, take into account the current margin settings. Letter-Perfect won't let you select a paper size that would cause overlapping margins. For example, if the left and right margins are both set at one inch, you can't define a paper width of two inches or less; after subtracting the space allowed for margins, there

```
Format: Paper Size/Type

Paper type and Orientation    Paper Size        Location     Font Type    Labels

3 X 10 Labels                 8.5" x 11"        Continuous   Portrait     3 x 10
4 X 1 Labels - Wide           4" x 1"           Continuous   Portrait     1 x 1
A4 Envelopes - Wide           8.58" x 4.33"     Manual       Landscape
A4 Labels                     8.27" x 11.69"    Continuous   Portrait     2 x 7
A4 Standard                   8.27" x 11.69"    Continuous   Portrait
A4 Standard - Wide            11.69" x 8.27"    Continuous   Landscape
Envelope - Wide               9.5" x 4"         Manual       Landscape
Half Sheet                    5.5" x 8.5"       Continuous   Portrait
Half Sheet - Wide             8.5" x 5.5"       Manual       Landscape
Standard                      8.22" x 12"       Continuous   Portrait
Standard                      8.5" x 11"        Continuous   Portrait
Standard                      8.5" x 14"        Continuous   Portrait
Standard - Wide               11" x 8.5"        Continuous   Landscape
Standard - Wide               14" x 8.5"        Continuous   Landscape
[ALL OTHERS]                  Width ≤ 8.5"      Manual
```

Width measurement

Width: 8.5"

FIGURE 2-8.   Creating a new paper size

would be no room for the text. This is one case where you must set new margins before you create the desired paper size.

You can select any size you want for the width or the height measurement, but you cannot create a paper size where both are greater than 8.5 inches. If you have WordPerfect 5.1 and you need to create a paper size where both measurements are greater than 8.5 inches, you must use the Paper Size/Type features of WordPerfect to create the size you want. Then, copy your WordPerfect printer file for use with LetterPerfect. Refer to Appendix C, "Information for WordPerfect Users," for more information on sharing printer files.

CENTERING TEXT ON THE PAGE

When you create brief documents, such as memos and letters, your text may not fill the entire page. If your text fills less than half the page, it will look unbalanced when printed. Fortunately, LetterPerfect includes a feature called "Center Page, Top to Bottom." This feature vertically centers your text on the page, so that the space above and below the text is more uniform.

To select this feature, first move to the top of the page, before the text. Press Format (SHIFT-F8), or choose Format from the Layout pull-down menu. Choose option **9**, Center Page (top to bottom), and then type **Y** for Yes to center the text vertically on the page. Finally, press Exit (F7) or click the right mouse button to return to your document. The actual text adjustment is made at the printer, so you won't see a difference until you view or print the document.

JUSTIFICATION AND LINE SPACING

Justification is a typesetting term that has been adopted into the world of word processing. In LetterPerfect, justification controls how words are distributed on a line. LetterPerfect also allows you to change the line spacing for all text or just one section of text. The Justification and Line Spacing features are both found on the LetterPerfect Format menu.

Changing the Text Justification

Figure 2-9 shows the four types of justification that you can choose for your documents. Left-justified text is aligned at the left margin, and the text lines wrap naturally near the right margin. Right-justified text is aligned at the right margin, with *ragged* text on the left. Center justification centers each line of text between the left and right margins, even when the text appears in paragraph form. Finally, full justification stretches each line so that the text extends to each margin; this produces a perfectly straight edge of text at both the left and right margins.

You can apply these formats to the entire text, or combine two or more types at different places in your document. Left justification is the standard LetterPerfect setting, but you can follow these steps to select a different type:

1. Move the text cursor to the top of the document, or to the place in the text where the new justification setting should take effect.

2. Press Format (SHIFT-F8), or select **F**ormat from the Layout pull-down menu.

3. Choose option **1**, **J**ustification, from the Format menu. This menu appears at the bottom of the screen:

    Justification: 1 Left; 2 Center; 3 Right; 4 Full: 0

LEFT JUSTIFICATION: The United States Library of Congress contains the largest motion picture collection in the world, with over 100,000 films. The American Museum of the Moving Arts is the only museum devoted to the motion picture arts.

RIGHT JUSTIFICATION: The United States Library of Congress contains the largest motion picture collection in the world, with over 100,000 films. The American Museum of the Moving Arts is the only museum devoted to the motion picture arts.

CENTER JUSTIFICATION: The United States Library of Congress contains the largest motion picture collection in the world, with over 100,000 films. The American Museum of the Moving Arts is the only museum devoted to the motion picture arts.

FULL JUSTIFICATION: The United States Library of Congress contains the largest motion picture collection in the world, with over 100,000 films. The American Museum of the Moving Arts is the only museum devoted to the motion picture arts.

FIGURE 2-9.   Types of text justification

4. For this example, select **4 Full**, to specify full justification. Then, press Exit (F7), or click the left mouse button, to return to the document screen.

All text that lies after the current cursor position, where full justification was selected, will extend to both the left and right margins. The effect of the Full Justification option is not visible at the regular document screen; you must choose the View Document option on the Print menu to see how the justified text will appear.

Changing the Line Spacing

Line spacing controls the vertical spacing of lines in your document, and you can change it as often as you want. Follow these steps to define line spacing for your text:

1. Move the text cursor to the top of the document, or to the place where the new line spacing should begin.

2. Press Format (SHIFT-F8), or select **Format** from the Layout pull-down menu.

3. Choose option **2**, Line Spacing. The cursor moves next to the Line Spacing option; type **2** to indicate double line spacing, and press ENTER. If you want a line spacing other than double, enter the appropriate number. You can enter any number, including decimal numbers such as **0.5**, **1.75**, or **3.5**.

4. Press Exit (F7) or click the right mouse button, to return to the main document screen. If you have text on the screen, you will immediately see the effect.

All text that lies below the current cursor position appears with the new line spacing. This setting remains active until you change it later in the document, or delete the invisible code that defines the format.

PARAGRAPH INDENTS AND TAB SETTINGS

Certain documents require paragraph indentation; this includes tabular indents for the first paragraph line, the indentation of paragraph margins, and hanging indents.

Figure 2-10 shows examples of these. LetterPerfect provides several features that let you create such indents, and it also allows you to redefine the tabular settings. This section explains these and other features.

Indenting with the TAB Key

This is the most common form of indentation—using the TAB key to indent the first line of a paragraph—and it's very easy to do.

1. Move the text cursor to the beginning of the paragraph that you want to indent.

2. Press TAB to indent the first line.

3. Press DOWN ARROW to move the cursor down a few lines. This will reformat the text in the paragraph.

That's all you need to do. If you decide that you want to remove the indent, move the cursor back to the first text character in the paragraph, and press BACKSPACE. This

---

TAB KEY INDENT: The United States Library of Congress contains the largest motion picture collection in the world, with over 100,000 films.

LEFT MARGIN INDENT: The United States Library of Congress contains the largest motion picture collection in the world, with over 100,000 films.

LEFT/RIGHT MARGIN INDENT: The United States Library of Congress contains the largest motion picture collection in the world, with over 100,000 films.

HANGING INDENT: The United States Library of Congress contains the largest motion picture collection in the world, with over 100,000 films.

FIGURE 2-10.   Examples of paragraph indentation

deletes the [Tab] code embedded in the text. If you prefer, you can press Reveal Codes (CTRL-R or ALT-F3) to see exactly where the [Tab] code is located, before you delete it.

Obviously, you can also use the TAB key to set up columns for tables. Later in this section, you'll have the opportunity to create a table with tabular columns.

Indenting Paragraph Margins

The TAB key only indents the first line of a paragraph, but the Left Indent (F4) and Right/Left Indent (SHIFT-F4) keys can indent the margins of an entire paragraph. These features allow you to offset passages of text from the main body of your document.

For example, you can use the Left Indent feature to indicate an item beneath a main topic. The Left/Right Indent is ideal for indenting a quotation from the main text. These steps will show you how to use the Left Indent and Left/Right Indent features:

1. Move the cursor to the beginning of the paragraph that you want to indent.

2. Press Left Indent (F4) to indent only the left margin of the paragraph, or press Left/Right Indent (SHIFT-F4) to indent both margins of the paragraph.

The Indent features are similar to the Tab feature because they use the current tab settings to determine how far to indent the text. You can define your own tab settings to specify different spacing. If you want to remove the paragraph indents, you can do so by moving to the beginning of the paragraph and pressing BACKSPACE to delete the codes.

Creating a Hanging Indent

A hanging indent is a little trickier than a regular paragraph indent. It involves two keystrokes: Left Indent (F4) and Margin Release (SHIFT-TAB). Follow these steps to create a hanging indent for a paragraph:

1. Move the text cursor to the beginning of the paragraph where the hanging indent should occur.

2. Press Left Indent (F4) to create the initial indent for the left margin of the paragraph.

3. Press Margin Release (SHIFT-TAB) to create the hanging indent. When you finish, your paragraph should look similar to this:

HANGING INDENT: The United States Library of Congress contains
    the largest motion picture collection in the world, with
    over 100,000 films.

This particular format can play tricks on your eyes, especially when the text cursor is on the first line of the paragraph. Sometimes it's difficult to tell whether your cursor is on one of the format codes, or actually on the text of the first line. You may want to display the Reveal Codes window when editing a paragraph with a hanging indent.

Defining Tab Settings

Tab settings determine the spacing for tab and paragraph indents, and also the spacing for hanging indents and margin releases. Under the default settings, tabs are predefined at half-inch increments. If you wish, you can define your own tab settings and place them anywhere in your document. This may be necessary if you need to create tables in LetterPerfect.

New tab settings are defined from the Format menu, and are normally set in relation to the left margin of the current document. In other words, if you set a tab at two inches from the left margin, and you later change your margins, the tab will still be located two inches from the left margin. LetterPerfect adjusts the tab positions to match the dimensions of the page, thus preventing some unpleasant surprises if you decide to change your margins.

LetterPerfect also allows you to select four different kinds of tabs: left-aligned, right-aligned, centered tabs, and decimal-aligned. Each type of tab will align text differently on the tab stop. A dot-leader enhancement allows you to insert a line of dots between tab stops. These steps will show you how to define your own tab settings, and will help you create the table shown in Figure 2-11.

1. From a clear LetterPerfect screen, press Format (SHIFT-F8), or select **F**ormat from the Layout pull-down menu.

2. Choose option **5**, **T**abs, from the Format menu. The Tab Set screen is displayed as shown here:

```
L....L....L....L....L....L....L....L....L....L....L....L....L....L....L....L...
!    ^    !    ^    !    ^    !    ^    !    ^    !    ^    !    ^    !    ^
0"       +1"       +2"       +3"       +4"       +5"       +6"       +7"
Delete EOL (clear tabs); Enter Number (set tab); Del (clear tab);
Type; Left; Center; Right; Decimal; .= Dot Leader; Press F7 when done.
```

The tab ruler shows the tabs that are currently set. Each *L* on the tab ruler indicates one left-aligned tab setting. The cursor is on *0*, which represents the left margin.

3. To clear the current tabs, move to the beginning of the tab ruler by pressing HOME, LEFT ARROW. Then, press CTRL-END to delete the tabs from the cursor position to the end of the ruler.

4. Now you're ready to define your own tab settings. To set a new tab, just type the number where the tab should be located and press ENTER. For example, type **3.5** and press ENTER. This sets a left-justified tab at 3.5 inches from the left margin.

5. Type **6** and press ENTER, to set a tab at 6 inches from the left margin. While the cursor is still on this tab, type **R** to change this to a **R**ight-aligned tab. Then, with the cursor still on the tab, type a period (.) to specify that you want a dotted-line, or dot-leader, between this and the previous tab setting.

6. Type **1** and press ENTER to set the next tab. While the cursor is still on the tab, type **C** to change it to a Centered tab. Type **2.5**, press ENTER, and type a **D**, to create a Decimal-aligned tab at 2.5 inches from the left margin.

7. Now you can accept these settings and create your table. Press Exit (F7) twice to return to the document editing screen. Press ENTER a few times to add some space at the top of the page.

8. Press TAB to move to the first column. Any text you type here will be centered over the tab stop, one inch from the left margin. Type the date, **9/8/91**.

9. Press TAB to move to the second column. This tab will align a number according to its decimal point, with the point over the tab stop. Type **23.47** as the first number in this column.

10. Press TAB to move to the third column. This is the left-aligned tab that you set. Type **Software** as the first entry for this column.

11. Press TAB to move to the last column. This is the right-aligned tab that you set. The text entered in this column will be aligned with the right edge at the tab stop. You will also notice a dot-leader between this column and the previous column. This appears because you typed a period when you defined this tab stop. Type **p. 19** as the text for this column.

12. Press ENTER to move to the next line. Using Figure 2-11 as a guide, type the rest of the text for the table. Remember to press TAB at the beginning of each line, to move to the first column.

Editing the Tab Settings

If you want to edit the tab settings that you've created, turn on Reveal Codes (CTRL-R or ALT-F3) and position the text cursor to the right of the [Tab Set:Rel;+1",+2.5",+3.5",+6"] code. Then, select option **5**, **Tabs**, from the Format menu. Figure 2-12 shows how the Tab Set screen should look. The current tab settings are displayed with your text above the tab ruler. You can press UP ARROW or DOWN ARROW to move to the next or previous tab stop on the ruler. With the cursor on a tab stop, you can press CTRL-RIGHT ARROW or CTRL-LEFT ARROW to reposition the tab. Or, press BACKSPACE to delete the tab.

As you make adjustments, the text above the tab ruler will move to show you the new tab settings. When you are finished editing the tabs, press Exit (F7) twice to

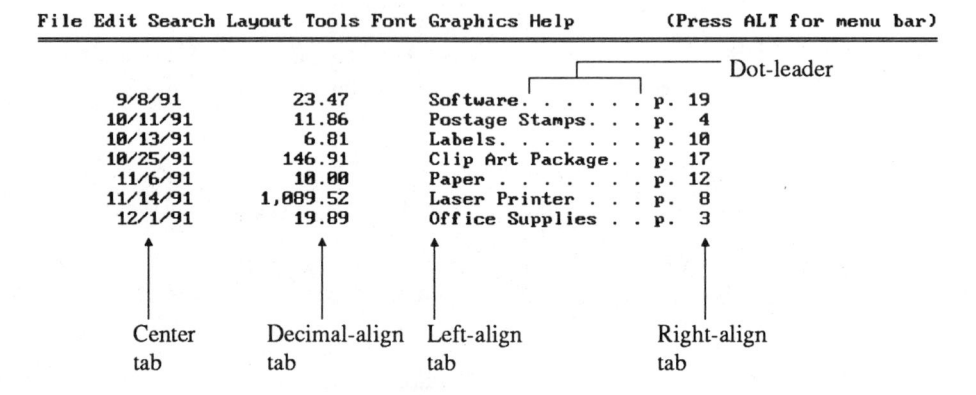

```
File Edit Search Layout Tools Font Graphics Help      (Press ALT for menu bar)
```
                                                                    ┌─── Dot-leader
        9/8/91   23.47   Software. . . . . . p. 19
       10/11/91   11.86   Postage Stamps. . . p. 4
       10/13/91   6.81   Labels. . . . . . . p. 10
       10/25/91   146.91   Clip Art Package. . p. 17
       11/6/91   10.00   Paper . . . . p. 12
       11/14/91   1,089.52   Laser Printer . . . p. 8
       12/1/91   19.89   Office Supplies . . p. 3
          ↑   ↑   ↑   ↑
          | | | |
        Center   Decimal-align Left-align   Right-align
         tab   tab   tab   tab

                                                        Pg 1 Ln 1" Pos 1"

FIGURE 2-11. A sample tabular table

return to the document screen. In the Reveal Codes window, you will see two [Tab Set:] codes. The code on the right contains the latest tab settings; the code on the left contains the old settings and may be deleted. Press Reveal Codes (CTRL-R or ALT-F3) again to restore the normal editing screen.

Setting Absolute Tabs

LetterPerfect usually adjusts the position of tabs when you change the margins of your document. If you wish, you can set the tabs according to absolute positions on the page, so that they are not adjusted for margin changes.

This is done by selecting **T**ype from the menu at the bottom of the Tab Set screen. Another menu appears with these options: **1 A**bsolute; **2 R**elative to Margin. Option 2 is the default for LetterPerfect; you can choose **1 A**bsolute to create tabs that are set according to the left edge of the page, instead of the left margin.

After you select the Absolute option, the tab ruler will change to indicate the new type. Now you can set the tabs that you want for your document. When you are finished, press Exit (F7) twice to return to the document editing screen.

```
     9/8/91          23.47     Software. . . . . . . p. 19
    10/11/91         11.86     Postage Stamps. . . p.  4
    10/13/91          6.81     Labels. . . . . . . . p. 10
    10/25/91        146.91     Clip Art Package. . p. 17
    11/6/91          10.00     Paper . . . . . . . . p. 12
    11/14/91      1,089.52     Laser Printer . . . p.  8
    12/1/91          19.89     Office Supplies . . p.  3
```

```
. . . . . . . . C . . . . . . . . . . . D . . . . . . . . L . . . . . . . . . . . . . . . . . . R . . . . . . . . . . . . . . .
!     ^     !     ^     !     ^     !     ^     !     ^     !     ^     !     ^     !     ^
0"        +1"        +2"        +3"        +4"        +5"        +6"        +7"
Delete EOL (clear tabs); Enter Number (set tab); Del (clear tab);
Type; Left; Center; Right; Decimal; .= Dot Leader; Press Exit when done.
```

FIGURE 2-12. Editing the tab settings

ADDING PAGE NUMBERS

It's easy to add page numbering to your document. Simply select where you want the page number to appear, and LetterPerfect automatically numbers the printed pages. Follow these steps to add page numbering to your document:

1. Move the text cursor to the top of the page where page numbering should begin.

2. Press Format (SHIFT-F8), or choose Format from the Layout pull-down menu. The Format menu is displayed.

3. Select option **7**, **P**age Numbering, from the Format menu. The Page Numbering screen, shown in Figure 2-13, appears. The numbers in the diagram represent the possible locations for page numbering: (**1**) top left, (**2**) top center, (**3**) top right, (**4**) bottom left, (**5**) bottom center, and (**6**) bottom right. The last option, **7** No Page Numbering, discontinues the numbering.

4. Type the number that indicates the page number position you want. For example, if you want the page numbers centered at the bottom of each page, select option **5** (bottom center).

5. The Format menu reappears, and the new page number position is displayed next to its entry on the menu. Press Exit (F7) or click the right mouse button to return to the main document editing screen.

The page numbers are not visible at the normal editing screen, but will be printed with the document pages. If you want to see the page numbers before you send your document to the printer, select the View Document option on the Print menu or simply press CTRL-P. While the View Document screen is displayed, you can press PGUP and PGDN to view each page.

You can discontinue page numbering by moving the text cursor to the bottom of the last page that should contain page numbering, and then choosing option **7** from the Page Numbering screen. However, unlike WordPerfect, you cannot display the page numbers as Roman numerals, and you cannot restart page numbering with a different number.

ADDING PAGE HEADERS AND FOOTERS

Many documents include running *headers* at the top of each page. Most books, for example, include headers to identify the name of the book and the title of the

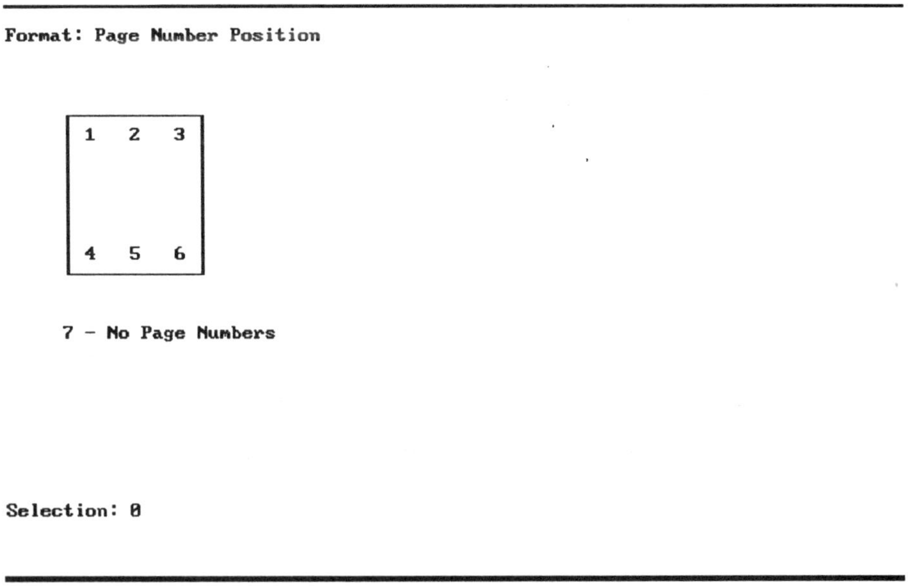

```
Format: Page Number Position

        ┌─────────────┐
        │ 1   2   3   │
        │             │
        │             │
        │ 4   5   6   │
        └─────────────┘

     7 - No Page Numbers




Selection: 0
```

FIGURE 2-13. The Page Numbering screen

current chapter. *Footers* are similar to headers, except they appear at the bottom of each page, rather than at the top.

LetterPerfect allows you to create one header and one footer per document page. You can define as many headers or footers as you want, but you can only display one of each on a single page. Headers and footers may contain a chapter or document title, page numbers, or other information that should appear at the top or bottom of each page. Since headers and footers are completely separate from the text in your document, you can select different formats for the headers and footers — such as margins and fonts — than what you've used for the main body of text.

Creating a Header or Footer

These steps will show you how to create a header in your document. To create a footer, select **2 F**ooter, instead of **1 H**eader, in step 4.

1. Move the text cursor to the beginning of your document, or to the top of the page where the header should begin.

2. Press Format (SHIFT-F8), or select Format from the Layout pull-down menu, to display the Format menu.

3. From the Format menu, choose option 6, Header/Footer. This menu appears at the bottom of the screen:

   ```
   Header: 2 Footer; 3 Suppress: 0
   ```

4. Choose 1 Header, and then select 2 Create, to create a header for your document. An editing screen appears, which is similar to the document editing screen.

5. Now, you can type text and insert formatting codes to create the document header. Remember, this information will appear at the top of every page in your document. After you have typed the text, press Exit (F7) twice to return to the document editing screen.

The header that you create will not be visible until you print the document or view it from the View Document screen. When you create a header or footer, Letter-Perfect will display it on every page, automatically adjusting the page to give the space needed for the header or footer text. An extra line space is added between the header or footer and the text on the page.

Most headers and footers are only one line long. In LetterPerfect, you can include as many lines as you need, but no header or footer can be longer than one page of text.

Page Numbering with Headers or Footers

The following steps will show you how to create a header with page numbering. When you include page numbering as part of a header or footer, you should *not* use the page numbering commands described in the previous section.

1. Move the text cursor to the beginning of your document, or to the beginning of the first page where the header should begin.

2. Press Format (SHIFT-F8), or select Format from the Layout pull-down menu, to display the Format menu.

3. From the Format menu, choose option 6, Header/Footer. Then, choose 1 Header and select option 2, Create. (Or, for footers, choose 2 Footer.) The editing screen appears for creating headers and footers.

4. Press Center (CTRL-C or SHIFT-F6) to center the text for the header. Then, type **LetterPerfect Document, p.** and press CTRL-V CTRL-B. The finished text should appear as "LetterPerfect Document, p. ^B". The ^B code will be displayed as the current page number on each page where the header appears.

5. Press Exit (F7) twice to return to the document editing screen.

Whenever you view or print the document, the ^B code inserts the current page number in the text of the header. The ^B code will do the same thing when included in a footer or even in regular text.

Turning Off a Header or Footer

The easiest way to turn off a header or footer is to remove the code from your document. You can use the Reveal Codes screen to help you find the code, and press BACKSPACE to delete it.

However, you may want to *suppress* the header or footer, so that it only appears on certain pages of your document. To do this,

1. Move the cursor to the beginning of the page where the header or footer should be discontinued.

2. Press Format (SHIFT-F8) and choose option **6**, Header/Footer, from the Format menu.

3. Select option **3**, Suppress, from the Header/Footer menu.

Another menu appears that lets you choose what you want to suppress: the header, the footer, or both. After you've made a selection, a "suppress" code is inserted into your document, which tells LetterPerfect to stop printing the header or footer.

DOCUMENT PAGINATION

Pagination prepares your document to be printed with the format settings you've defined. Some word processors require you to select a special command that paginates your document after you are finished creating it. Other word processors paginate only when you send your document to the printer.

Fortunately, LetterPerfect is a *document-oriented* word processor. This means that as you type text and insert format commands, LetterPerfect is reformatting the entire document to reflect the changes that you make. Thus, your text lines, indents, and tab settings will be formatted on the screen as they will appear when printed. You won't have to guess where a text line will wrap or where a page will end. LetterPerfect automatically shows these on the screen.

Soft Page Breaks

When the text you are typing fills the current page, LetterPerfect displays a single dotted-line on the screen. Figure 2-14 shows how this will appear. This is called a *soft page break* ([SPg]). "Soft" means that LetterPerfect automatically inserts this command as needed. In other words, LetterPerfect knows when the text fills the current page and inserts a soft page break that can shift with each reformatting of your document. If you add or delete text, LetterPerfect will adjust the placement of the soft page break, so that the page ending will change according to how you manipulate your document. Your text is correctly formatted on the pages no matter what you add or delete.

Hard Page Breaks

Sometimes, you will want to begin the next page even though text does not fill the current page. You can insert a *hard page break* by pressing CTRL-ENTER. This inserts an invisible [HPg] code into your text that is displayed as a double line, as shown in Figure 2-15. This instructs LetterPerfect to end the current page and start the next one. "Hard" means that this command is inserted by the person who creates the document. Unlike the soft page command, the hard page break remains exactly where it is placed in the text. If you add or delete text, the hard page is reformatted with the text preceding it, but the page break always remains where you placed it.

EXERCISE: CREATING A RÉSUMÉ

This exercise will give you some practice with the features discussed in the previous sections. You will create a business résumé and save it to a file on disk. The finished

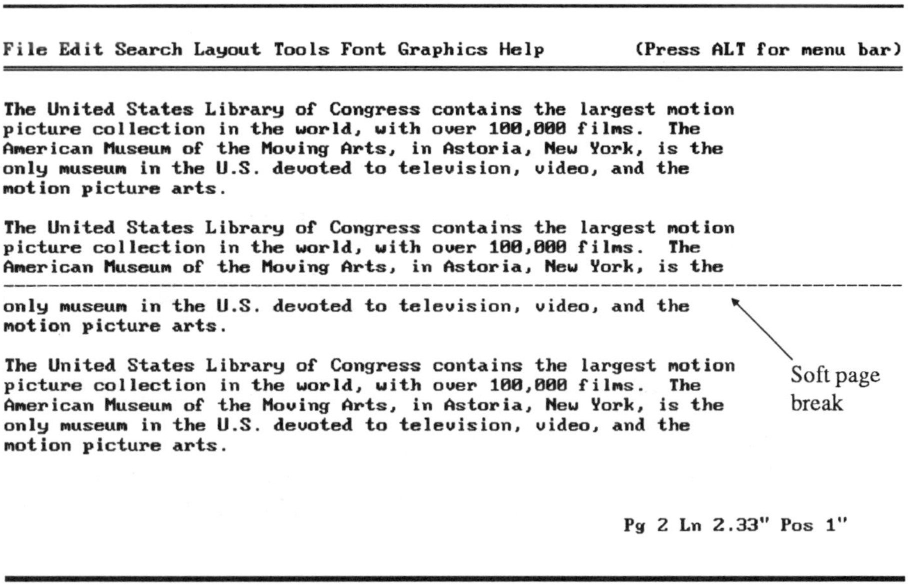

FIGURE 2-14. A soft page break

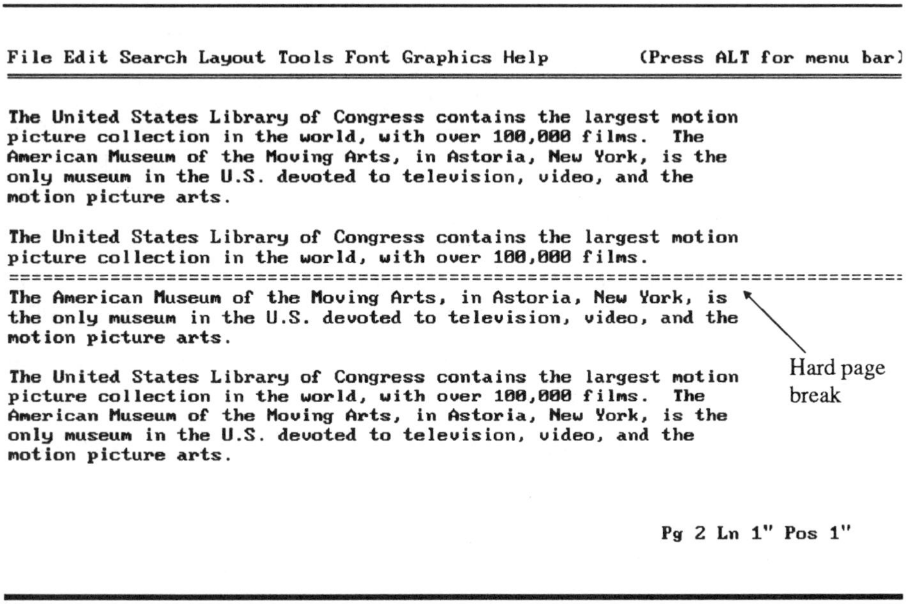

FIGURE 2-15. A hard page break

résumé is shown in Figure 2-16. If you want, you can substitute your own text for the information provided here. Before you begin, make sure you clear the screen.

1. First, you must center the person's name at the top of the page. Press Center (CTRL-C or SHIFT-F6), or choose Center from the Layout pull-down menu. The text cursor moves to the center of the page.

2. Press Bold (CTRL-B or F6), type **WILLIAM J. RATHE**, and press Bold again to turn off the attribute. Press ENTER three times.

3. The next two lines will include Mr. Rathe's address and phone numbers for work and home. Type **92 Spencer Road**.

4. Before you complete the address, you'll enter one of the phone numbers. Press Flush Right (ALT-F6), or select **Flush Right** from the **Layout** pull-down menu. Type **Work: (415) 555-3481**, and press ENTER to move to the next line.

5. Complete the address by typing **Berkeley, CA 94710**. Select the Flush Right feature again, and type the text for the second phone number, **Home: (415) 555-1284**. Press ENTER four times. Your screen should look like Figure 2-17.

6. Now you will define tab settings for the résumé. Press Format (SHIFT-F8) and choose option **5, Tabs**. You can also choose Format from the Layout pull-down menu, and then select **Tabs**.

7. Press HOME, LEFT ARROW and then CTRL-END, to delete the current tab settings. Type **2** and press ENTER to set a tab at the two-inch mark. Type **2.5** and press ENTER to set a tab at 2.5 inches. Press Exit (F7) twice, or click the right mouse button, to return to the document screen.

8. Press Bold (CTRL-B or F6), and type **EDUCATION:** as the first heading in the résumé. Press Bold (CTRL-B or F6) again, to turn off the Bold attribute.

9. Press TAB to move to the first tab stop, and type **University of Calif., Berkeley, CA**. Press ENTER to move to the next line.

10. Press TAB twice to indent the second line beneath the first. Then, type **B.A. - Psychology, 1978**. Press ENTER twice.

11. Press TAB, and type **Ranglin' Bros. Clown College, Orlando, FL**. Press ENTER to move to the next line. Press TAB twice and type **Graduated with Big Top Honors, 1983**. Press ENTER, press TAB twice, and type **Recipient, Golden Bozo Award**. Press ENTER twice.

WILLIAM J. RATHE

92 Spencer Road   Work: (415) 555-3481
Berkeley, CA 94710   Home: (415) 555-1284

EDUCATION: University of Calif., Berkeley, CA
                   B.A. - Psychology, 1978

                   Ranglin' Bros. Clown College, Orlando, FL
                   Graduated with Big Top Honors, 1983
                   Recipient, Golden Bozo Award

                   University of Calif., Los Angeles, CA
                   M.A. - Motion Picture Arts, 1981

EXPERIENCE: PARTY SHACK CATERING, INC., Berkeley, CA
1987 - Present

                   Creative Director, Children's Party Division.
                   Responsible for clowns, jugglers, and trained animal acts.
                   Performance experience as "Spunky the Magic Clown."

1983 - 1987   TRAPP'S BONANZA ARCADE, Orlando, FL

                   Manager, Orlando Group. Responsible for the operation of
                   three successful arcade/pizza parlor restaurants.
                   Implemented new programs for better service and quality,
                   resulting in a 20% increase of revenues during the first year.

1981 - 1982   WESTON COMMUNICATIONS GROUP, Los Angeles, CA

                   Entertainment Critic for radio station, K103.5 FM.
                   Researched clubs, concerts, movies, and swap meets in Los
                   Angeles County area. Presented on-air commentary.

FIGURE 2-16.   The completed résumé

```
File Edit Search Layout Tools Font Graphics Help      (Press ALT for menu bar)
                        WILLIAM J. RATHE

92 Spencer Road                          Work: (415) 555-3481
Berkeley, CA  94710                      Home: (415) 555-1284












                                              Pg 1 Ln 2.33" Pos 1"
```

FIGURE 2-17.   Creating the résumé

12. Press TAB, type **University of Calif., Los Angeles, CA**, and press ENTER to move to the next line. Press TAB twice and type **M.A. - Motion Picture Arts, 1981.** Press ENTER three times to begin the work experience block of text.

13. Press Bold (CTRL-B or F6), and type **EXPERIENCE:** as the second heading in the résumé. Press Bold again to turn off the Bold attribute.

14. Press TAB and type **PARTY SHACK CATERING, INC., Berkeley, CA**. Press ENTER to move to the next line.

15. Type **1987 - Present**, and then press ENTER. Press Left Indent (F4) and type **Creative Director, Children's Party Division. Responsible for clowns, jugglers, and trained animal acts. Performance experience as "Spunky the Magic Clown."** Then, press ENTER twice.

16. Press CTRL-P to preview the résumé at the View Document screen. When you're finished viewing the résumé, press Exit (F7) to return to the document screen.

17. Save the document by pressing Save (F10) or selecting **S**ave from the **F**ile pull-down menu. Type **resume.doc** as the document name, and press ENTER to save the file.

Although this is a simple résumé, you can easily adapt it to suit your own needs. If you wish, finish creating the résumé shown in Figure 2-16. Or, you can substitute the text in this example for information regarding your own education and work experience.

SUMMARY

In this chapter you learned about creating a new document layout. You can now define new margins, select paper sizes for printing, and change tab settings. You also know how to set up page numbering, change headers and footers, line spacing, and justification. You've also created a basic document that may serve as a model for your own résumé, if you choose to make one.

The information in this chapter shows how to select the features that define how your document pages are formatted. In the next chapter, you'll learn about the features that affect the appearance and placement of text.

chapter 3

SPECIAL FEATURES FOR TEXT

Selecting Fonts and Text Attributes
Aligning Text
Using the Date Features
Placing Endnotes into Your Document
Hyphenation
Inserting Special Characters
Summary

Margins, line spacing, tabs, and paper size set the stage for your document. But you don't actually have a document until you type something. Letter-Perfect includes features that let you format and enhance the appearance of your text. You can select different typefaces and choose text attributes, such as boldface and italics. Other features let you align titles and headlines, insert the date, and place endnotes that are automatically numbered and printed at the end of your document.

The following sections will show you how to use the various text features of LetterPerfect. You will learn how to select typefaces, align text, and use the date features. You'll learn about LetterPerfect's hyphenation capabilities, the Characters feature, and you'll insert endnotes into a document.

SELECTING FONTS AND TEXT ATTRIBUTES

If your printer can produce different fonts, LetterPerfect provides the features that let you select them for your documents. Fonts allow you to print your text with different *typefaces*, such as Times Roman, Helvetica, and Courier. Text attributes include enhancements such as boldface, underlining, and italics. Fonts and attributes can help communicate your message and improve the appearance of your documents.

You can select fonts—referred to as *base fonts* in LetterPerfect—and text attributes as often as you need them. These can be applied to any text in your documents, including headers, footers, and endnotes. In this section, you will learn more about the font features of LetterPerfect.

Fonts, Text Attributes, and Your Printer

The number and type of fonts available to you depends on the capabilities of your printer. Text attributes, too, are limited by your printer's abilities. Generally, dot-matrix and ink-jet printers provide limited font capabilities, while most laser printers allow you to use *downloadable soft fonts* from files on diskettes. Regardless of your printer type, LetterPerfect attempts to make full use of the features that your printer supports.

Before you continue with this section, make sure you have installed and selected the correct printer. If you have not already done so, refer to Chapter 7 for more information about setting up a printer for use with LetterPerfect.

Selecting a New Font

Part of creating an attractive document includes the careful use of fonts. Letter-Perfect lets you change the fonts as often as you wish, but make sure you don't overdo it. Common design principles suggest that no more than two or three typefaces should be used in a single document.

Depending on whether you used the function keys or the pull-down menus, the Font menu will appear either at the bottom of the screen, or as a pull-down menu. This is the menu that appears when you press the Font function key:

```
1 Bold; 2 Underline; 3 Normal; 4 Base Font; 5 Italc; 6 Suprscpt; 7 Subscpt: 0
```

and this is the Font menu that appears when you use the pull-down menus:

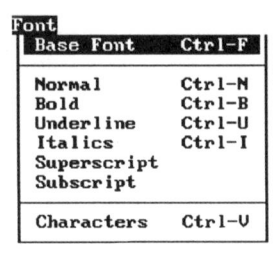

```
Font
 Base Font    Ctrl-F

 Normal       Ctrl-N
 Bold         Ctrl-B
 Underline    Ctrl-U
 Italics      Ctrl-I
 Superscript
 Subscript

 Characters   Ctrl-V
```

When you're ready to select a new font, follow these steps:

1. Move the text cursor to the place in the document where the font change should begin.

2. Press Font (CTRL-F8), or choose Font from the pull-down menu.

3. Select the Base Font option from the menu and a list of the fonts that your printer can produce is displayed. This screen may appear as shown in Figure 3-1. Your font list will be different, depending on your printer's capabilities.

4. Use the arrow keys to move the highlighted bar to the font you want to select and choose option **1**, **S**elect from the menu. If you are using a mouse, you can simply move the mouse pointer to the font you want, and double-click the left mouse button.

note — If you have a PostScript printer installed, you will be prompted to enter a point size, after selecting the font name. A *point* is a typesetting measurement that determines the height of a particular font; there are 72 points per one inch.

After you select the font, you are returned to the document editing screen. Now, the text that lies after the current cursor position will be printed with the new font. LetterPerfect will reformat your text to account for the font change. If you wish, you can select the View Document feature to see how your document will look when printed, but this display is limited. You will need to print the document to check the final results.

The Fast Key for selecting a base font is CTRL-F. You can press this key, instead of Font (CTRL-F8), option **4**, to display and select from a list of available fonts.

```
Base Font
* Courier 10cpi
  Courier 10cpi Bold
  Courier 10cpi Italic
  Courier 12cpi
  Courier 12cpi Bold
  Courier 12cpi Italic
  Line Printer 16.67cpi




1 Select; N Name search: 1
```

FIGURE 3-1. Selecting a base font

Selecting Text Attributes

You can apply different attributes to your text, including bold, underline, italics, superscript, and subscript. When you select a text attribute, it is inserted as a *code pair*. This means that two codes will be placed in your document: the first code turns on the attribute, the second code turns it off.

For example, if you choose the Bold attribute, a pair of codes is inserted as [Bold] [bold] into your document. The cursor is conveniently placed between the codes so you can type the text. Of course, these codes are only visible in the Reveal Codes window, but if you keep your eye on the status line, the number after the Pos label shows the text attributes at the current cursor position.

LetterPerfect will let you select attributes for bold, underline, italics, superscript, and subscript, but your printer must have the ability to produce these attributes before you can actually print them. Follow these steps to choose text attributes:

1. Move your cursor to the place where the new attribute should begin.

2. Press Font (CTRL-F8), or select Font from the pull-down menu. The Font menu appears on the screen.

3. Select one of the attributes—**Bold**, **Underline**, **Italic**, **Superscript**, or **Subscript**.

4. Now, type the text that should be printed with that attribute.

5. When you are finished typing the text, press the RIGHT ARROW key once or twice to move the cursor past the text that you've typed. Or, simply select Normal from the Font menu. This will move the cursor beyond the boundaries of the paired codes, where you can type regular text.

If you are familiar with LetterPerfect's Block feature, you can apply any of these attributes to text that is already in your document. First, press Block (ALT-F4 or F12) to define a section of your text. Then, choose the desired attribute from the Font menu, and the defined text is displayed with that attribute.

There are also keyboard commands that allow you to select text attributes without displaying the Font menu. These keys are Bold (CTRL-B or F6), Underline (CTRL-U or F8), and Italics (CTRL-I). When you press these keys, you select the bold, underline, and italics attributes, just as if you had chosen them from the Font menu. After you type the desired text, you can press the key again to turn off the attribute.

ALIGNING TEXT

Your text is aligned according to the justification setting described in Chapter 2. Left justification is the most common text alignment. However, there will be times when you want to center headlines or align the current date at the right edge of the page. For these situations, you don't want to redefine justification for the entire text, just for one or two lines.

You can use the Center and Flush Right features to center text or align it at the right margin. You can select these features before typing text, or apply them to text that is already in your document.

Centering Text Between Margins

The Center feature positions a line of text precisely between the left and right margins of your document. Before you select this format, move the cursor to a new line. Then press Center (CTRL-C or SHIFT-F6) or choose Center from the Layout pull-down menu. The text cursor will move to the center of the page, where you can type a line of text.

As you type the text, LetterPerfect adjusts the position so that the line is centered between the left and right margins. Press ENTER to end the centered line and move the cursor to the next line.

If you want to center a line of text that is already in your document, move to the beginning of the line and press Center or choose Center from the Layout pull-down menu. The text will appear misaligned, until you press DOWN ARROW to move the cursor to the next line. This will reformat and center the text.

Aligning Text at the Right Margin

The Flush Right feature positions text against the right margin. Make sure you are at the beginning of the line before you select this feature. Then, press Flush Right (ALT-F6), or choose Flush Right from the Layout pull-down menu. The text cursor moves to the right edge of the page, and you can type the text that should be aligned there. As you type the text, LetterPerfect adjusts the text so that it is set against the right margin. Press ENTER, and the cursor moves to the next line.

You can "flush-right" a line of text that is already in your document by moving the cursor to the beginning of the line and pressing Flush Right (ALT-F6). At first, the text will move past the right edge of the screen. But when you press DOWN ARROW, the document is reformatted and the text is aligned at the right margin.

USING THE DATE FEATURES

If your computer keeps track of the current time and date, you can use the Date features to insert the date into your document. There are two ways to do this; you can instruct LetterPerfect to type the date for you, or you can insert a special code that always displays the current date whenever your document is retrieved or printed.

Inserting Today's Date into Your Text

If you follow these steps, LetterPerfect takes the date stored in your computer, and inserts it as text, at the current cursor position.

1. First, move the cursor to the place in your document where the date should be typed.

2. Then, press Date/Outline (SHIFT-F5), and choose option **1**, Date **T**ext, or simply press the Fast Key, CTRL-D. If you prefer to use the pull-down menus, choose Date Text from the Tools menu.

Inserting a Date Code

The Date Code feature also displays the date in your document. But if you insert a date code instead of date text, the current date will always be displayed whenever you retrieve or print your document.

1. Move the text cursor to the place where the date should be inserted.

2. Press Date/Outline (SHIFT-F5) and choose option **2,** Date **C**ode. If you prefer the pull-down menus over the function keys, choose Date Code from the Tools menu. The date is inserted into the document.

From the normal document editing screen, it may appear that LetterPerfect has just typed the date. Actually, a special date code was inserted instead. This code will always check the date stored in the computer and display it as part of the document. This feature is useful for form letters, memo formats, or other documents that should always display the current date.

Changing the Date Format

Stored with the LetterPerfect program is a language resource file (WP.LRS) that determines how the date is displayed. If you want LetterPerfect to insert the date with a different format, you must retrieve and edit the .LRS file.

The following steps will show you how to edit the WP.LRS file for the U.S. version of LetterPerfect. If you are familiar with the Notebook program from WordPerfect Library/WordPerfect Office, you will recognize the .LRS file as a Notebook file. Make sure you clear the screen before you attempt these steps.

1. From a clear LetterPerfect screen, press Retrieve (SHIFT-F10), and LetterPerfect prompts you with "Document to be retrieved:". Type **WP.LRS** and press ENTER to retrieve the WP.LRS file. You may need to include a complete path name before

you can retrieve the file. For example, if your LetterPerfect program files are stored on the A drive, you might need to type **A:\WP.LRS** and press ENTER, when prompted for the file name.

2. The file appears on your screen, but you may find it confusing. You'll see several strange codes, but don't worry—they're supposed to be there. Press Search (F2) to display the → Srch: prompt. Enter **US^R** as the search criterion (type **US** and then press CTRL-V CTRL-R). Press Search (F2) again to initiate the search.

3. The cursor will stop after the "US^R" line, as shown in Figure 3-2. This is is the beginning of the U.S. language record. The line that reads "3 1, 4" is the date format line, which determines how the text is displayed when you use the date features.

    You can edit this line to change the format of the date. You can even add a text phrase as part of the format. See Table 3-1 for a list of the numbers you can include in the format, and what they represent.

4. When you are finished editing the date line, use the Save feature to save the WP.LRS file. When prompted about replacing the existing file, type **Y** for Yes.

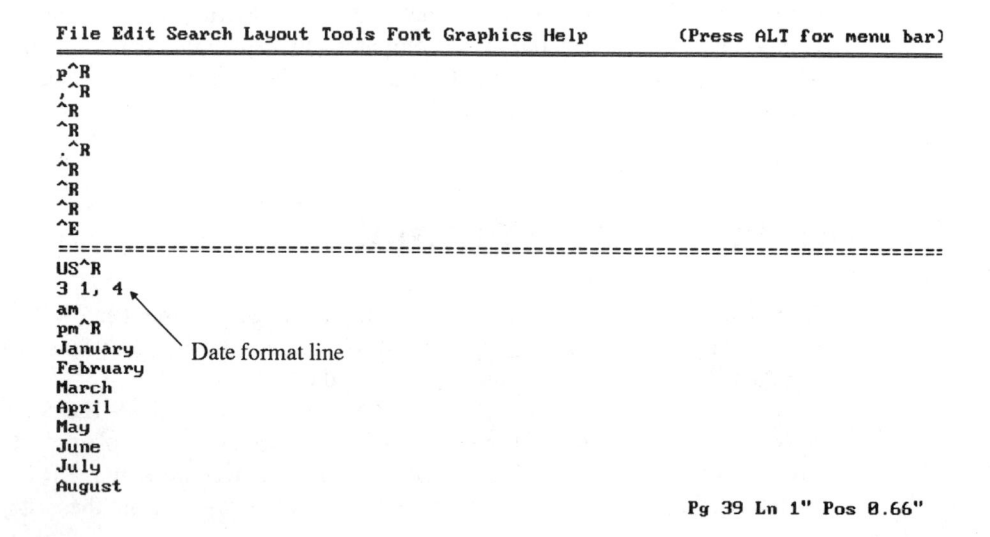

```
 File Edit Search Layout Tools Font Graphics Help      (Press ALT for menu bar)
p^R
,^R
^R
^R
.^R
^R
^R
^R
^E
================================================================================
US^R
3 1, 4
am
pm^R
January     Date format line
February
March
April
May
June
July
August
                                                              Pg 39 Ln 1" Pos 0.66"
```

FIGURE 3-2.   Editing the date format

5. At this point, you need to exit LetterPerfect, and then start it again to reset the date format with the new file. When you start LetterPerfect again, press Date/Outline (SHIFT-F5), and choose option **1**, Date **T**ext, or option **2**, Date **C**ode, and the date will be inserted with the new format.

If the date format does not display as you edited it, make sure you have the right language selected. Press Language (ALT-F8) to display the Language prompt at the bottom of the screen. Type **US** and press ENTER.

The WP.LRS file contains other information that controls some of the display settings in LetterPerfect. Be very careful not to disturb any other information while you are editing the file.

Character	Displays
1	Day of the month
2	Month as a number
3	Month as a word
4	Four-digit year
5	Two-digit year
6	Week day as a word
7	Current hour, 24-hour clock
8	Current hour, 12-hour clock
9	Current minute
0	"am" or "pm" after time
% or $	For numbers that are less than 10, the % character inserts a leading zero and the $ character inserts a leading space. Also abbreviates month/day names to 3 characters.

Examples

3 1, 4	=	June 23, 1991
2/1/5	=	6/23/91
%2–%1–5 8:90	=	06-23-91 5:48pm

TABLE 3-1. Numbers/Characters for the Date Format

PLACING ENDNOTES INTO YOUR DOCUMENT

LetterPerfect does not allow you to create footnotes, as you can in WordPerfect. But it does allow endnotes, which are more common for student papers and personal documents. Endnotes are simply references in your text that refer to a list of notes at the end of the document. Endnotes are easy to add to your text, and are automatically numbered as you create them.

Creating a New Endnote

Before you create an endnote, make sure the text cursor is located at the position in the text where the endnote reference should appear. Then, press the Fast Key, CTRL-E, or press Endnote (CTRL-F7) and select option **1**, to begin a new endnote. If you prefer the pull-down menus, choose Endnote **C**reate from the **L**ayout menu.

It may seem that the text for your document has disappeared. Actually, LetterPerfect has switched to a blank editing screen where you can type the text for the endnote. At this screen, you can also select different fonts and text attributes. Figure 3-3 shows a sample endnote.

When you are finished typing the text, press Exit (F7), or click the right mouse button, to return to the main document editing screen. You will see the endnote reference number in your text. The number may appear as regular text, but it will be printed as superscript text, assuming that your printer is capable of printing this attribute.

When you print the document, all endnotes are compiled in a list at the end of the text. Although the endnotes are not visible from the normal editing screen, you can select the View Document feature to examine the document before you print it.

Editing Endnotes

You can edit a endnote by moving the text cursor before the endnote reference. Then, press Endnote (CTRL-F7) and choose option **2**, **E**dit. LetterPerfect will ask you to verify the endnote number that you want to edit. If the number is correct, press ENTER; if the number is incorrect, type the right number and press ENTER.

The text of the endnote is displayed on the editing screen. Make any necessary changes to the text, then press Exit (F7) to return to the main editing screen. The

```
File Edit Search Layout Tools Font [Graphics] Help       (Press ALT for menu bar)
1.  Information on film museums and libraries provided by Howard
    J. Saunders, Marquee Magazine, March 1991.




Endnote:  Press F7 when done                      Pg 1 Ln 1.17" Pos 5.7"
```

FIGURE 3-3.   Creating an endnote

new endnote will appear in the printed document. If you want to remove an endnote, simply delete the reference from the text.

HYPHENATION

There are some formatting commands that you can use to manually hyphenate the text in your document. In addition, LetterPerfect can automatically hyphenate text if a special file, known as the *hyphenation module*, is installed with the program files. This section explains how to insert hyphen characters, and how to set up LetterPerfect so that it can automatically hyphenate your text.

Manual Hyphenation

There are four characters that you can insert as part of your text, to indicate how words should be hyphenated or broken. These characters tell LetterPerfect where and how to wrap the lines in your document; the result is a form of text hyphenation that does not require the hyphenation module described in the upcoming section, "Automatic Hyphenation."

HYPHEN CHARACTER The hyphen character appears as a dash between two or more words, and is printed as an actual text character. You should insert the hyphen character for phrases such as "two-story house," "ten-year-old daughter," and hyphenated names such as "Barney-Wells." If LetterPerfect needs to hyphenate, it will break the word after the hyphen character. You can insert this as you are typing or editing text; simply press the - character found at the top of your keyboard, or on the numeric keypad. This character is also called the minus symbol.

SOFT HYPHEN The soft hyphen is quite different from the hyphen character. This type of hyphen is inserted to indicate where a word should be broken, and remains invisible, until it becomes necessary to hyphenate the word. To insert the character, first move the cursor to the place in the word where it should be broken, if hyphenation is necessary. Then, hold down the CTRL key and press – (the minus key). You won't see the character on your screen, but you can press Reveal Codes (CTRL-R or ALT-F3) to view the soft hyphen.

HARD HYPHEN A hard hyphen is similar to the hyphen character, but is considered to be a text character, not an actual hyphen. This allows you to create a hyphenated word that will not be broken if hyphenation is necessary. The word will simply be wrapped to the next line. To insert this character, press and release the HOME key, and then press – (the minus key).

For example, assume you need to insert a double dash into your document. If you type two hyphen characters, LetterPerfect may split them as the text is wrapped for the paragraph. But you can press the HOME key, and then press –, followed by another –, and a double dash is inserted that cannot be broken when the text is wrapped. This character appears as [–] in the Reveal Codes window.

INVISIBLE SOFT RETURN This character is similar to the soft hyphen, but invisible soft returns do not hyphenate text. Instead, they help LetterPerfect to know where text should be broken, if necessary. The most common use for this character is for compound words that are separated by a slash, such as he/she, yes/no, and backward/forward. These words do not require a hyphen, but, if both words cannot fit on the current line, they should be broken after the slash character.

To insert an invisible soft return, place the text cursor after the slash character and press HOME, ENTER. An [ISRt] code is inserted into your text, which may be seen while the Reveal Codes window is displayed.

Automatic Hyphenation

LetterPerfect does not include direct hyphenation features such as those found in WordPerfect. However, LetterPerfect will automatically hyphenate your text if you have the correct *hyphenation module* installed. The module is a separate disk file that provides LetterPerfect with the information it needs to hyphenate text. This file must be installed on the diskette or directory where the LetterPerfect program files are located.

For the U.S. release of LetterPerfect, the hyphenation module is named WP{WP}US.HYC. This file is not included with LetterPerfect. If you own WordPerfect 5.1, the hyphenation module is already installed with your Speller files, and you can copy it to your LetterPerfect directory. If you do not have the file, you can order a hyphenation module diskette from WordPerfect Corporation; their telephone number is listed in your LetterPerfect manual. Once the module is copied to your program diskette or directory, LetterPerfect will hyphenate your documents as they are retrieved or reformatted on the screen.

Sometimes, LetterPerfect will find a word that should be hyphenated, but it doesn't know where the word should be broken. This often occurs with very long words or technical terms. In this case, LetterPerfect will ask you to position the hyphen yourself. For example, suppose the word "Revolution" is found in your text and LetterPerfect doesn't know where it should be hyphenated (actually, LetterPerfect would know, but this is just an example). You are prompted with "Position hyphen; Press ENTER Revo-lution." This prompt asks you to position the hyphen yourself. You can press LEFT ARROW or RIGHT ARROW to position the hyphen for the displayed word. Then press ENTER to accept it.

LetterPerfect displays this prompt only when necessary; in most cases, you will not need to manually position the hyphen for words that should be broken.

INSERTING SPECIAL CHARACTERS

Many people need to create documents with foreign characters or special symbols. For some word processors this just isn't possible, but in LetterPerfect you can include accented characters and special symbols in your documents. And you can print these characters with any printer capable of producing graphic images.

Composing Accented Characters

You can insert foreign accented characters in your text with LetterPerfect's Characters feature. Assume you want to insert these characters into your text: é, ü, Ç, and è. You begin by pressing Characters (CTRL-V or CTRL-2), or choosing Characters from the Font pull-down menu. Then, type the two characters from the keyboard that will create the accented character. For example, press Characters (CTRL-V or CTRL-2), type **e'** and press ENTER. This inserts the *é* character in your document.

The following steps show you how to create a few other accented characters. The Characters key is listed in the exercise, but you can either press Characters (CTRL-V or CTRL-2) or choose Characters from the Font pull-down menu, to select the feature.

1. Press Characters (CTRL-V or CTRL-2) and type **u"** to create the *ü* character.

2. Press Characters (CTRL-V or CTRL-2) and type **C,** (type *C* and a comma) to create the *Ç* character.

3. Press Characters (CTRL-V or CTRL-2) and type **e`** to create the *è* character.

Feel free to experiment with different letters and accent marks on the keyboard. After you press Characters or select Characters from the Font pull-down menu, type two characters from the keyboard to test the results.

Using the WordPerfect Character Sets

If you have a copy of WordPerfect 5.1, and have enough space on your disk, you can copy the WP.DRS file to your LetterPerfect directory and access up to 1,200 extended characters, including the Math Symbols set and several foreign language character sets. For more information about inserting these extended characters, refer to the Characters section of your LetterPerfect Reference manual.

SUMMARY

LetterPerfect includes many useful features for changing the appearance of your text, and arranging text lines on the screen. You can choose different fonts and text attributes from the Font menus, align text with the Center and Flush Right features, and insert the date. Other text features allow you to create endnotes, compose special characters, and insert manual hyphenation.

In the next chapter, you will learn more about editing your text, and you'll learn how to edit the codes that create the document format.

chapter 4

EDITING A DOCUMENT

Using the Block Feature
Deleting and Restoring Text
Moving and Copying Text
Searching and Replacing Text
Editing Document Codes
Initial Codes for Documents
Exercise: Editing the Party Shack Flyer
Summary

After you've created the format and entered the text, your document may still need some modifications. Perhaps you need to add new text. You might want to change margins, select new fonts, or just rearrange the order of your paragraphs. LetterPerfect lets you revise and edit your documents with features for deleting, moving, and copying text. You can also search for specific words or phrases, and, if you wish, replace them with different text. In addition, the Reveal Codes feature allows you to edit the invisible formatting codes in your document.

USING THE BLOCK FEATURE

An important part of editing is selecting what you want to change. Sometimes you don't want to move an entire sentence; perhaps only one phrase should be moved.

LetterPerfect's Block feature lets you define exactly what you want to delete, move, or copy. You can also use the Block feature to apply attributes, such as bold or italics, to a specific section of your text. You don't always need to block your text before performing an editing task, but many editing features are easier to use when a block of text is defined.

The process of selecting or defining a block of text is quite simple. The following illustration shows how a block is defined.

Begin

The United States Library of Congress contains the largest motion picture collection in the world, with over 100,000 files. The American Museum of the Moving Arts, in Astoria, New York, is the only museum in the U.S. devoted to television, video, and the motion picture arts.

End

To begin, move the cursor to the first text character that should be included in the block. Then, use the Block feature to highlight the text you want to change. Once the block is defined, you can choose an editing feature or attribute for the text. The actual process varies depending on whether you are using the keyboard or the mouse to define the block.

Defining a Block with the Keyboard

The following steps will show you how to define a block with the cursor arrow keys and the Block (ALT-F4 or F12) function key. If you are using a mouse with LetterPerfect, refer to the next section, "Defining a Block with the Mouse." You'll want to type a few sentences, or retrieve a document, before you try these steps.

1. Move the text cursor to the first text character that should be included in the block. For example, if you are moving a group of words, move the text cursor to the first letter of the first word.

2. Press Block (ALT-F4 or F12), or choose **Block** from the **Edit** pull-down menu. A "Block on" message flashes in the lower-left corner of the screen to let you know that Block is now active.

3. Use the arrow keys to move the text cursor just past the last character that should be included in the block. As you do this, the characters in the block will be highlighted. Figure 4-1 shows an example of a highlighted block of text.

Once a block is defined, you can select an editing feature to manipulate the text. Later in this section, you will use the Block feature to apply a font attribute to your text. For now, just press Cancel (F1 or ESC) to cancel the block.

Defining a Block with the Mouse

If you are using a mouse with LetterPerfect, you'll find that it's very easy to define a block of text. The following steps will show you how:

1. Move the mouse pointer to the first text character that should be included in the block.

2. Press and hold the left mouse button. Then move the mouse pointer to the right of the last character that should be included in the block. As you move the mouse, the text is highlighted, indicating the block.

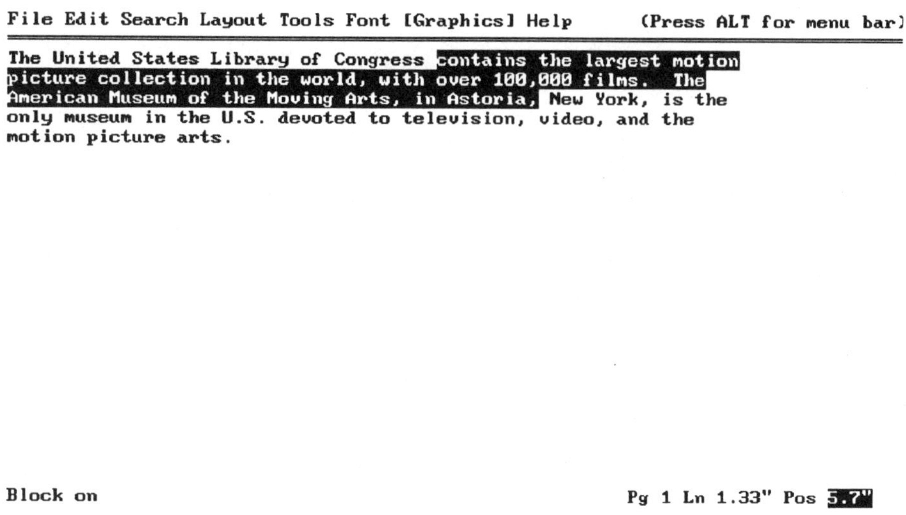

```
File Edit Search Layout Tools Font [Graphics] Help      (Press ALT for menu bar)
The United States Library of Congress contains the largest motion
picture collection in the world, with over 100,000 films. The
American Museum of the Moving Arts, in Astoria, New York, is the
only museum in the U.S. devoted to television, video, and the
motion picture arts.
```

Block on   Pg 1 Ln 1.33" Pos 5.7"

FIGURE 4-1.   Blocking text in LetterPerfect

3. When you've highlighted the text you want to block, release the mouse button.

Now, you can select different editing features or text attributes to change the highlighted text. Later in this section, you will use the Block feature to apply a font attribute to the text. For now, you'll want to cancel the Block feature. If your mouse has two buttons, click both buttons simultaneously to cancel the block. If your mouse has three buttons, cancel the block by clicking the center button.

Applying Attributes to a Block

In Chapter 3, you learned how to select different attributes for text, such as italics, boldface, and underlining. Generally, it's best to select these attributes as you are typing the text. However, you'll often need to italicize or underline text that is already on your screen; you don't want to delete the text, select an attribute, and then retype it.

The Block feature makes it possible for you to apply the attributes to any text on your screen. Simply block the text and choose the attribute you want. To test this, you will retrieve the PARTY.DOC file that you created earlier. Make sure the screen is clear before you continue (F7, N, N).

1. Press Retrieve (SHIFT-F10). At the "Document to be retrieved: " prompt, type **party.doc** and press ENTER.

2. Move the text cursor to the beginning of the headline, "GREETINGS FROM THE PARTY SHACK!". If you are using the keyboard, press Block (ALT-F4 or F12). If you are using a mouse, move the mouse pointer to the beginning of the headline and hold down the left mouse button. Move the text cursor or mouse pointer to the end of the current line, after the exclamation point. If you are using a mouse, release the left mouse button when the cursor is at the end of the line.

3. The text is now blocked. Press Bold (CTRL-B or F6) or choose **B**old from the Font pull-down menu. If you wish, you can press Underline (CTRL-U or F8) instead, or select a different attribute from the Font pull-down menu.

After you select the attribute, it is applied to the blocked text, and the Block feature is automatically turned off. You can follow this procedure to apply attributes such as boldface, underlining, italics, and superscript to your text. However, you cannot use the Block feature to change the base font of your text. This must be done manually at every point in your document where the font should change, as described in Chapter 3.

Before you continue, you should save the PARTY.DOC document and clear the screen. To do so, press Exit (F7) or choose Exit from the File pull-down menu. LetterPerfect prompts you with "Save document? Yes (No)". Type **Y** for Yes, and press ENTER to accept the PARTY.DOC name. You will be asked whether you want to replace the existing file on disk; type **Y** for Yes. Now, you are asked whether you want to exit LetterPerfect. Type **N** for No. The document is saved and the screen is cleared.

Tips and Tricks for the Block Feature

While the Block feature is turned on, you can type a character from the keyboard to extend the block to the next occurrence of that character. For example, assume you want to define a block from the cursor position to the end of the current sentence. Simply turn on the Block feature by pressing Block (ALT-F4 or F12) or by choosing **Block** from the **Edit** pull-down menu. Then, type a period (.) and the text is highlighted from the cursor position to the next period character, which is most likely the end of the sentence. You aren't limited to the period character; you can type any text key to extend the block to the next occurrence of that character.

After you choose an editing feature or a text attribute, the defined block is automatically turned off. Sometimes, you'll want to reblock the text and select another feature. LetterPerfect provides a way to jump back to the previous position, and reblock the text with only two keystrokes. This is especially useful if you want to apply more than one text attribute to the same section of text.

This is the procedure. After you've blocked some text and selected a text attribute, the block will be turned off. Press Block (ALT-F4 or F12), or choose **Block** from the **Edit** menu to turn on the Block feature again. Then, press Go To (CTRL-HOME) twice. This causes the cursor to jump back to its original position, before the block was defined. The same text will be highlighted, and you can choose another editing feature or text attribute.

DELETING AND RESTORING TEXT

One of the most important editing tasks is deleting unwanted text. There are different ways to remove text characters, words, paragraphs, and even formatting codes from your document; you can delete text with keyboard commands or with the Move feature. If you change your mind, you can restore deleted text with LetterPerfect's Undelete feature.

Using the Delete Keys

There are several keystrokes that allow you to remove items from your document. Some keys delete one character at a time, while others delete a word or an entire line. Table 4-1 lists the keys you can press to delete text and codes.

Pressing BACKSPACE deletes the text character that is to the left of the cursor position. If you hold down the BACKSPACE key, the cursor will move left continuously, deleting characters as it moves. DEL deletes the character at the cursor position, and if you hold down the DEL key, characters are deleted to the right of the cursor. These keystrokes may be used alone or with the Block feature to delete a section of your text.

As you use BACKSPACE and DEL, you may run into a formatting code; LetterPerfect will ask you whether you want to delete the code. If so, you can type **Y** for Yes, and the code will be removed from your document. If you type **N** for No, the code will remain in your document and the text cursor will move to the other side of the code.

Press CTRL-BACKSPACE to delete the word at the cursor position. You can also press HOME, then press BACKSPACE, to delete the word that is to the left of the cursor. Pressing HOME, then DEL, deletes the word that is to the right of the cursor.

Press CTRL-END to delete from the cursor position to the right margin. This is called *delete to end of line*. Press CTRL-PGDN to delete the text from the cursor position to the end of the current page.

If you want to try these keystrokes yourself, type a few sentences on your screen, and follow these steps:

Key	Action
BACKSPACE	Delete left of cursor
DEL	Delete at cursor
CTRL-BACKSPACE	Delete word at cursor
HOME, BACKSPACE	Delete word left of cursor
HOME, DELETE	Delete word right of cursor
CTRL-END	Delete to the end of line
CTRL-PGDN	Delete to the end of page

TABLE 4-1.   LetterPerfect Delete Keys

1. Move the text cursor to a word on your screen. Press CTRL-BACKSPACE to delete the word.

2. Now, move the text cursor to the middle of a sentence in the text. Press CTRL-END to delete the text from the cursor position to the right margin or end of the current line.

3. Finally, move the text cursor to the middle of the text on the page. Press CTRL-PGDN and LetterPerfect prompts you with "Delete remainder of page? No (Yes)". Type **Y** for Yes, and the text between the cursor and the end of the page is deleted.

The Delete keys allow you to quickly remove unwanted text from your document. The next section shows how to use the Block feature with these keystrokes to delete a specific section of text. Before you continue, clear the screen; press Exit (F7) and type **n** twice.

Deleting a Block of Text

So far, you've learned how to delete characters, words, and text lines with keyboard commands. However, you can also use the Block feature to define and delete a section of text from your document. The following steps will show you how to select and delete a block of text.

1. Press Retrieve (SHIFT-F10). At the "Document to be retrieved: " prompt, type **party.doc** and press ENTER.

2. Using the keyboard or mouse, define a block to highlight the phrase "Certified with the renowned Crockett Institute of Fine Party Cuisine," in the second paragraph.

3. Press BACKSPACE or DEL, or choose **D**elete from the Edit pull-down menu. Figure 4-2 shows how your screen will appear.

4. LetterPerfect prompts you with, "Delete Block? No (Yes)". Type **Y**, or click on Yes with the mouse, to delete the highlighted block of text.

The blocked text is removed from your document. For now, keep the PARTY.DOC file on your screen, and later, you'll use the Undelete feature to restore the text that you've deleted.

```
File Edit Search Layout Tools Font [Graphics] Help     (Press ALT for menu bar)
                        GREETINGS FROM THE PARTY SHACK!

The Party Shack offers complete catering services for all your
entertainment needs.  Our creative directors have the perfect
ideas for every occasion:  birthday parties, weddings, holidays--
we can even bring Spunky the Magic Clown and twelve trained
dachshunds to add some excitement to a boring dinner party!

Why cook?  Our chefs can do it for you!  Certified with the
renowned Crockett Institute of Fine Party Cuisine, we can create
the most exotic and creative dishes, suitable for any backyard
barbecue or corporate Christmas party.

And now is the best time to get acquainted with our services.  If
you plan a party before July 31st, we'll give you a 10% discount
on all party favors!  So drop by the Party Shack, where there's
always a party going on!




Delete Block? No (Yes)
```

FIGURE 4-2.   Deleting a block of text

Using the Move Key to Delete Text

In addition to the Delete keys, you can also use LetterPerfect's Move feature to delete a sentence, paragraph, or block of text. In the following steps, you will use the Move (CTRL-F4) key to delete a paragraph from the text. The PARTY.DOC file should already be on your screen from the previous exercise.

1. Move the text cursor to the last paragraph on the screen, the one that begins "And now is the best time...". It doesn't matter where the cursor is located; just make sure that it lies within the boundaries of the paragraph.

2. Press Move (CTRL-F4), and a menu is displayed with four options.

3. Choose option **2**, **P**aragraph to select the paragraph where the cursor is currently located. After you make the selection, the paragraph is highlighted.

4. Another menu appears with the Move, Copy, and Delete options. Choose option **3**, **D**elete, to delete the paragraph.

That's all you need to do. In Step 3, you could have selected **1 S**entence or **3 B**lock, instead of **2 P**aragraph, to delete the current sentence or block of text.

You can also use the pull-down menus to delete a sentence or paragraph. Just choose Select Sentence or Select Paragraph from the Edit pull-down menu. After you make a selection, the text is highlighted. You will be prompted to define a block; then a menu appears with three options: Move, Copy, and Delete. Select the Delete option; the highlighted text is removed, and the block is turned off.

In the next section, you will use LetterPerfect's Undelete feature to restore the text that you've deleted.

Restoring Deleted Text

Everyone makes mistakes. Sometimes you'll delete a sentence or paragraph and then realize that you shouldn't have. Fortunately, LetterPerfect remembers the last three deletions that you made, and can return any of them to your document.

LetterPerfect considers one deletion to be everything you deleted at one time. If you move the cursor, and type new text or select a menu item, you've ended the current deletion. For example, you can delete a long word by pressing BACKSPACE for each letter, and LetterPerfect considers the entire word as one deletion. However, if you use BACKSPACE to delete part of a word, move the text cursor, and then continue deleting the word with BACKSPACE, you have made two deletions. LetterPerfect can remember only the last three things you deleted; if you make a fourth deletion, the first deletion is removed from the list of things you can restore.

In the following steps, you will learn how to use the Undelete feature to restore deleted text. The PARTY.DOC file should still be on your screen, after deleting text in the previous section.

1. Move the text cursor to the bottom of your document, at the place where you deleted the last paragraph.

2. Press Cancel (F1 or ESC), or choose Undelete from the Edit pull-down menu. The most recent deletion appears at the current cursor position. In this case, the paragraph you deleted is highlighted in your document, but it is not yet restored.

3. The Undelete menu appears at the bottom of the screen, as shown in Figure 4-3. Choose option **1**, **R**estore, to restore the highlighted text.

4. Now, you need to restore the block of text that you previously deleted. Move the cursor after the sentence "Our chefs can do it for you!", in the second paragraph.

5. Press Cancel (F1 or ESC), or choose Undelete from the Edit pull-down menu. Although this text has already been restored to the screen, the paragraph appears again because it was the most recent deletion.

```
File Edit Search Layout Tools Font Graphics Help        (Press ALT for menu bar)
                          GREETINGS FROM THE PARTY SHACK!

The Party Shack offers complete catering services for all your
entertainment needs.  Our creative directors have the perfect
ideas for every occasion:  birthday parties, weddings, holidays--
we can even bring Spunky the Magic Clown and twelve trained
dachshunds to add some excitement to a boring dinner party!

Why cook?  Our chefs can do it for you!   we can create the most
exotic and creative dishes, suitable for any backyard barbecue or
corporate Christmas party.

And now is the best time to get acquainted with our services.  If
you plan a party before July 31st, we'll give you a 10% discount
on all party favors!  So drop by the Party Shack, where there's
always a party going on!



Undelete: 1 Restore; 2 Previous Deletion: 0
```

FIGURE 4-3.   Restoring a deleted paragraph

6. Choose option **2, P**revious Deletion, to view the first text you deleted. The previously deleted text is now displayed at the cursor position, but it is not yet restored. Choose **1 R**estore, to restore this to your document.

Now your text should appear as it did when you first retrieved the PARTY.DOC file. If you wish, save this revised version of the file.

The Undelete feature can also restore any formatting codes that you have deleted from your text. When you restore text or codes, keep in mind that LetterPerfect does not automatically return the deleted text to its original position. It's important to remember that restored text or codes are inserted at the current cursor position.

MOVING AND COPYING TEXT

One of the greatest advantages of word processing is the ability to rearrange the text in your document. You can also make copies of any section of text and move it to another location. The following information explains how to use the Move and Copy features of LetterPerfect. Before you continue, clear the screen and retrieve the RESUME.DOC file that you created in Chapter 2.

Moving a Block of Text

The following instructions show how to move a block of text. In this exercise, you will use the résumé document that you created in Chapter 2, but you can apply the same procedure to move the text in any document.

1. Use the Block feature to highlight the text you want to move. For this example, block the second paragraph under the "EDUCATION" heading. When you finish defining the block, your screen should look like Figure 4-4.

Notice that the block begins at the beginning of the first line of the paragraph, and ends with the text cursor on the first line of the following paragraph. This block is

```
File Edit Search Layout Tools Font [Graphics] Help      (Press ALT for menu bar)
                         WILLIAM J. RATHE

92 Spencer Road                     Work: (415) 555-3481
Berkeley, CA  94710                 Home: (415) 555-1284


EDUCATION:         University of California, Berkeley
                   B.A. - Psychology, 1978

                   Ranglin' Bros. Clown College, Orlando, FL.
                   Graduated with Big Top Honors, 1983
                   Recipient, Golden Bozo Award

    _              University of California, Los Angeles
                   M.A. - Theater/Motion Picture Arts, 1981

EXPERIENCE:        PARTY SHACK CATERING, INC., Berkeley, CA
1987 - Present
                   Entertainment Director, Children's Party
Block on                                         Pg 1 Ln 3.5" Pos
```

FIGURE 4-4.   Moving a block of text

defined to include the line space beneath the paragraph, so that there is no extra space after the paragraph is moved.

2. Press Move (CTRL-F4) and select **1 Move**, or choose **Move (Cut)** from the **Edit** pull-down menu. The blocked text is removed from the screen. A message appears at the bottom of the screen, "Move cursor; press **Enter** to retrieve".

3. Move the cursor to the location where the text should be moved. In this case, move the cursor to the line immediately above the "EXPERIENCE" heading.

4. Press ENTER, or choose **Paste Block** from the **Edit** pull-down menu. You can also press the Fast Key for "paste block," CTRL-A. The block is moved to the new location.

Your résumé is now complete. If you wish, use the Save feature to save the edited version of the résumé and replace the previous RESUME.DOC file. Then, clear the screen.

LetterPerfect wins the prize for versatility; there are also a few other ways to move and copy text. These perform the same basic functions, but present different ways to do the tasks. If you choose **M**ove (Cut) from the **E**dit pull-down menu or press the Fast Key, CTRL-M, without first blocking some text, you will have the opportunity to define a block. Also, if you press Move (CTRL-F4) without first defining a block, a menu appears that lets you select what you want to move—a sentence, a paragraph, or a block.

Copying a Block of Text

The Copy feature makes a copy of a text block and leaves the original text in place. The following steps show how to copy a section of text that has been defined with the Block feature. You will probably want to type some text, or retrieve a sample file before you continue.

1. Using the keyboard or mouse, define a block around the text you want to copy.

2. Press Move (CTRL-F4) and select **2 Copy**, or choose **Copy** from the **Edit** pull-down menu. A copy of the blocked text is stored in your computer's memory.

3. A message appears at the bottom of the screen, "Move cursor; press **Enter** to retrieve". Move the cursor to the location where the text should be copied.

4. Press ENTER, or choose **Paste Block** from the **Edit** pull-down menu. The copy is inserted at the cursor location.

The copy that you made will remain stored in your computer's memory until you copy or move something else. You can press Retrieve (SHIFT-F10) or select **R**etrieve from the **F**ile pull-down menu to retrieve the copy again. A message appears at the bottom of the screen, "Document to be retrieved: ". If you simply press ENTER, without typing a file name, LetterPerfect will retrieve the copy of the text from memory, and insert it at the cursor position. This also works after you've moved a block of text.

note
If you choose Copy from the Edit pull-down menu without first blocking some text, you will have the opportunity to define a block.

Using the Fast Keys to Move and Copy

The previous sections explain how to move and copy text after you've defined a block of text. LetterPerfect also provides two Fast Keys for moving and copying text. The Fast Keys perform the same tasks as described earlier, but the procedure is slightly different. (Note that the Block feature is not used in the following instructions.) These steps will show you how to use the Move (CTRL-M) and Copy (CTRL-K) Fast Keys.

1. To move text, press Move (CTRL-M). To copy text, press Copy (CTRL-K).

2. A message at the bottom of the screen reads "Position to top corner of text; press **Enter**". This tells you to move the cursor to the first character of the text you want to move or copy. Then, press ENTER.

3. The message at the bottom of the screen changes to read "Position to bottom corner of text; press **Enter**". Move your cursor to the end of the section of text that should be moved or copied. Then, press ENTER.

4. LetterPerfect prompts you with "Move cursor; press **Enter** to retrieve". Position your cursor at the place in your document where the text should be located. Then, press ENTER to move it there.

As described in previous sections, you can also use the Block feature to define a section of text, and then press Move (CTRL-M) or Copy (CTRL-K) to manipulate it. These steps have shown that if you don't first define a block, LetterPerfect will prompt you to do so before it moves or copies your text.

SEARCHING AND REPLACING TEXT

Sometimes you need to find one specific word—or every occurrence of a word—in your document. LetterPerfect's Search feature can help you locate text by searching through the entire text, including headers, footers, and endnotes. You can also search for formatting codes, such as tab settings or margin changes. The Replace feature lets you locate *and* replace words, phrases, or codes. Both features can assist you with document editing.

Searching for Text and Codes

LetterPerfect allows you to search forward or backward through the text of your document. When you use the Search feature, the search begins from the cursor position and continues to the end or to the beginning of the text. The direction of the search depends on whether you select the Forward Search or Backward Search feature.

The following steps explain how to search for text. (In the example, it is assumed that the cursor is at the beginning of the document, and that you wish to search from the cursor position to the end of the text.)

1. Press **Forward Search** (F2), or choose **Forward** from the Search pull-down menu. The "→ Srch:" message appears at the bottom of the screen, where you may type the text or enter the codes.

2. Type the text you want to find. This is known as the *search criterion*. If the search criterion contains capital letters, only the words with identical capitalization will match. Words without capital letters will match all words, regardless of capitalization. For example, if you type *The* as the text to find, the search will match only "The". However, if you type *the*, the search finds both "*the*" and "*The*", or even "*tHe*" and "*thE*", if they exist in the document.

3. Do not press ENTER after typing the text, as this will insert the Hard Return ([HRt]) code into the search criterion. Instead, press **Forward Search** (F2) again, or choose **Forward** from the Search pull-down menu to initiate the search. If the search criterion is found, the cursor will move to it.

note If the text or code is not in the document, a "Not Found" message will appear at the bottom of the screen.

4. You can continue searching for the specified text by pressing Forward Search (F2). You will see the search criterion displayed after the "→ Srch:" prompt. Then, press F2 again to search for the next occurrence of the search criterion.

The Forward Search command searches the text between the cursor position and the bottom of the document. If your cursor is not at the beginning of the text, you can press Backward Search (SHIFT-F2), or choose **B**ackward from the Search pull-down menu to search the text between the cursor position and the beginning of the document.

Also, while the "Srch:" prompt is displayed at the bottom of the screen, you can press DOWN ARROW or UP ARROW to change the direction of the search, either forward ("→ Srch:") or backward ("← Srch:")

If you want to find a formatting code instead of text, press Format (SHIFT-F8) while the "Srch:" prompt is displayed. Then, choose any feature from the menu that appears at the bottom of the screen. You can also press function keys, such as Bold (CTRL-B or F6), to search for text attribute codes.

Replacing Text and Codes

Like the Search feature, the Replace feature allows you to find specific words and phrases. But it also gives you the opportunity to replace them with something else. This can be useful when, for example, you create a report with several references to an accounting figure or an historical date. If you need to change that reference, you can use the Replace feature to correct the information, rather than edit each occurrence of the figure or date.

Once you perform a replace operation, you cannot "undo" it; therefore, you should save your document before you choose to replace any text. Follow these steps to replace text in your document:

1. Press Replace (ALT-F2) or choose **R**eplace from the Search pull-down menu. LetterPerfect prompts you with "w/Confirm? No (Yes)". Choose Yes if you want the opportunity to accept or reject each replacement; choose No to instruct Letter-Perfect to perform each replacement without confirmation.

2. The "→Srch:" message appears at the bottom of the screen, where you can enter a search criterion. Type the text or enter the codes that you want to replace.

3. Press Search (F2) again, or select **F**orward from the Search pull-down menu. LetterPerfect prompts you with "Replace with:". Now, type the text or enter the codes that should replace the search criterion.

4. Press Search (F2) once again, or select **Forward** from the Search pull-down menu. LetterPerfect will replace each match of the search criterion with the specified text or codes.

Be careful with the Replace feature. If you aren't careful you could create some serious mistakes. For example, assume you want to replace the word "the" with the word "those." Since you are searching for a single word, you need to type spaces before and after the search and replacement text. Otherwise, words like *the*re, ga*the*r, and brea*the* will become *those*re, ga*those*r, and brea*those*, respectively.

If you do insert spaces as part of the search criterion, make sure you include them in the replacement text also. Remember, the replacement text replaces everything that matches the search criterion.

EDITING DOCUMENT CODES

In Chapter 2, you were introduced to the concept of document codes. Whenever you select a formatting feature or choose an attribute for text, you insert a code into the text of your document. There are codes for margin and tab settings, font changes, text attributes, justification, and date formats. Other features in LetterPerfect, such as endnotes and graphics, also insert codes into your text. The codes help LetterPerfect format your document so that it will print correctly when it's sent to the printer.

When you create simple documents, you probably won't need to worry about these invisible codes. But when you want to edit complex documents, you'll need to see where the codes are located. Figure 4-5 shows how the codes affect the format of a sample document. Codes are normally invisible on the document editing screen, but LetterPerfect includes a feature called Reveal Codes that allows you to view and edit the formatting codes in your document. Before you continue, clear the screen.

Editing with Reveal Codes

LetterPerfect's Reveal Codes feature displays a window that shows where the codes are in your document. Retrieve the RESUME.DOC file that you created earlier to test this feature. After you've retrieved the file, press Reveal Codes (CTRL-R or ALT-F3) or choose **R**eveal Codes from the **E**dit pull-down menu. Your screen will look similar to Figure 4-6.

Footer code to begin
footer on this page

The United States Library of Congress contains the largest motion picture collection in the world, with over 100,000 films.

Double line spacing → The United States Library of Congress contains the largest motion picture collection in the world, with over 100,000 films.

Single line spacing → The United States Library of Congress contains the largest motion picture collection in the world, with over 100,000 films. The American Museum of the Moving Arts, in Astoria, New York, is the only museum in the U.S. devoted to television, video, and the motion picture arts.

Indent → The United States Library of Congress contains the largest motion picture collection in the world, with over 100,000 films. The American Museum of the Moving Arts, in Astoria, New York, is the only museum in the U.S. devoted to television, video, and the motion picture arts.

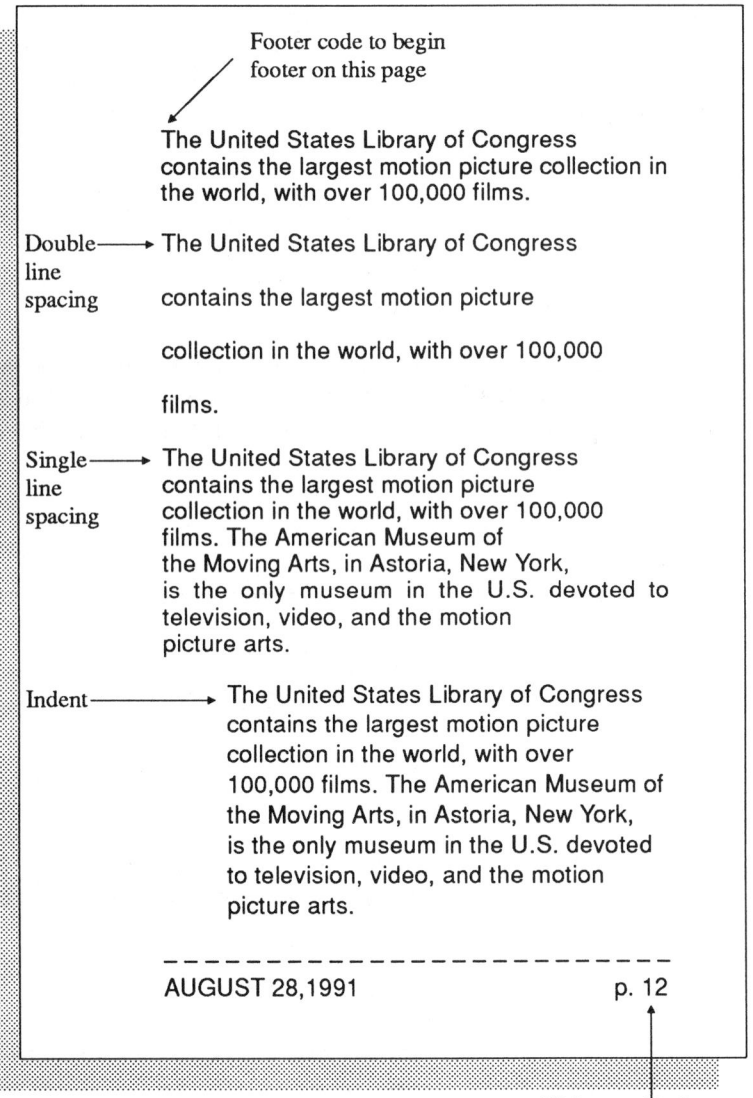

AUGUST 28, 1991   p. 12

^B inserted in footer text to display current page number

FIGURE 4-5.   Formatting codes are placed in the text

Notice that the screen is divided by a bar, which displays triangles where the tab stops are set. Square brackets on the bar show the current margin settings. If you see a French bracket ({ or }), it indicates a margin that is located on a defined tab stop. The area above the bar shows your document as it normally appears on the document screen. The area below the bar is the Reveal Codes window. This shows your text with the formatting codes.

In the Reveal Codes window, the text cursor appears as a *reverse video* highlight. You can move the cursor, type new text, or use the Delete keys to remove text and codes.

note: When the Reveal Codes window is displayed, LetterPerfect will let you delete codes without prompting you about the deletion.

Any changes you make are immediately displayed in the text at the top half of the screen. When you are finished editing the codes, press Reveal Codes (CTRL-R or ALT-F3), or choose **Reveal Codes** from the **Edit** menu to restore the normal document editing screen.

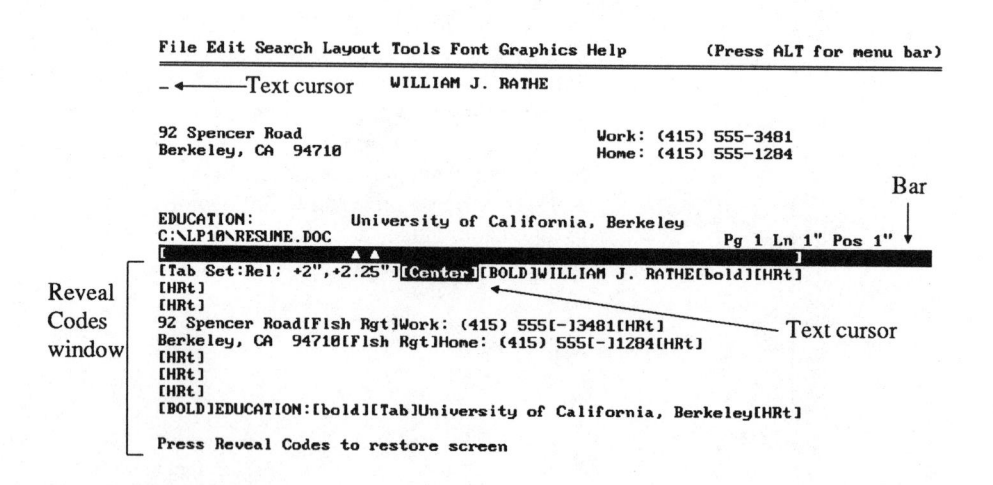

FIGURE 4-6. The Reveal Codes window

LetterPerfect Codes

Table 4-2 shows the formatting codes that may appear while the Reveal Codes window is displayed. Most of these codes are inserted as you select features, but many of them are automatically inserted by LetterPerfect, as necessary, to format your text. Remember, each code is treated as a single character in your document.

WordPerfect Codes

You can retrieve WordPerfect 5.1 documents into LetterPerfect, perform editing tasks, and save documents without converting to a different format. This is possible because WordPerfect 5.1 documents are fully compatible with LetterPerfect. However, not all WordPerfect features are available in LetterPerfect; some codes may be converted or temporarily ignored. WordPerfect codes that are *not* supported by LetterPerfect are displayed in French brackets (such as {Tbl Off}) in the Reveal Codes window.

For example, assume you've created a document that includes footnotes in the text. When you view this document in WordPerfect, the footnote code may appear in Reveal Codes like this:

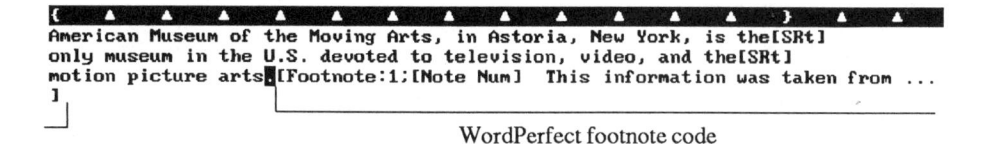

```
American Museum of the Moving Arts, in Astoria, New York, is the[SRt]
only museum in the U.S. devoted to television, video, and the[SRt]
motion picture arts.[Footnote:1;[Note Num]  This information was taken from ...
]
```

WordPerfect footnote code

LetterPerfect does not have a footnote feature. So, if you retrieve the WordPerfect document into LetterPerfect, the footnote code is converted to an endnote, and appears like this in Reveal Codes:

```
picture collection in the world, with over 100,000 films.  The[SRt]
American Museum of the Moving Arts, in Astoria, New York, is the[SRt]
only museum in the U.S. devoted to television, video, and the[SRt]
motion picture arts.[Endnote/WP Footnote:1;[Note Num]  This information was take
n from ... ]
```

Converted footnote code

It's important to note that the code is converted as an [Endnote/WP Footnote] code. LetterPerfect still recognizes it as a WordPerfect footnote, but it doesn't

Code	Feature	Keystroke
[ ]	Hard Space	HOME, SPACEBAR
[-]	Hyphen Character	-
[Block]	Beginning of Block	ALT-F4
[Bold] [bold]	Bold on/off	F6 or CTRL-B
[Center]	Align text at Center	SHIFT-F6 or CTRL-C
[Center Pg]	Center text Vertically on page	SHIFT-F8, 9
[Cntr Tab]	Tab to Center Tab Stop	TAB
[CNTR TAB]	Fixed Center Tab	HOME, SHIFT-F6
[Date:]	Date/Time Code	SHIFT-F5, 2
[Dec Tab]	Tab to Decimal-align Tab Stop	TAB
[DEC TAB]	Fixed Decimal-align Tab	CTRL-F6
[Dorm HRt]	Dormant Hard Return*	
[DSRt]	Deletable Soft Return*	
[Endnote:]	Endnote	CTRL-F7 or CTRL-E
[Fig Box:]	Graphic Figure Box	ALT-F9, 1 or CTRL-G
[Fig Opt:]	Border Y/N, Figure Option	ALT-F9, 1, 5
[Flsh Rgt]	Right-aligned text	ALT-F6
[Font]	Font Change	CTRL-F8, 4 or CTRL-F
[Footer A:]	Document Footer	SHIFT-F8, 6, 2
[Header A:]	Document Header	SHIFT-F8, 6, 1
[HPg]	Hard Page Command	CTRL-ENTER
[HRt]	Hard Return	ENTER
[HRt-SPg]	Hard Return/Soft Page Break*	
[→Indent]	Indents Left Paragraph Margin	F4
[→Indent←]	Indents Both Paragraph Margins	SHIFT-F4
[ISRt]	Invisible Soft Return	HOME, ENTER
[Italc] [italc]	Italics On/Off	CTRL-F8, 5 or CTRL-I

TABLE 4-2. LetterPerfect Codes

Code	Feature	Keystroke
[Just]	Text Justification	SHIFT-F8, 1
[L/R Mar]	Left/Right Margin setting	SHIFT-F8, 4
[Lang:]	Language Selection	ALT-F8
[Ln Spacing:]	Line Spacing	SHIFT-F8, 2
[←Mar Rel]	Left Margin Release	SHIFT-TAB
[Mrg:]	Merge Code	SHIFT-F9
[Note Num]	Endnote number*	
[Outline Off]	Turn off Outline Mode	SHIFT-F5, 4
[Outline On]	Turn on Outline Mode	SHIFT-F5, 3
[Paper Sz/Typ:]	Paper Size/Type selection	SHIFT-F8, 8
[Par Num:]	Numbering Code for Outline*	
[Pg Numbering:]	Page Numbering	SHIFT-F8, 7
[Rgt Tab]	Tab to Right-align Tab Stop	TAB
[RGT TAB]	Fixed Right-align Tab	HOME, ALT-F6
[SPg]	Soft Page Break*	
[SRt]	Soft Return*	
[Subscpt] [subscpt]	Subscripted text	CTRL-F8, 7
[Suppress]	Suppress Header or Footer	SHIFT-F8, 6, 3
[Suprscpt] [suprscpt]	Superscripted text	CTRL-F8, 6
[T/B Mar]	Top/Bottom Margins	SHIFT-F8, 3
[Tab]	Tab to Left-align Tab Stop	TAB
[TAB]	Fixed Left-align Tab	HOME, TAB
[Tab Set]	Tabular Definition	SHIFT-F8, 5
[Und] [und]	Underline On/Off	CTRL-F8, 2 or CTRL-U
[Unknown]	Non-LetterPerfect Code or WP 5.0 Code*	

* There is no keystroke that will insert this code into your document. This code is inserted by LetterPerfect as needed.

TABLE 4-2. LetterPerfect Codes (*continued*)

support the feature, so the footnote is formatted and printed as an endnote. If you save the document and retrieve it into WordPerfect, the footnote will be restored to the text.

Sometimes WordPerfect codes can't be converted, and so LetterPerfect simply ignores them. Again, the codes are not deleted, they're just displayed in French brackets to indicate that the feature is not supported in LetterPerfect. Suppose you've used WordPerfect's Table feature to create a document.

Figure 4-7 shows how one table appears on the WordPerfect Reveal Codes screen. You will notice that the table begins with a [Tbl Def:] code, and that [Row] and [Cell] codes define the structure of the table. Finally, a [Tbl Off] code ends the table. If you were to retrieve this document into LetterPerfect, it would appear as shown in Figure 4-8. The structure is similar in Reveal Codes, but the table codes appear as {Tbl Def}, {Row}, {Cell}, and {Tbl Off}. The French brackets indicate that these features were carried over from WordPerfect 5.1.

Notice that the text above the Reveal Codes bar is not formatted as a table because the Table feature is not supported by LetterPerfect. You can still edit the text, but you can't change the structure of the table. Of course, you can delete any of the table codes, but that would destroy the table structure. After you edit, you can save your changes and retrieve the file into WordPerfect 5.1. If you didn't delete any table codes, the table will appear in its original form.

DATE	ITEM	ORDER #	PRICE
10/14	Office Supplies (General)	1516	37.50
10/19	Copy Paper & Toner Cartridges	1517	287.00
10/30	Pens, Note Pads, FAX Paper	1519	42.50
11/06	Business Cards (Reprint for NGA)	1527	200.00
11/09	Printer Ribbons x 12	1521	32.00

Doc 1 Pg 1 Ln 1" Pos 1"

[Tbl Def:I;4,1.03",3.63",0.925",0.925"]
[Row][Cell]DATE[Cell]ITEM[Cell]ORDER #[Cell]PRICE
[Row][Cell]10/14[Cell] Office Supplies (General)[Cell]1516[Cell]37.50
[Row][Cell]10/19[Cell] Copy Paper & Toner Cartridges[Cell]1517[Cell]287.00
[Row][Cell]10/30[Cell] Pens, Note Pads, FAX Paper[Cell]1519[Cell]42.50
[Row][Cell]11/06[Cell] Business Cards (Reprint for NGA)[Cell]1527[Cell]200.00
[Row][Cell]11/09[Cell] Printer Ribbons x 12[Cell]1521[Cell]32.00[Tbl Off]

Press Reveal Codes to restore screen

FIGURE 4-7. A WordPerfect 5.1 table

Chapter 4 Editing a Document 105

```
File Edit Search Layout Tools Font Graphics Help        (Press ALT for menu bar)
DATE
ITEM
ORDER #
PRICE
10/14
  Office Supplies (General)
1516
37.50
E:\DOCUMENT\BOOK\REPORT.51                              Pg 1 Ln 1" Pos 1"
{  ▲    ▲    ▲    ▲    ▲    ▲    ▲    ▲    ▲    ▲    ▲    }    ▲    ▲
{Tbl Def}
{Row}{Cell}DATE{Cell}ITEM{Cell}ORDER #{Cell}PRICE
{Row}{Cell}10/14{Cell}   Office Supplies (General){Cell}1516{Cell}37.50
{Row}{Cell}10/19{Cell}   Copy Paper & Toner Cartridges{Cell}1517{Cell}287.00
{Row}{Cell}10/30{Cell}   Pens, Note Pads, FAX Paper{Cell}1519{Cell}42.50
{Row}{Cell}11/06{Cell}   Business Cards (Reprint for NGA){Cell}1527{Cell}200.00
{Row}{Cell}11/09{Cell}   Printer Ribbons x 12{Cell}1521{Cell}32.00{Tbl Off}



Press Reveal Codes to restore screen
```

FIGURE 4-8. Retrieving a table into LetterPerfect

An appendix in the LetterPerfect manual lists all WordPerfect codes, and explains those that are supported in LetterPerfect. Consult this appendix for the complete list of WordPerfect codes.

INITIAL CODES FOR DOCUMENTS

In Chapter 2, you learned how to create a new layout by inserting the proper formatting codes into your document. This is a powerful way to create a document layout, but there are a few disadvantages to this system. Sometimes, editing is difficult because you have to make sure that any new text is inserted after the right formatting codes. However, when the formatting codes are mixed with your text, it's easy to forget where they are. You may accidentally delete a line spacing code, or place text before the margin code that should affect it.

The Reveal Codes feature can prevent these problems, but sometimes it would be better to apply format settings to the entire document, without worrying about whether they're in the right place. LetterPerfect includes a feature that lets you do just that. The Document Initial Codes feature lets you create a document layout that applies to the entire document. Instead of placing formatting codes into your text, you create the layout at the Initial Codes screen, where the formatting commands will stay out of your way. You can return to this screen at any time and edit the format—so you don't need to search through your document to find the right codes.

Creating a Format at the Initial Codes Screen

Until now, you have inserted formatting codes directly into your text. LetterPerfect's Document Initial Codes feature allows you to set up default codes for the current document. These include the formats that should be applied to all text in your document, such as paper size and margins. The following exercise will show you how to set up a document format with the Document Initial Codes feature. Make sure you clear the screen before continuing.

1. Press Format (SHIFT-F8) or choose **Format** from the Layout pull-down menu. Then, choose the Document Initial Codes/Base Font option from the Format menu. The following menu appears:

```
1 Initial Codes; 2 Initial Base Font: 0
```

2. Choose option **1**, Initial Codes, to display the screen shown in Figure 4-9. This is the Document Initial Codes screen. Here, you can select format settings and insert the codes that should be applied to all text in your document.

note Figure 4-9 shows the two codes that LetterPerfect automatically inserts as part of the standard format. The [Just:Left] code indicates left justification for the text lines. The {W/O On} code applies Widow/Orphan protection for your text, preventing a single word from being wrapped alone, at the bottom or top of a page. LetterPerfect inserts the {W/O On} code for you, because there is no such option on the LetterPerfect menus.

3. Press the LEFT ARROW key once, to move the text cursor to highlight the {W/O On} code. Press BACKSPACE to delete the Justification code.

4. Press Format (SHIFT-F8). Choose **1**, Justification, and select option **4**, Full.

5. The Format menu should still be displayed. Choose **2**, Line Spacing. Type **2** and press ENTER to select double line spacing. Press Exit (F7) to return to the Initial Codes screen.

```
File Edit Search Layout Tools Font Graphics Help      (Press ALT for menu bar
```

```
Initial Codes:  Press F7 when done                         Ln 1" Pos 1"
[Just:Left]{W/O On}
```

FIGURE 4-9.   The Document Initial Codes screen

```
File Edit Search Layout Tools Font Graphics Help      (Press ALT for menu bar
```

```
Initial Codes:  Press F7 when done                         Ln 1" Pos 1"
[Just:Full][Ln Spacing:2]{W/O On}
```

FIGURE 4-10.   Editing the initial document codes

6. Your screen should look like Figure 4-10. Press Exit (F7) twice to return to the main document editing screen.

7. Now, type a paragraph of text. It doesn't have to be very long; a few lines will do. If you wish, you can just copy the text shown in Figure 4-11.

8. Press Reveal Codes (CTRL-R or ALT-F3) or select **R**eveal Codes from the **E**dit pull-down menu.

The codes that you entered under Document Initial Codes will affect your document, but they will not be visible when you display the Reveal Codes window. Obviously, this could be confusing if you didn't know the format was already defined. However, if you don't need to change tabs, margins, and line spacing throughout your entire document, the Document Initial Codes feature will make it easier to edit the format, and will keep excess codes out of your way.

For example, suppose you've already defined margin settings at the Document Initial Codes screen, and decide you want to change them. You don't need to search through your document to find the Margin Set code. Just select the Document Initial

```
File Edit Search Layout Tools Font Graphics Help        (Press ALT for menu bar)
The United States Library of Congress contains the largest motion

picture collection in the world, with over 100,000 films.  The

American Museum of the Moving Arts, in Astoria, New York, is the

only museum in the U.S. devoted to television, video, and the

motion picture arts.
                                                         Pg 1 Ln 1" Pos 1"
{    ▲    ▲    ▲    ▲    ▲    ▲    ▲    ▲    ▲    ▲    }    ▲    ▲
The United States Library of Congress contains the largest motion[SRt]
picture collection in the world, with over 100,000 films.  The[SRt]
American Museum of the Moving Arts, in Astoria, New York, is the[SRt]
only museum in the U.S. devoted to television, video, and the[SRt]
motion picture arts.




Press Reveal Codes to restore screen
```

FIGURE 4-11. Initial codes are not seen in Reveal Codes

Codes feature again, and the code is displayed. Then, delete it and insert a new Margin Set code.

Another option from the Document Initial Codes/Base Font feature also allows you to select a font that affects all text in the document—including headers, footers, and endnotes. Press Format (SHIFT-F8) and select the Document Initial Codes/Base Font feature. Option 2, Initial Base Font, lets you select a default font for the document. Select this option and a list of available fonts is displayed. You can select one for the entire document.

Copying Document Codes to the Initial Codes Screen

If your document layout is already defined, you can use the Block and Move features to transfer the formatting codes from the Reveal Codes window to the Document Initial Codes screen. Move only the codes that should apply to all text in your document, such as paper size, margin settings, and line spacing.

You don't need to transfer formatting codes to the Document Initial Codes screen, but it does condense the format of your document, and can prevent important codes from being deleted accidentally. This is also important for merging files together, when you don't want the formatting codes to be mixed with the text. In Chapter 11, you'll use the Document Initial Codes feature to store formatting codes for mass-mailing documents.

EXERCISE: EDITING THE PARTY SHACK FLYER

Now that you've learned about the editing features of LetterPerfect, you are ready to edit your own document. In the following exercise, you will edit the layout and text of the Party Shack flyer, and you'll also add a table to the document. Before you begin, make sure the screen is clear.

Editing the Document Layout

Follow these steps to center the text on the page and add a header and footer to the document format:

1. Press Retrieve (SHIFT-F10) or choose **Retrieve** from the **File** pull-down menu. Type **party.doc** and press ENTER to retrieve the Party Shack flyer that you created earlier.

2. You need to insert a formatting code that will center the document text on the current page. Press the HOME key twice, and then press the UP ARROW key, to move the cursor to the beginning of the text.

3. Press Format (SHIFT-F8) or choose **Format** from the **Layout** pull-down menu. Select option **9**, Center Page, from the Format menu, and type **Y** for Yes.

4. The Format menu should still be displayed on the screen. Now, you will create a header that contains a horizontal line for the top of the page. Choose option **6**, Header/Footer, and select **1** Header. A menu appears with three options for headers and footers. Choose option **2**, Create to create a new header.

5. At the Header screen, type the underscore character (SHIFT - −) 64 times. This should create a line that extends from the left margin to the right margin.

6. You'll want to copy the line you just created. This will save you the trouble of typing the underscore character 64 times when you create the footer in the next step. Press Block (ALT-F4 or F12) and then press HOME, LEFT ARROW to block the entire line. Press Move (CTRL-F4) and select **2** Copy to copy the blocked line.

7. Note the "Press Enter to retrieve" message at the bottom of the screen. Since you don't want to immediately retrieve the copy, press Cancel (F1 or ESC) to cancel the message. The copied text is still stored in memory. Press Exit (F7) to return to the Format menu.

8. Now, you'll create a footer that contains the date and the horizontal line that you copied at the Header screen. Select option **6**, Header/Footer again. Then, choose **2** Footer and **2** Create.

9. At the Footer screen, press Center (CTRL-C or SHIFT-F6), or select **Center** from the **Layout** menu. Press Date (SHIFT-F5) and select option **1**, Date Text, or choose Date Text from the **Tools** pull-down menu.

10. Press ENTER to move to the next line. Now, press Retrieve (SHIFT-F10) or select **Retrieve** from the **File** pull-down menu. At the "Document to be retrieved" prompt, simply press ENTER to retrieve the underscore characters that you copied from the header. Then, press Exit (F7) twice to return to the main editing screen.

11. If you wish, press Print (SHIFT-F7) and select option **3**, View Document, or simply press the Fast Key, CTRL-P.

Your document is displayed as it will be printed. When you are finished viewing the document, press Exit (F7) to return to the main editing screen.

Editing the Text

Now, you will rearrange the headline at the top of the page, and add some additional text to the flyer.

1. Move the text cursor to the word "GREETINGS". Press CTRL-BACKSPACE to delete the word, and type **SUMMER SAVINGS!** to replace it. Press ENTER after "SUMMER SAVINGS!" to divide the headline into two lines.

2. Press Center (CTRL-C or SHIFT-F6), or select Center from the Layout pull-down menu to center the second line between the margins. Press DOWN ARROW to move to the next line. Your document should now look like Figure 4-12.

```
File Edit Search Layout Tools Font Graphics Help        (Press ALT for menu bar)

                           SUMMER SAVINGS!
                          FROM THE PARTY SHACK!

  The Party Shack offers complete catering services for all your
  entertainment needs.  Our creative directors have the perfect
  ideas for every occasion:  birthday parties, weddings, holidays--
  we can even bring Spunky the Magic Clown and twelve trained
  dachshunds to add some excitement to a boring dinner party!

  Why cook?  Our chefs can do it for you!  Certified with the
  renowned Crockett Institute of Fine Party Cuisine, we can create
  the most exotic and creative dishes, suitable for any backyard
  barbecue or corporate Christmas party.

  And now is the best time to get acquainted with our services.  If
  you plan a party before July 31st, we'll give you a 10% discount
  on all party favors!  So drop by the Party Shack, where there's
  always a party going on!



  C:\LP10\PARTY.DOC                              Pg 1 Ln 1.67" Pos 1"
```

FIGURE 4-12.   Editing the flyer headlines

3. Move the cursor to the end of the second paragraph, and add the following sentence: **In fact, why not visit our store and sample these tasty treats:**

4. Next, move the cursor to the last paragraph and edit the second sentence to read: "If you plan a party before July 31st, we'll give you a **25%** discount on all party favors **and a 10% discount on catering services!**" (the bold text represents the changes you'll need to make).

Creating a Table

You've just added a sentence to the second paragraph that refers to a list of "tasty treats." The following steps will show you how to create the table of items that the catering company can deliver:

1. Move the cursor to the end of the last sentence in the second paragraph. Press ENTER three times to add space between the paragraphs.

2. Press Format (SHIFT-F8) or choose Format from the Layout pull-down menu. Select option **5**, **T**abs, and the Tab screen is displayed.

3. Press HOME, LEFT ARROW to move to the left edge of the tab ruler, and press CTRL-END to delete the current tab settings. Type **0.5** and press ENTER to set a tab one half-inch from the left margin. Then, type **3.5** and press ENTER to set another tab. Press Exit (F7) twice to return to the main editing screen.

4. Press TAB and type **Taco Kabobs**. Press TAB again to move to the second column, and type **Gummi Bear Flambé**. The accented *e* is inserted by pressing CTRL-V, and typing e'. Press ENTER twice to move to the next line in the table.

5. Press TAB and type **Curried Moose**. Press TAB again, and type **Seafood Pasta with Raisins**. Press ENTER twice to move to the next line of the table.

6. Enter the last two lines of the table, as shown in Figure 4-13. Press ENTER twice to end the table.

7. Press Save (F10) or select Save from the File pull-down menu. Press ENTER to accept the displayed file name, and type **Y** for Yes when prompted about replacing the original file.

8. Press Print (SHIFT-F7) and choose option **3**, **V**iew Document, or simply press the Fast Key, CTRL-P. The completed flyer should look similar to the example shown in Figure 4-14.

Chapter 4 Editing a Document 113

```
File Edit Search Layout Tools Font Graphics Help    (Press ALT for menu bar)
```
Why cook? Our chefs can do it for you! Certified with the
renowned Crockett Institute of Fine Party Cuisine, we can create
the most exotic and creative dishes, suitable for any backyard
barbecue or corporate Christmas party. In fact, why not visit
our store and sample these tasty treats:

  Taco Kabobs   Gummi Bear Flambé

  Curried Moose   Seafood Pasta with Raisins

  Peanut Butter Surprise   M & M Chicken

  Oysters Jeff   Homemade Ice Cream

And now is the best time to get acquainted with our services. If
you plan a party before July 31st, we'll give you a 25% discount
on all party favors and a 10% discount on catering services! So
drop by the Party Shack, where there's always a party going on!

C:\LP10\PARTY.DOC   Pg 1 Ln 5.5" Pos 1"

FIGURE 4-13.   Creating a table

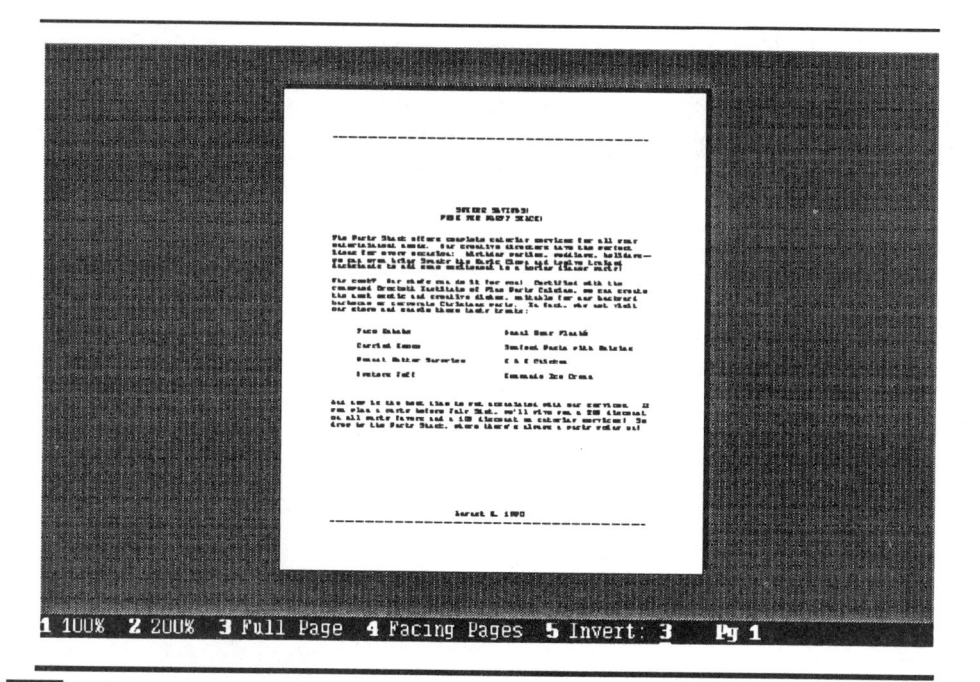

FIGURE 4-14.   Viewing the PARTY.DOC flyer

When you are finished viewing your document, press Exit (F7) or click the right mouse button to return to the normal editing screen. It doesn't matter if your document doesn't look exactly like the illustrations shown here; what's important is that you've had the opportunity to practice the editing features.

SUMMARY

In this chapter, you've learned about the features and commands that allow you to make changes to your text. You know how to delete text with the keys on your keyboard and with LetterPerfect's Move feature. Simply define a block and use the Move (CTRL-F4) key, the pull-down menus, or the Fast Keys to manipulate the text. If you select these features without first defining a block, you will be prompted to select what you want to move or copy.

LetterPerfect includes features that let you search for specific words and phrases and replace them with other text. You can use the Reveal Codes feature to edit the invisible formatting codes in your document. The Document Initial Codes screen can make editing easier by storing in one place the codes that affect the entire document.

Now that you've completed the first four chapters of this book, you can create most of the documents that you will need. In the next chapter, you'll learn how to use LetterPerfect's Speller to correct typing errors and the Thesaurus to enhance your writing with a broader vocabulary.

chapter 5

USING THE SPELLER AND THESAURUS

Using the Speller
Speller Dictionaries
Using the Thesaurus
Summary

If you are a writer, you probably feel comfortable with your ability to spell words correctly—at least, that's what most people would expect. Unfortunately, spelling errors creep into most documents, regardless of the writer's abilities. In the professional world, editors find and correct the errors of spelling, grammar, and content. However, an editor may not be available to you.

LetterPerfect includes two utility features, the Speller and Thesaurus, that can act as your own personal editor. They can't improve your grammar or turn poor writing into a literary masterpiece. But the Speller can correct misspelled words and typing errors, and the Thesaurus can help you find the perfect word for the message you need to convey. It's important to remember that these features are tools to help you create better documents, but they do not eliminate the need for good old-fashioned editing.

USING THE SPELLER

The LetterPerfect Speller includes an 80,000-word dictionary that can check every word in your document and correct the spelling errors. You can also add words to a supplementary dictionary file and customize the speller for your own projects.

note The LetterPerfect Speller and Thesaurus utilities require special files that are installed during program installation. If you decided not to install the Speller or Thesaurus files, the LetterPerfect program cannot access these features. See Appendix A for information about the complete installation of LetterPerfect.

Correcting Spelling Errors

When you run the Speller, it highlights the words that are not found in its dictionary, and it displays a list of possible corrections. Then, you can choose a replacement word, ignore the word, or edit the text.

The following exercise will show you how to use the LetterPerfect Speller. Before you begin, clear the screen. First, you'll need some text on the screen—with spelling errors, of course.

1. Type the following paragraph at the main LetterPerfect screen:

   Caldwell Industries offers a fundamental combination of quality manufacturing and dynamic marketing. We beleive our company woll produce the the product you envision, and we look forward to meeting with you on August 10th. Then, we woll discuss our future plans.

   The text of this paragraph contains spelling errors that you'll correct in the following steps. Make sure you type the text exactly as it is shown.

2. Now you're ready to spell-check the document. Press Spell (CTRL-S or CTRL-F2), or select Spell from the Tools pull-down menu. Your screen is divided into two sections, as shown in Figure 5-1. Your text appears above the ruler. The lower half of the screen displays possible replacement words (we'll explain shortly why none are displayed in this example), and a menu with options for the Speller.

3. The word "Caldwell" is highlighted as the first misspelling in the document. However, "Caldwell" is not really misspelled; it is a proper name and is not found in the LetterPerfect spelling dictionary. In this case, choose option **2**, Skip. This

Chapter 5   Using the Speller and Thesaurus   117

><mark>Caldwell</mark> Industries offers a fundamental combination of quality manufacturing
>and dynamic marketing. We beleive our company woll produce the the product
>you envision, and we look forward to meeting with you on August 10th. Then,
>we woll discuss our future plans.


```
                                                              Pg 1 Ln 1" Pos 1"
[   ▲    ▲    ▲    ▲    ▲    ▲    ▲    ▲    ▲   ▲   ▲   ▲   ▲   ▲   ]
```
The
Speller
window

Not Found: 1 Skip Once; 2 Skip; 3 Add; 4 Edit; 5 Look Up; 6 Ignore Numbers: 0

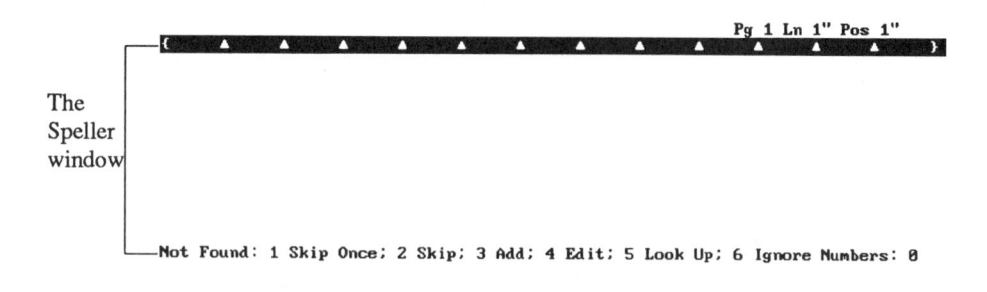

FIGURE 5-1.   The Speller screen

tells LetterPerfect to ignore this word during this spell-check of your entire document. If you want to ignore only this occurrence of the word, choose option **1**, Skip Once.

4. The Speller then stops at the word "beleive", which is misspelled. Notice, in Figure 5-2, that possible replacement words are displayed beneath the ruler on the screen. Type **A** to choose "believe", and LetterPerfect replaces "beleive" with the correct spelling.

5. Next, the word "woll" is highlighted. This is obviously a typing error, and a long list of replacement words appears in the Speller window. Type **C** to select the correct spelling, "will". The word is replaced.

6. Now, the Speller stops at a double word. In this case the word "the" was accidentally typed twice. As shown in Figure 5-3, the menu at the bottom of the screen changes to handle this situation. Choose option **3**, Delete 2nd, to remove the second occurrence of "the".

7. The last highlight is on "10th". This isn't really a word because it has text characters and numbers combined. So, the Speller highlights it and asks you what you want to do. If you have other numbers like this in your document, you can choose option **6**, Ignore Numbers, to skip each one. Otherwise, simply choose option **2**, Skip.

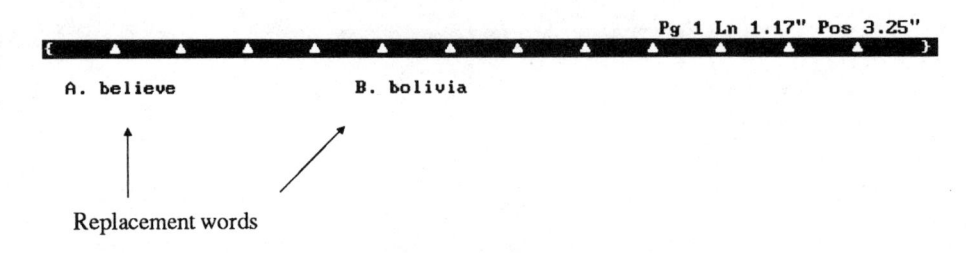

```
Caldwell Industries offers a fundamental combination of quality manufacturing
and dynamic marketing.  We beleive our company woll produce the the product
you envision, and we look forward to meeting with you on August 10th.  Then,
we woll discuss our future plans.




                                              Pg 1 Ln 1.17" Pos 3.25"
{   ▲   ▲   ▲   ▲   ▲   ▲   ▲   ▲   ▲   ▲   ▲   ▲   }
  A. believe          B. bolivia
                ↑          ↗
                 Replacement words

Not Found: 1 Skip Once; 2 Skip; 3 Add; 4 Edit; 5 Look Up; 6 Ignore Numbers: 0
```

FIGURE 5-2.   The Speller suggests replacement words

```
Caldwell Industries offers a fundamental combination of quality manufacturing
and dynamic marketing.  We believe our company will produce the the product
you envision, and we look forward to meeting with you on August 10th.  Then,
we woll discuss our future plans.
                                                         |
                                                    Double word


                                              Pg 1 Ln 1.17" Pos 6"
{   ▲   ▲   ▲   ▲   ▲   ▲   ▲   ▲   ▲   ▲   ▲   ▲   }




Double Word: 1 2 Skip; 3 Delete 2nd; 4 Edit; 5 Disable Double Word Checking
```

FIGURE 5-3.   Checking for double words

The Speller is finished checking the text, and displays the number of words in the document at the bottom of the screen. Press the SPACEBAR to return to the normal editing screen.

When the Speller finds a misspelled word, it searches its dictionary to find possible replacement words. First, it displays words that match the characters of the original word. Then, it displays words that have similar phonetic sounds. This is why "bolivia" was displayed next to "believe" when you corrected the first misspelling.

note During the exercise, you may have noticed that replacement words are displayed without capitalization; however, if the misspelled word is capitalized, the Speller will also capitalize the replacement.

The Speller also automatically corrects additional misspellings of the same word; you may have noticed that "will" was misspelled twice in the original text of the example, but the Speller stopped only at the first occurrence of the word. You only need to correct the first misspelling and LetterPerfect does the rest.

It's a good idea to save your document before you run the Speller, because you can't undo the effects of a spell-check. Then, after you spell-check a document, make sure you read the text to verify that everything is correct, and save the document again. Before you continue, save the document on your screen by pressing Save (F10). Then, type **proposal.doc** and press ENTER. You will need this file to test the Thesaurus feature later in this chapter.

Spell-Checking a Page or Block

The LetterPerfect Speller automatically checks the entire document for misspelled or unrecognized words. However, suppose you're making changes to only one page of a document that's already been checked; if your text covers many pages, you may not want to check the entire document again. Instead, you can use the Block (ALT-F4 or F12) feature, described in Chapter 4, to highlight only the text you want to check. Then, press Spell (CTRL-2 or CTRL-F2) to do a spell-check on the block.

SPELLER DICTIONARIES

The LetterPerfect Speller compares your text with the words stored in a dictionary file, which is specific to a particular language. Your copy of LetterPerfect probably includes the English version of the Speller dictionary; dictionary files are also available for other languages (more about these later in the chapter).

You can also create your own supplemental dictionary file, which contains words not found in the standard dictionary. These may include names, technical terms, or professional jargon. The following explains how to create a supplemental dictionary file, and how to install and use a foreign-language dictionary.

Creating Your Own Dictionaries

Occasionally, the Speller will stop on words that aren't necessarily misspelled; they're just not in the Speller dictionary. This often happens with names and professional terms. When the Speller highlights these types of words, you can choose option **3**, Add, from the Speller menu, to insert them into a supplemental dictionary file. Then, the next time you use the Speller, it won't stop on those words.

The supplemental dictionary file, called WP{WP}US.SUP, is automatically created the first time you add a word while using the Speller. This is simply a LetterPerfect document file with a list of the words that you've added. If you haven't already added words while spell-checking, you can create the file yourself. For example, clear the screen (F7, N, N), and follow these steps to create a supplemental dictionary file:

1. Type your first name on the first line of the screen and press ENTER to move to the next line.

2. Type your last name and press ENTER.

3. Now, save the file. Press Save (F10) or choose Save from the File pull-down menu.

4. When prompted with "Document to be saved: ", type the drive and path name where the LetterPerfect program files are stored, followed by the name **wp{wp}us.sup**. Then, press ENTER.

    For example, if you are running the LetterPerfect program from drive A, type **a:wp{wp}us.sup** and press ENTER. If you are running the program from a hard disk directory called *C:\ LP10,* type **c:\lp10\wp{wp}us.sup** and press ENTER.

The supplemental dictionary file is saved. Now, whenever you check a document, the Speller will recognize your first and last names as words that are spelled correctly. You can retrieve the supplemental dictionary file into LetterPerfect and easily edit or add to the list. When you are finished editing the file, make sure you save it and replace the original supplemental dictionary file. Then, clear the screen.

Foreign-Language Dictionaries

WordPerfect Corporation has developed Speller dictionaries for over 20 foreign languages, including French, Spanish, German, and even Russian. Contact your software dealer or the WordPerfect Corporation Orders Department for information on ordering a foreign-language dictionary file.

Each Speller dictionary file is named according to the language it supports. For example, the English dictionary file is named WP{WP}*US*.LEX, the Norwegian dictionary is called WP{WP}*NO*.LEX, and WP{WP}*IT*.LEX is the name of the Italian dictionary file. Once you have the dictionary file that you want to use, it must be installed to the directory where your LetterPerfect program files are located. Each foreign-language Speller diskette contains an installation program (LMINSTAL.EXE) that can help you copy the file.

After the dictionary file is copied to your program directory, you need to insert a code into your text that tells LetterPerfect which dictionary the Speller should use for the current document. This is done with the Language feature:

1. Press HOME, HOME, UP ARROW to move the text cursor to the beginning of the document.

2. Press Language (ALT-F8), or choose Language from the Layout pull-down menu. LetterPerfect prompts you with "Language: ".

3. At this point, you need to type a two-letter code that indicates which language dictionary you want to use. Type the code (such as, *IT* for *IT*alian) and press ENTER. If you aren't sure what you should type, press Help (F3 or F1) at the prompt to display a help screen with all the language codes, and then press SPACEBAR to return to your document.

LetterPerfect inserts the [Lang:] code into your text. Also inserted is a decimal-align character code, [Decml/Align Char:], which determines the number alignment character for the chosen language. You can view both codes by pressing Reveal Codes (CTRL-R or ALT-F3). The language setting is stored with your text when you save your document. Clear the screen, and LetterPerfect returns to the default language setting.

The Language feature also affects the way dates are inserted into your document with the Date/Outline (SHIFT-F5) key. If, for example, you change the language to *FR* for *FR*ench, the date "July 30, 1991" is inserted as "30 juillet 1991" when you use the Date features.

note: The Language feature also determines which Thesaurus file LetterPerfect will look for when you press CTRL-T or ALT-F1 or choose Thesaurus from the Tools pull-down menu.

USING THE THESAURUS

The Thesaurus can help find the right words for the message you want to deliver. The Thesaurus can also help you check the context of the words you've used. For example, assume you've typed the sentence, "As the morning poured calmly, the harbor feigned peace." Is *feigned* the correct word for this sentence? Does it suggest the intended meaning? You can use the Thesaurus to display synonyms and antonyms of a word, and this will help you decide whether or not you've used it correctly.

Finding the Right Word

In the following exercise, you'll learn how to replace a word in your document with a synonym from the Thesaurus. If you are running LetterPerfect on a double-floppy system, replace the diskette in drive B with your working copy of the LetterPerfect "Utilities/Images" diskette. This diskette contains the Thesaurus utility file.

1. Press Retrieve (SHIFT-F10) or choose **Retrieve** from the **File** pull-down menu. At the "Document to be retrieved:" prompt, type **proposal.doc** and press ENTER. This retrieves the text that you typed earlier in this chapter.

2. Assume that you want to find a better word for the first sentence on your screen. Move the cursor to the word "fundamental".

3. Press CTRL-T or ALT-F1 or choose **Thesaurus** from the **Tools** pull-down menu. The Thesaurus window appears on your screen, as shown in Figure 5-4.

4. Suppose you want to replace "fundamental" with the word "vital". Select option **1**, Replace Word, from the menu at the bottom of the screen. You are prompted to "Press letter for word." Type **D** to select "vital", and it replaces the original word.

That's all you need to do. When you're looking for common words, the Thesaurus is really quite simple to use. Languages can be complex, however, and many words may share the same or similar meanings. In this example, you found the word you

Chapter 5   Using the Speller and Thesaurus   123

```
Caldwell Industries offers a fundamental combination of quality manufacturing
and dynamic marketing.  We believe our company will produce the product you
envision, and we look forward to meeting with you on August 10th.  Then, we
will discuss our future plans.
  ┌fundamental=(a)────────────┬─────────────────────┬─────────────────────┐
  │ 1 A ·central              │                     │                     │
  │   B ·integral             │                     │                     │
  │                           │                     │                     │
  │ 2 C ·essential            │                     │                     │
  │   D ·vital                │                     │                     │
  │                           │                     │                     │
  │ 3 E ·basic                │                     │                     │
  │   F ·primary              │                     │                     │
  │                           │                     │                     │
  │fundamental-(n)────────────│                     │                     │
  │ 4 G ·basic                │                     │                     │
  │   H ·principle            │                     │                     │
  │                           │                     │                     │
  │ 5 I ·requirement          │                     │                     │
  │                           │                     │                     │
  │                           │                     │                     │
  └───────────────────────────┴─────────────────────┴─────────────────────┘
1 Replace Word; 2 Look Up Word; 3 Clear Column: 0
```

FIGURE 5-4.   Using the Thesaurus

needed from the list of synonyms for "fundamental", but sometimes you may need to explore further to find the right word. The next section will show you how to navigate through the Thesaurus window, and display synonyms for several levels of words.

Navigating Through the Thesaurus Menus

The Thesaurus window includes three columns that may display additional synonyms for the highlighted word in your document. Sometimes, antonyms are also displayed. A menu at the bottom of the screen provides options for the Thesaurus feature. Refer to Figure 5-5 for a diagram of the different parts of the display.

Select letters (A, B, C, and so on) appear next to the words in one of the columns. These allow you to select a word to replace the highlighted word, or view more synonyms. The words with dots next to them are called *headwords*, meaning that

```
                Caldwell Industries offers a vital combination of quality manufacturing and
                dynamic marketing. We believe our company will  produce  the product you
                envision, and we look forward to meeting with you on August 18th. Then, we
                will discuss our future plans.
                ┌produce=(v)────────┬create=(v)────────┬construct=(v)──────┐
                │ 1 ┌·construct     │ 1   ·develop     │ 1 A ·assemble     │
                │   │·manufacture   │     ·invent      │   B ·make         │
                │   │·manifest      │                  │                   │
                │   │·present       │ 2   ·devise      │ 2 C ·build        │
                │   │·compose       │                  │   D ·erect        │
Headwords ──────┤   │·create        │ 3   ·establish   │         ▲         │
                │   │·spawn         │                  │         │         │
                │   │·provide       │ 4   ·construct   │         │         │
                │   │·yield         │                  │    Select letters │
                │   │·accomplish    │ 5   ·generate    │                   │
                │   └·generate      │     ·make        │                   │
                │produce=(n)────────│                  │                   │
                │ 2   ·harvest      │                  │                   │
                │                   │                  │                   │
                │      Column 1     │     Column 2     │     Column 3      │
                │ 1 Replace Word; 2 Look Up Word; 3 Clear Column: 0        │
                └─────────────────────────────────────────────────────────┘
                                         Menu
```

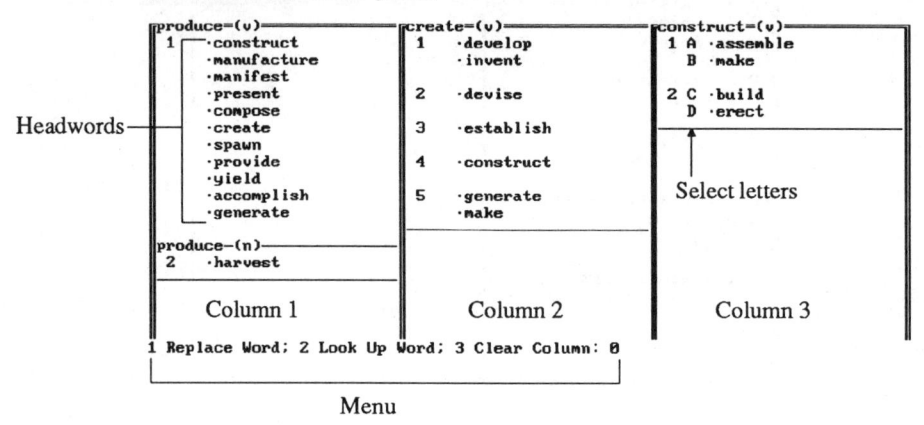

FIGURE 5-5. The Thesaurus window

these words are headings for an additional list of synonyms. You've already learned how to replace a word in your document with a displayed synonym. To view more synonyms from the list, simply type one of the select letters, and additional words are displayed in the next column. You will notice that the select letters also move to the new column, again enabling you to choose.

You can press LEFT ARROW or RIGHT ARROW to move the select letters to the previous column or to the next column, so you can select from any of the word lists. Choose option **3**, Clear Column, from the Thesaurus menu to clear the column where the select letters are positioned. After you choose option **1**, Replace, and select a letter, the highlighted word in your document is replaced and the document screen is restored. Press Exit (F7) or Cancel (F1 or ESC) to return to the normal editing screen, without replacing a word.

The following steps will give you some practice with the different Thesaurus options. The PROPOSAL.DOC text should still be on your screen. In this example, the phrase "produce the product" sounds a little awkward, so let's find a replacement.

1. Move the text cursor to the word "produce" in the second sentence. Press CTRL-T or ALT-F1 or choose Thesaurus from the Tools pull-down menu. A list of synonyms for the word "produce" appears.

2. Type **F** to display synonyms for the word "create" in the second column. These appear as shown in Figure 5-6. Notice that the select letters have also moved to the second column.

3. Assume that the word "construct" is close to the meaning you want. Type **E** to display synonyms for that word. These will appear in the third column.

4. None of the words for "construct" seem right, so choose option **3**, Clear Column, from the menu at the bottom of the screen. The "construct" column is cleared and the select letters move back to column two.

5. Choose option **1**, Replace, from the Thesaurus menu. Type **A** to replace "produce" with "develop". After you select a replacement word, the Thesaurus window is removed from the screen.

```
Caldwell Industries offers a vital combination of quality manufacturing and
dynamic marketing.  We believe our company will produce the product you
envision, and we look forward to meeting with you on August 10th.  Then, we
will discuss our future plans.
  ┌produce=(v)════════════════╤create=(v)═══════════════╤
  │ 1    ·construct           │ 1 A  ·develop           │
  │      ·manufacture         │   B  ·invent            │
  │      ·manifest            │                         │
  │      ·present             │ 2 C  ·devise            │
  │      ·compose             │                         │
  │      ·create              │ 3 D  ·establish         │
  │      ·spawn               │                         │
  │      ·provide             │ 4 E  ·construct         │
  │      ·yield               │                         │
  │      ·accomplish          │ 5 F  ·generate          │
  │      ·generate            │   G  ·make              │
  │                           │                         │
  │produce-(n)────────────────┤                         │
  │ 2    ·harvest             │                         │
  │                           │                         │
  │                           │                         │
  │                           │                         │
  │                           │                         │
  1 Replace Word; 2 Look Up Word; 3 Clear Column: 0
```

FIGURE 5-6.   Displaying synonyms for *create*

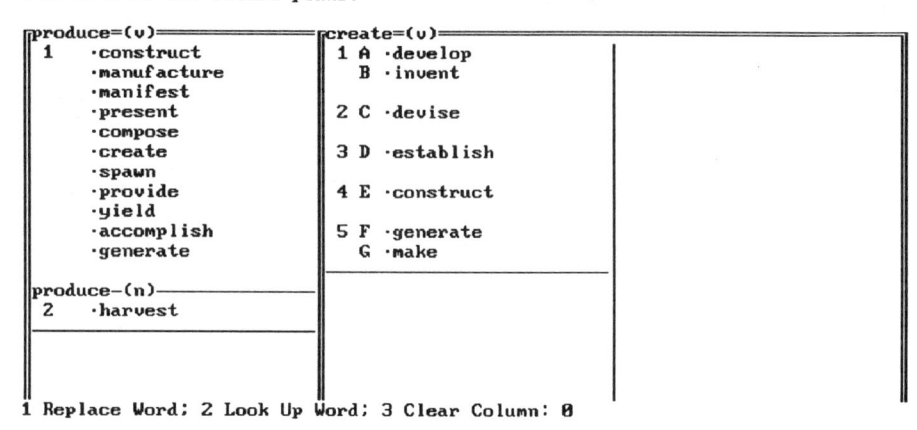

Sometimes, you will want to choose option **2**, Look Up Word, to display the synonyms of a word that is not on the screen. If you wish, move your cursor to other words in your text and use the Thesaurus feature to find synonyms for them. If you want to exit the Thesaurus without replacing a word, press Exit (F7) or Cancel (F1 or ESC).

Before you continue, you should save this document again, and clear the screen. The Thesaurus is not difficult to use, but since so many words are interrelated, you can go through several different levels before finding the precise word.

SUMMARY

The LetterPerfect Speller can check the text in your document and help you correct misspelled or unrecognized words. You can customize the Speller by creating a supplemental dictionary file; this is a LetterPerfect file that contains words you've added while using the Speller. You can also retrieve the supplemental dictionary file into LetterPerfect and add or edit words in the list. Then resave the document under the same name.

The LetterPerfect Thesaurus can help you find alternate words to improve the vocabulary in your documents. When you use the Thesaurus, synonyms—and sometimes antonyms—are displayed for the word that your cursor is on. You can replace the word in your document or look up additional synonyms for the words displayed in the Thesaurus window.

chapter 6

USING THE GRAPHICS FEATURES

Inserting a Graphic Image
Editing a Graphic Image
Exercise: Adding Graphics to the Party Shack Flyer
Drawing Lines and Boxes
Summary

A few years ago, a typed manuscript was the standard design for college papers, letters, and common business documents. Sophisticated word processors now allow multiple fonts, elaborate text arrangements, and of course, graphics. This is important because people expect more than just words on a page. Sometimes, graphics are the most effective way to communicate your message. You may need to include a graph with the text of your scientific paper, a map that shows how to get to the local baseball field, or an illustration for your club newsletter.

LetterPerfect makes it easy to get started with graphics. Over 25 graphic images are included with your program files, some of which are shown in Figure 6-1. You can insert any of these illustrations into the text of your documents. LetterPerfect does not have any drawing capabilities, but you can insert pictures and graphs from many popular programs, including PC Paintbrush, Lotus 1-2-3, and DrawPerfect. Consult your LetterPerfect manual for a complete list of the types of graphics files that can be included in your documents.

FIGURE 6-1. LetterPerfect graphic images

If you are familiar with the graphic capabilities of WordPerfect, you'll feel at ease with the similar features found in LetterPerfect.

INSERTING A GRAPHIC IMAGE

When you're ready to insert a graphic image into your document, you specify the file name and LetterPerfect creates a *figure box* for the image. A figure box determines the location and size of the illustration in the document. Figure 6-2 shows an example of this. You also indicate whether you want a border for the figure box, and whether the text of your document is formatted around or printed over the graphic image.

FIGURE 6-2.   Graphic files are inserted into figure boxes

Creating a Figure Box

The following exercise explains how to create a figure box and insert a graphic image into your text. If you wish, you can retrieve or create a document before performing the steps.

This exercise assumes that when you installed the LetterPerfect program files, you also installed the LetterPerfect Graphic Images in your program directory. If you have not installed these graphic files, you should run the Installation program again and install these files before continuing here.

1. Move the text cursor to the beginning of the line or paragraph where the graphic image should appear. The cursor should be at the left margin of the text.

2. Press Graphics (ALT-F9) and select option **1**, **Create**, or choose **Create** from the Graphics pull-down menu. If you prefer to use the Fast Key, simply press CTRL-G. Figure 6-3 shows the Graphics Definition screen that appears. This is where you can define the figure box for your graphic image.

3. Choose option **1**, **Filename**, and the "Enter filename:" prompt appears at the bottom of the screen. If you are running LetterPerfect on a hard disk system, type **c:\lp10\printr-3.wpg** and press ENTER, to retrieve the graphic image of a laser printer that was installed with your program files. (If you are running LetterPerfect on a double-floppy system, place the "Utilities/Images" diskette in drive B, type **b:printr-3.wpg**, and press ENTER.)

4. Now, you will select a position for the figure box. Choose option **2**, **Horizontal Position**. This menu appears at the bottom of the screen:

```
Horizontal Position: 1 Left; 2 Right; 3 Center; 4 Full: 0
```

5. Choose option **1**, **Left**, from the menu, to position the figure box at the left margin of the text.

```
Graphics Definition
     1 - Filename
     2 - Horizontal Position   Right
     3 - Size                  3.25" wide x 3.25" (high)
     4 - Wrap Text Around Box  Yes
     5 - Border                Yes
         Note: Each time you specify a border option,
               a figure option code ([Fig Opt]) is inserted
               in your document.  This code affects all
               subsequent figures until LetterPerfect
               encounters another figure option code.




Selection: 0
```

FIGURE 6-3. The Graphics Definition screen

Chapter 6   Using the Graphics Features   131

6. Select option **3**, Size, to define the size of the box. The Size menu appears with four options:

   `1 Set Width/Auto Height; 2 Set Height/Auto Width; 3 Set Both; 4 Auto Both: 0`

7. Choose option **1**, Set Width/Auto Height. A message appears at the bottom of the screen, prompting you to enter a width measurement for the figure box. Type **2.5"** and press ENTER. Since this is the Set Width/Auto Height option, you enter the width, and LetterPerfect automatically adjusts the height for the graphic image specified under the Filename option.

8. Press Exit (F7), or click the right mouse button to return to the main document screen. Press DOWN ARROW to reformat your text. If you already have text on the screen, you will notice the outline of the figure box, as shown in Figure 6-4. The actual graphic image is not visible from the main screen, so you'll have to preview the document.

```
File Edit Search Layout Tools Font Graphics Help        (Press ALT for menu bar)
┌─FIG 1─────────────────┐  How can I export a PlanPerfect [3.0]
│                       │  graph to WordPerfect 5.0?
│                       │
│                       │  A special graphic output "driver"
│                       │  exports PlanPerfect 3.0 graphs to a
│                       │  file format that WordPerfect 5.0 can
│                       │  handle.  This driver is called the
│                       │  GSS*CGM Metafile Driver.
│     Outline of        │
│     figure box        │  To install the driver from within
│                       │  PlanPerfect, press the Graph key, Alt-
│                       │  F9, then type 1 to select Output
│                       │  Devices.  The Graphic Device Drivers
│                       │  screen is displayed.  The message at
│                       │  the bottom of the screen should say
└───────────────────────┘  
"Graphics Display."  If you installed PlanPerfect correctly, the
graphics display driver for your monitor should be already
selected.  Press an Arrow (Cursor) key to change the message to
"Graphics Output," and you can select the Metafile driver.

Insert the PlanPerfect Graphics 1 diskette into drive A:  (If you
have a double-floppy system, insert the diskette into drive B:),
C:\FILES\PL50Q8A.DOC                              Pg 1 Ln 1.17" Pos 3.67"
```

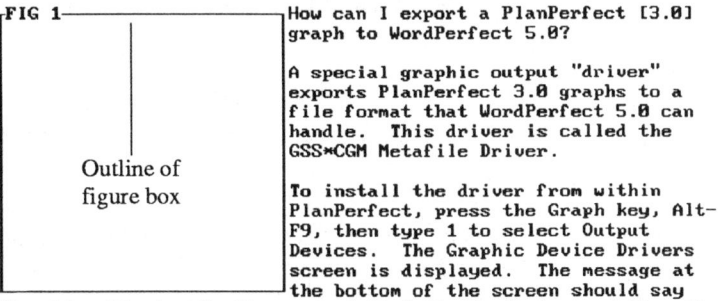

FIGURE 6-4.   A figure box outline appears on the text screen

132 LetterPerfect Made Easy

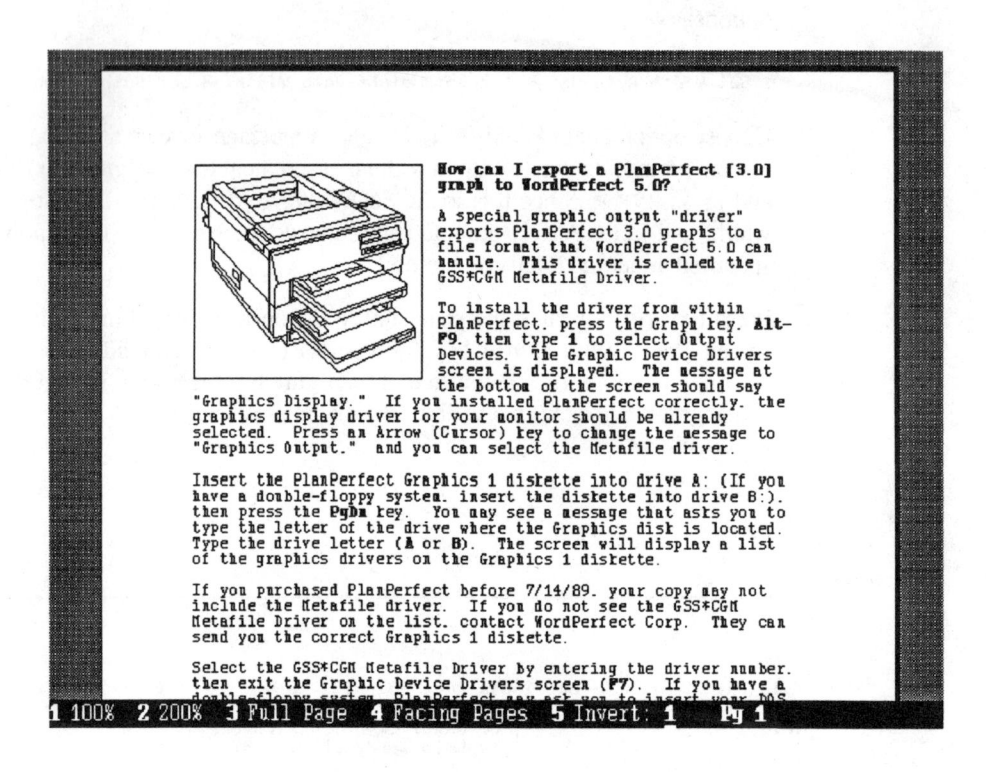

FIGURE 6-5.   Viewing your document with the graphic image

9. Press CTRL-P to preview the document. Your screen will look similar to the display in Figure 6-5. When you are finished viewing the document, press Exit (F7) to return to the main editing screen.

The graphic image is now incorporated into your document file. For now, keep this document on the screen; in the next section, you'll edit the figure box.

When you create a graphic image in LetterPerfect, a figure box code (such as [Fig Box:1;PRINTR-3.WPG]) is inserted at the current cursor position; you can view this code with the Reveal Codes feature (CTRL-R or ALT-F3). The figure box is attached to the current paragraph of text. This means that as you move, copy, or delete the text of your document, any graphic images will stay with the paragraph of text where they were placed.

note — If you retrieve a large graphic file into a figure box, the size of your document file will increase considerably.

Sizing the Figure Box

The Size option on the Graphics Definition menu provides complete control over the size of the figure box. In the previous exercise, you selected **1**, Set **W**idth/Auto Height to specify a width, and LetterPerfect figured out the height measurement for you. Option **2**, Set **H**eight/Auto Width, requires you to enter a height measurement, and LetterPerfect automatically calculates the width. Option **3**, Set **B**oth, lets you enter specific measurements for both the width and height; in this case, Letter-Perfect will not make any adjustments to the sizes you enter, unless you enter a measurement that is larger than the dimensions of the page. The last option, Auto Both, resets the width and height of the figure box to the measurements recommended by the LetterPerfect program.

After you enter a size, the measurement appears after the Size option on the menu (for example, 2.5" wide x 2.31" (high)).

note — If the word *high* or *wide* appears in parentheses, then LetterPerfect has automatically calculated this measurement for you.

Shortcuts for Inserting Graphics

You've already learned how to insert graphics by pressing Graphics (ALT-F9, 1 or CTRL-G), or by selecting the Create option from the Graphics menu. Each of these methods displays the Graphics Definition screen, where you can specify the file name and define the settings for a figure box.

LetterPerfect also provides two shortcuts that quickly insert a graphic image when you don't want to define each figure box setting. You can retrieve a graphic file with either Retrieve (SHIFT-F10), or from the List Files screen, and it will be retrieved as a figure box.

For example, move your cursor to the beginning of the paragraph where a graphic image should be inserted. Press Retrieve (SHIFT-F10), type **c:\lp10\printr-3.wpg** or **b:printr-3.wpg**, and press ENTER. When you retrieve the file, Letter-Perfect recognizes it as a graphic image, and places it into a figure box. LetterPerfect takes care of the graphic settings for you; you won't even see the Graphics Definition screen.

Likewise, you can press List Files (F5) to view a directory of files. Move the cursor to highlight a graphic file and choose option **1**, **R**etrieve. Again, LetterPerfect recognizes the graphic file and creates a figure box with the image.

When you retrieve a graphic file in this manner, LetterPerfect uses the standard graphic settings to create the figure box. That is, the figure box has a width of 3.5 inches, is horizontally positioned at the right margin, borders are turned on, and the text is wrapped around the box. The height of the box is automatically adjusted for the graphic image that you've retrieved. If you want to change any of these settings, you must edit the figure boxes as described later in this chapter.

note Not all graphic files can be retrieved into LetterPerfect. Refer to your LetterPerfect manual for a complete list of the graphic file formats that LetterPerfect supports.

Figure Box Numbering

As you create more figure boxes, you will notice that each is numbered consecutively, similar to the way endnotes are numbered. You can insert up to 100 figure boxes for each page of text, with an unlimited number of figure boxes for the entire document. However, the actual number of figure boxes is limited by the amount of memory available in your computer and printer. Each figure box is automatically assigned a unique number, allowing you to select a specific figure box when you need to change any of the graphic images.

EDITING A GRAPHIC IMAGE

LetterPerfect lets you edit the settings that create a figure box. You can select a different file name, change the size of the box, and turn the border on or off. You can also reposition the figure box by selecting a different horizontal alignment.

Since LetterPerfect does not include any graphic drawing tools, you cannot edit the actual graphic image—just the figure box that holds the image. Any editing of the drawing or graph itself must be done in the program that originally created the image.

Editing the Figure Box Settings

All graphic editing is performed at the Graphics Definition screen—the same screen where you originally created the figure box. In the following exercise, you'll learn how to edit the graphic image that you created earlier.

1. Press Graphics (ALT-F9) and select option 2, Edit, or choose Edit from the Graphics pull-down menu. LetterPerfect prompts you with "Figure number?", followed by a number. Since you only have one figure box in this document, type 1 and press ENTER.

note
When you choose to edit a figure box, LetterPerfect automatically displays the number of the next figure box code, which falls to the right of the text cursor. If you do not want to edit the figure box indicated by the number, simply type a different number and press ENTER.

If the code for the figure box you want to edit is located to the right of the text cursor, then its number is displayed after the "Figure number?" prompt. If the figure box code is at the left of the text cursor, then the next figure box number is displayed.

2. After you enter the number of the figure box you want to edit, the Graphics Definition screen is displayed. Now you can select any of the features from the menu, and change the file name, horizontal position, and size of the figure box.

3. When you are finished editing the figure box settings, press Exit (F7) to return to the main document screen and update the edited graphic image.

It's important to note that figure boxes are always numbered in sequential order. If you move a paragraph of text that contains a figure box, the graphic image is also moved and the text is reformatted to reflect the change. The following sections also explain important information about editing figure boxes. Before you continue, clear the screen (F7, N, N).

Adjusting for the Edited Graphic Image

When you insert graphic images into your document, LetterPerfect will always try to use the settings you have defined. But if you select measurements for width and height that are greater than the dimensions of the page, LetterPerfect will use the maximum possible measurement. If, for example, you create a figure box that is 8.5 inches wide, but your page is 8.5 inches wide with one-inch margins at each side, LetterPerfect changes your width measurement to 6.5 inches or less.

Likewise, if you choose Horizontal Position/Full, and then try to change the width of the figure box, LetterPerfect ignores the attempt. "Full" horizontal placement means that the figure box will extend the full width of the page, and this overrides the width definition under the Size option.

LetterPerfect also adjusts the width and height measurements for whatever is contained in the figure box. For example, if you edit a figure box and specify a different file name, the figure box will be resized for the dimensions of the new graphic image. There is, however, one exception to this case; if you select the Size option from the Graphics Definition screen and define both width and height measurements with the Set Both option, the figure box will not be resized to fit the graphic image. Instead, the graphic image will be stretched or squashed to fit the exact measurements that you have entered for the size of the figure box.

Why Does the Graphic Image Jump to the Next Page?

When a figure box is located near the bottom of a page, and you increase the size of the box through editing, it is possible that the graphic will be moved to the following page. This happens because the figure box is too large to fit on the current page. The [Fig Box] code remains at the same location in the text, but the graphic image is "bumped" to the next page, and the text is reformatted around it. You can fix this by turning on Reveal Codes (CTRL-R or ALT-F3), and using Block (ALT-F4 or F12) to move the [Fig Box] code to the previous paragraph in the text. You may need to experiment with this until you discover how far to move the code above the bottom of the page.

EXERCISE: ADDING GRAPHICS TO THE PARTY SHACK FLYER

In previous chapters, you created a flyer for a catering business. The text for this flyer should be completed, and now you'll add a few graphic images to make it more visually interesting. If you have not yet created the Party Shack flyer, refer to Chapters 1 through 4 for instructions on creating this document. Then, follow these steps to insert illustrations for the flyer, as shown in Figure 6-6.

1. From a clear screen, press Retrieve (SHIFT-F10) or select **R**etrieve from the File pull-down menu. Type **party.doc** and press ENTER to retrieve the document.

2. With the text cursor at the beginning of your document, press ENTER twice to add space above the headline of the flyer.

Chapter 6　　　　　　　　　　　　　　　　Using the Graphics Features　　137

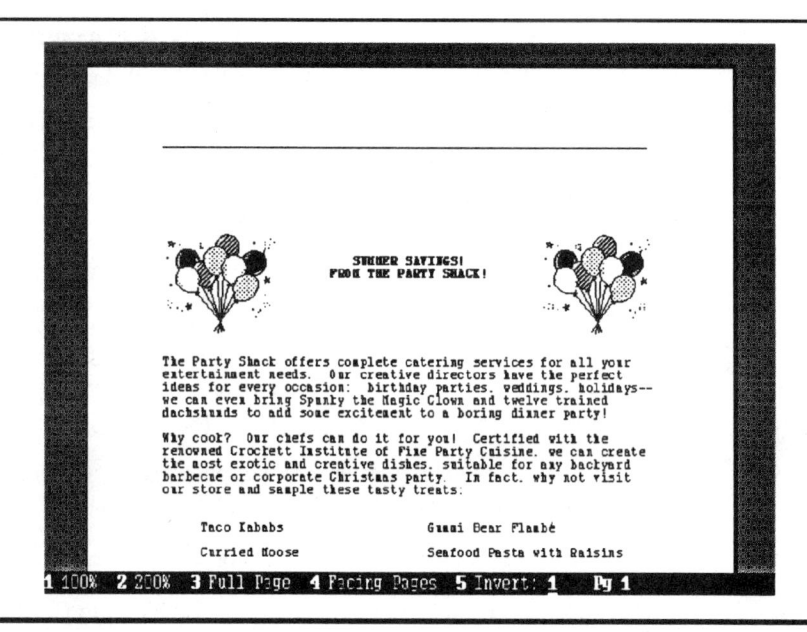

FIGURE 6-6.　　Graphics in the PARTY.DOC flyer

3. Press HOME, HOME, UP ARROW to move the cursor back to the top of the document. This is where you will insert the graphic images.

4. Press Graphics (ALT-F9) and select option **1**, Create, or choose Create from the Graphics pull-down menu. If you prefer to use the Fast Key, simply press CTRL-G.

5. The Graphics Definition screen appears. Choose the first option, **Filename**. If you are running LetterPerfect from a hard disk, type **c:\lp10\balloons.wpg** as the file name and press ENTER. If you are running LetterPerfect on a double-floppy system, insert the "Utilities/Images" diskette into drive B, type **b:balloons.wpg**, and press ENTER. The graphic image of balloons is retrieved into the graphics box.

6. Next, choose option **2**, **Horizontal Position**. Select option **1**, **Left**, from the menu that appears at the bottom of the screen.

7. Select option **3**, **Size**, and choose **1**, Set Width/Auto Height. Type **1.5"** as the width for the box, and press ENTER. LetterPerfect automatically adjusts the height.

8. Now, select option, **5**, **Border**. You don't want a border around the graphics box, so choose **No**.

9. The first box is finished. Press Exit (F7) or click the right mouse button to return to the main document screen, where you'll see the top of the figure box outline.

10. Press the DOWN ARROW key to reformat the text. Move the text cursor down to the word "The," in the first sentence; make sure the cursor is on the capital *T*. Notice that as you move the cursor, an outline of the graphics box is drawn to show you where the image falls in relation to your text.

11. Press ENTER four times to add some space between the graphics box and the text. Press HOME, HOME, UP ARROW to move the text cursor to the top of the document.

12. Now you're ready to create the second graphics box. Press Graphics (ALT-F9) and select option **1**, **Create**, or choose Create from the Graphics pull-down menu. If you prefer to use the Fast Key, simply press CTRL-G.

13. Choose option **1**, **Filename**, from the Graphics Definition menu. Type either **c:\lp10\balloons.wpg** or **b:balloons.wpg** and press ENTER.

14. Select option **2**, **Horizontal Position**, and choose option **2**, **Right**.

15. Select option **3**, **Size**, and choose option **1**, **Set Width/Auto Height**. Type **1.5"** and press ENTER for the width of the box.

note: In the first graphics box that you created, you turned off the graphics box borders by selecting No for option **5**, **Borders**. This placed a [Fig Opt:Borders Off] code in your text to specify that you don't want borders. This setting will affect any figure boxes that are placed after this code, until you select a new border setting. You will notice that this option is already set to No when you create the second graphics box, because its border setting is affected by the [Fig Opt:Border Off] code from the first graphics box.

16. Press Exit (F7) or click the right mouse button to return to the main document screen. Press DOWN ARROW about ten times to move the text cursor to the first paragraph. This will also reformat the text and adjust the figure box outlines, as shown in Figure 6-7.

17. Press the Fast Key (CTRL-P) or press Print (SHIFT-F7) and choose option **3**, **View Document**. This will display your document with the graphic images that you just created. Figure 6-8 shows how the flyer may appear on your screen.

When you're finished viewing the document, press Exit (F7) to return to the main document screen. You'll probably want to save this document, so press Save (F10) or choose Save from the File pull-down menu. The original file name, PARTY.DOC will appear after the "Document to be saved: " prompt. Press ENTER to accept this name and LetterPerfect asks if you want to replace the original file. Type **Y** for Yes,

Chapter 6 Using the Graphics Features 139

```
File Edit Search Layout Tools Font Graphics Help        (Press ALT for menu bar)
  ┌FIG 1────────┐                              ┌FIG 2────────┐
  │             │        SUMMER SAVINGS!       │             │
  │             │       FROM THE PARTY SHACK!  │             │
  │             │                              │             │
  │             │                              │             │
  └─────────────┘                              └─────────────┘

The Party Shack offers complete catering services for all your
entertainment needs.  Our creative directors have the perfect
ideas for every occasion:  birthday parties, weddings, holidays--
we can even bring Spunky the Magic Clown and twelve trained
dachshunds to add some excitement to a boring dinner party!

Why cook?  Our chefs can do it for you!  Certified with the
renowned Crockett Institute of Fine Party Cuisine, we can create
the most exotic and creative dishes, suitable for any backyard
barbecue or corporate Christmas party.  In fact, why not visit
our store and sample these tasty treats:

C:\LP10\PARTY.DOC                              Pg 1 Ln 1.33" Pos 2.8"
```

FIGURE 6-7.   Inserting figure boxes into the flyer

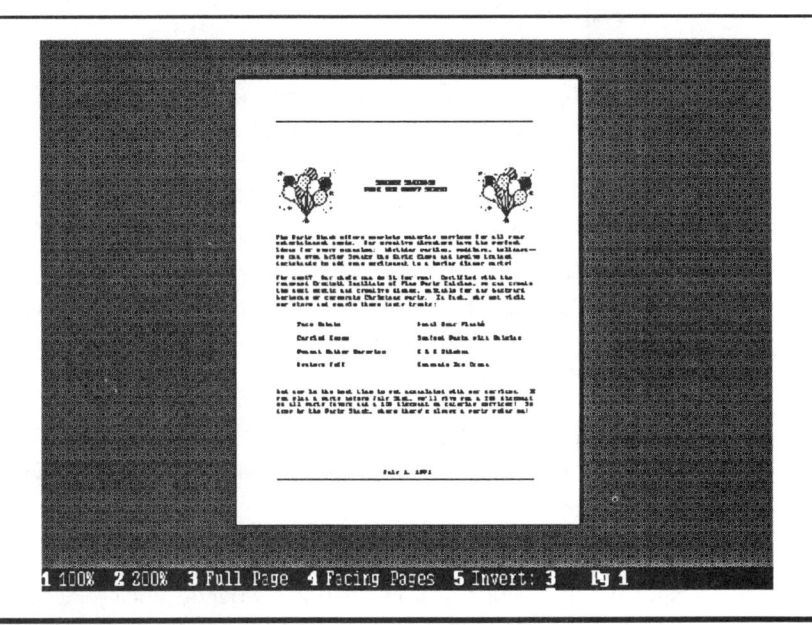

FIGURE 6-8.   The completed Party Shack flyer

and the new document is saved. If you wish, print the document (SHIFT-F7, 1). Before you continue, you should also clear the screen.

DRAWING LINES AND BOXES

You can use LetterPerfect's Line Draw feature to create lines, boxes, and borders. You can select from ten different line styles, or draw lines with a specific text character or symbol. Although somewhat limited, this feature provides a quick way to draw diagrams and lines in your documents.

The following exercise will acquaint you with the Line Draw feature. When the Line Draw mode is active, you can move the text cursor to draw lines. You will create two boxes on the screen, select different line styles, and then insert text. If you wish, look ahead to Figure 6-11 to see the finished boxes. Clear your screen before you perform the steps.

1. The text cursor should be at the top of a clear screen. Press Line Draw (CTRL-F3) or select **Line Draw** from the **Tools** pull-down menu. The following menu appears at the bottom of the screen:

   1 |; 2 ||; 3 *; 4 Change; 5 Erase; 6 Move: 1

   This menu provides different options for drawing lines. Options 1 through 3 display the different line styles that you can select. Option 4 lets you select additional line styles. Option 5 lets you erase a line, and option 6 lets you move the cursor without drawing or erasing a line. After you select an option, its number appears at the end of the menu.

2. Choose option **1** to select the single-line style. Then, press RIGHT ARROW to move the cursor to the right. As you move the cursor, a line is drawn; this will become the top of the first box. Continue to press RIGHT ARROW until the cursor stops at the right margin.

   note: The arrows at each end of the line indicate the beginning and end of the line. These arrows are inserted for display purposes only; they will not appear on the printed document.

3. Press DOWN ARROW twice to draw the side of the box. Then, press LEFT ARROW until the cursor stops at the left margin of your document. As you draw, your screen will look like Figure 6-9.

```
File Edit Search Layout Tools Font Graphics Help     (Press ALT for menu bar)
```

```
1 |; 2 ‖; 3 *; 4 Change; 5 Erase; 6 Move: 1          Ln 1.33" Pos 4.6"
```

FIGURE 6-9.   Drawing a box with Line Draw

4. When the cursor stops at the left margin, press UP ARROW twice to complete the box. Now, you're ready to draw a second box.

5. Choose option **6, M**ove, from the menu at the bottom of the screen. This option allows you to move the cursor without drawing a line. Press DOWN ARROW 4 times, and then press RIGHT ARROW 19 times. This places the cursor at the position where the second box will begin.

6. Choose option **2** to select the double-line style. Press RIGHT ARROW 27 times to create the top edge of the box. If you move the cursor too far, choose option **5**, Erase, move the cursor back, and then choose option **2** to continue drawing.

7. Press DOWN ARROW 9 times to create the side of the box.

8. Press LEFT ARROW 27 times to draw the bottom edge, and press UP ARROW until the lines connect at the top corner of the box. Your screen should now look like Figure 6-10.

9. Choose option **6, M**ove. Press DOWN ARROW once, and then press LEFT ARROW twice. This moves the cursor outside of the box. Now, you're going to create a shadow. This is simply a thicker line at two edges of the box.

142 LetterPerfect Made Easy

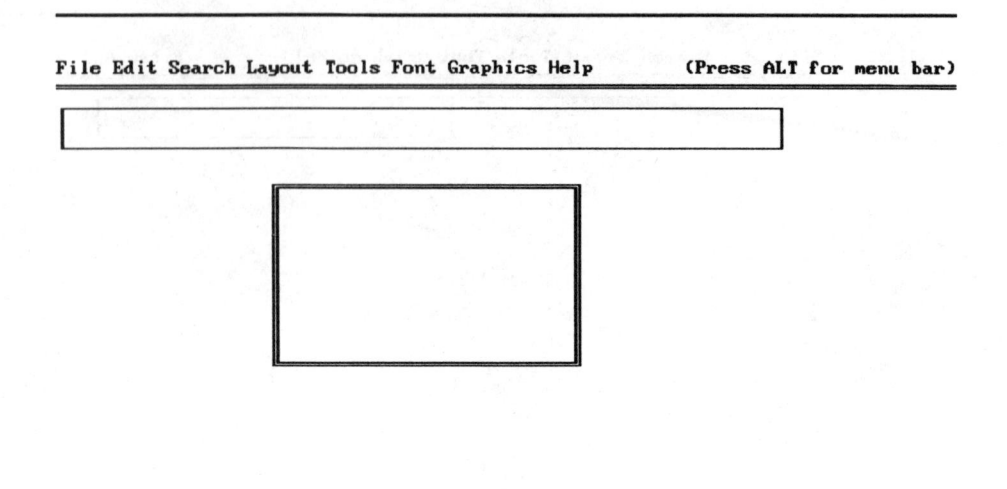

```
File Edit Search Layout Tools Font Graphics Help    (Press ALT for menu bar)
```

1 |; 2 ‖; 3 *; 4 Change; 5 Erase; 6 Move: 2   Ln 1.67" Pos 2.9"

FIGURE 6-10. The finished boxes

10. To create the shadow, you need to select a different line style. Options 1 and 2 on the Line Draw menu are the standard line style types. However, you can change the line style for option 3. Choose option **4**, Change, and this menu appears at the bottom of the screen:

    1 ; 2 ; 3 ; 4 ; 5 ; 6 |; 7 |; 8 ■; 9 Other: 0

11. Select line style **4** from the menu to draw a thicker line. The Line Draw menu reappears. Notice that the line style you selected is now displayed as option 3 on the menu. Press DOWN ARROW 9 times to create the shadow at the left edge of the box.

12. You need to change the line style again for the shadow at the bottom edge. Choose **4** Change, and select line style **8**. Press RIGHT ARROW 28 times to create the shadow at the bottom edge of the box.

13. You've completed the two boxes and are now finished with the Line Draw feature. Press Exit (F7) or click the right mouse button to return to the text editing mode.

14. Now you're ready to insert some text into the boxes. Press HOME, HOME, UP ARROW to move the text cursor to the top of the document. Then, press DOWN ARROW once.

Press RIGHT ARROW 10 times to move the cursor to the place where the text will begin in the first box.

15. When you use the Line Draw feature, LetterPerfect inserts text spaces to fill the empty areas between the lines on your screen. Because of this, you must select the Typeover mode to type text over the spaces inside the boxes. Press INS (Insert) and the "Typeover" message appears at the lower-left corner of the screen.

16. Type **FASHION BARGAINS AT YOUR ARMY SURPLUS STORE!!**. Because of the Typeover mode, the text you type is written over the spaces in the box.

note If Typeover mode were not active, the text would be inserted into the line of spaces, and would push the edge of the box off the screen until LetterPerfect wrapped the line.

17. Press LEFT ARROW 29 times to move the text cursor back until it is located between the words "BARGAINS" and "AT". Then press DOWN ARROW 5 times to move the cursor into the second box.

18. The Typeover mode should still be active. Type **Urban Modeling**. Press LEFT ARROW 8 times, press DOWN ARROW twice, and then type **by** as the next line of text.

19. Press LEFT ARROW 7 times, press DOWN ARROW twice, and type **Gunther Beck**. Now you're finished with the text. Press INS (Insert) to turn off the Typeover mode.

Your screen should now look like Figure 6-11. This is just one example of what you can do with Line Draw. Figure 6-12 shows other examples. As you experiment with the different options, remember that Line Draw fills empty areas with text spaces. If you want to insert text into the line-draw boxes, exit the Line Draw mode, and then use the Typeover mode to type the text.

Sometimes, you may want to draw lines with a particular character. You can do this by pressing Line Draw (CTRL-F3) to display the Line Draw menu, and choosing option **4**, Change. This displays the line style options. Select option **9** Other and LetterPerfect prompts you with "Solid character: ". Type any character from the keyboard (for example, #, @, or X), and this becomes the line style for option **3** on the Line Draw menu. Select option **3** and you can draw lines with the character you typed.

You can use the Line Draw feature to draw lines around existing text, such as tables created with tabs. However, if you try to draw lines around paragraph text, the lines will not fall correctly. Also, the Line Draw characters are meant to be printed with a nonproportional font (one in which all text characters are the same width when printed). Line Draw works fine with fonts such as Courier; however, if you select a proportional font for the document, your lines may not print correctly.

144   **LetterPerfect Made Easy**

File Edit Search Layout Tools Font Graphics Help   (Press ALT for menu bar)

FASHION BARGAINS AT YOUR ARMY SURPLUS STORE!!

Urban Modeling

by

Gunther Beck_

Pg 1 Ln 2.67" Pos 4.9"

FIGURE 6-11.   Inserting text into the boxes

File Edit Search Layout Tools Font Graphics Help   (Press ALT for menu bar)

LESSON 12.5: LINEAR REGRESSION ——————————————————————————— Horizontal line

In this lesson, you will learn how to perform linear regression analysis. PlanPerfect's Regression Table feature returns the regression output data to a specified block. A column of dependent values (the Y variable) must be specified...

PRESIDENT ←——— Organization chart

V.P.s   V.P.s

Date	Description	Qty.	Price	Total
7/25	Printer Ribbons	6	@ $9	$54
8/15	Paper Supplies	8/500	@ $5	$40

←——— Table

E:\DOCUMENT\BOOK\LDEX.DOC   Pg 1 Ln 1.33" Pos 1"

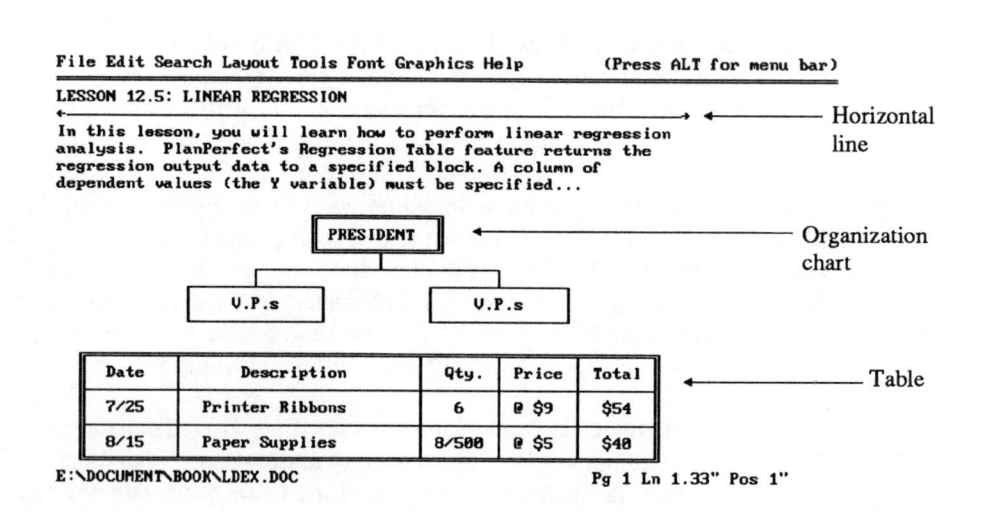

FIGURE 6-12.   Examples of Line Draw figures

SUMMARY

Now you know how to use the graphics features of LetterPerfect. Although not as elaborate as the features of some other programs, LetterPerfect's graphics features are easy to use and allow you to incorporate a wide variety of graphic images into your documents.

Graphic images are inserted into your text with a figure box. You define the size of the box and where it should be placed in relation to the current line of text. You specify the file name of a graphic image, and it becomes part of the current document. You can retrieve graphics files from most of the major graphics programs, use the graphic images provided with the LetterPerfect program, or create your own graphic images with DrawPerfect.

LetterPerfect can't actually edit the lines and shapes that make up the graphic image—that must be done with the program on which the original image was made—but it does allow you to edit the settings that create the figure box.

You've also learned how to use the Line Draw feature to create lines, borders, and boxes. You can draw a chart or diagram, then select the Typeover mode to insert text into the boxes or borders that you've drawn.

chapter 7

PRINTING YOUR DOCUMENTS

Your Printer and LetterPerfect
Previewing a Document
Printing Your Document
Options for Printing
Summary

L etterPerfect inherits some powerful printing features from its big brother, WordPerfect. Once LetterPerfect is set up to work with your printer, the rest is easy. A Document Preview feature lets you see everything as it will print—before you send anything to the printer. Then, you can print the entire document or only specific pages.

In this chapter, you will learn how to install your printer for use with LetterPerfect. You will also learn how to print your documents and choose printing options.

YOUR PRINTER AND LETTERPERFECT

There are several hundred printers available for PC computers, and it's likely that LetterPerfect supports the printer you own. Generally, there are four types of printers: dot-matrix printers, plotters, daisy-wheel printers, and laser printers. LetterPerfect uses different methods of communication for each printer type. Before you can send documents to your printer, special printer files must be installed with the LetterPerfect program files.

In addition, LetterPerfect formats text according to the capabilities of the current printer. Your documents are closely linked to the printer that is selected when you create the layout, and printer information is saved with your document files. This is important because it ensures that font changes, line spacing, and other format settings will be tailored for your printer, thus producing the best quality documents possible.

Installing Your Printer

When you install the LetterPerfect program, a menu option allows you to install printer files. During the printer installation process, a file with an .ALL extension may be copied to your LetterPerfect directory. This file contains information that allows LetterPerfect to communicate with your printer, as well as with other similar printers. The Installation Program uses information in the .ALL file to create a *printer driver* for your particular printer. Printer drivers are files that allow LetterPerfect to communicate directly with your printer; the names of these files end with a .PRS extension.

If you did not select a printer when you installed the LetterPerfect program, the following exercise will show you how to copy the correct files to your LetterPerfect directory. You can have more than one printer installed, so these steps will also help you install additional printers.

note If you are running LetterPerfect from a floppy-drive system, keep in mind that your disk space is very limited. You may have enough disk space for only one set of printer files.

1. Exit any programs that are currently running. Insert the LetterPerfect Install/Utilities 1 diskette into drive A.

2. At the DOS prompt, type **a:** and press ENTER to change the default drive to A.

3. Type **install** to start the LetterPerfect Installation program. Type **Y** for Yes when prompted about continuing with the installation. Type the appropriate response (**Y** or **N**) for any additional prompts until the main installation screen appears.

4. Choose option **3, Printer,** to install a new printer. First you are prompted with "Install from: A:\"; press ENTER to accept this. Then, you are prompted with "Install LetterPerfect to: ", followed by a suggested path name. You can enter a new path

Chapter 7   Printing Your Documents ≡ 149

name, or simply press ENTER to accept the displayed location. For example, if your LetterPerfect program files were installed in C:\LP10, you would type **c:\lp10** and press ENTER.

5. A message on the screen asks you to replace the diskette in drive A with the diskette marked "Printer 1." Remove the Install/Utilities diskette from the A drive, and insert the Printer 1 disk. Then, press ENTER.

6. A list of printers is displayed on the screen, as shown in Figure 7-1. If you don't see your printer on the list, press PGDN or PGUP until the name appears.

note If you know the name of the printer you want to select, choose Name Search from the menu at the bottom of the screen, and type your printer's name. It will be displayed on the screen; then, press ENTER to continue.

7. Type the number that is to the right of your printer name on the list. Press ENTER to accept the number, and LetterPerfect will ask you whether you want to continue with the selection. Type **Y** for Yes, and the printer files are installed.

```
 1 *Acer LP-76
 2 *AEG Olympia Compact RO
 3 *AEG Olympia ESW 2000
 4 *AEG Olympia Laserstar 6
 5 *AEG Olympia Laserstar 6e
 6  AEG Olympia NP 136-24
 7  AEG Olympia NP 136 SE
 8  AEG Olympia NP 30
 9  AEG Olympia NP 80-24
10  AEG Olympia NP 80 SE
11  AEG Olympia NPC 136-24
12 *AEG Olympia Startype
13 *AGFA Compugraphic 9400PS
14  Alphacom Alphapro 101
15  Alps Allegro 24
16 *Alps Allegro 24 (Additional)
17  Alps ALQ200 (18 pin)
18  Alps ALQ200 (24 pin)
19  Alps ALQ224e
20 *Alps ALQ224e (Additional)
21  Alps ALQ300 (18 pin)
22  Alps ALQ300 (24 pin)
```

```
Printers marked with '*' are
not included with shipping
disks. Select printer for
more information.

If you do not see your printer
listed, press F3 for Help.
```

N Name Search; PgDn More Printers; PgUp Previous Screen; F3 Help; F7 Exit;
Selection: 0

FIGURE 7-1.   Installing a printer from the list

If the information for the printer you selected is not on the Printer 1 diskette, you will be prompted to insert the Printer 2 diskette in drive A.

8. LetterPerfect prompts you with "Do you want to install another printer? No (Yes)". Type **N** for No, to continue, or type **Y** to select another printer.

When you are finished, the LetterPerfect program is started and the appropriate printer files are installed to your LetterPerfect directory or disk. When the installation process is completed, your screen will look similar to this:

```
Installation Complete.

When you want to run LetterPerfect, change to the LetterPerfect directory,
type LP, and press Enter.


C:\>
```

Start the LetterPerfect program, and the latest printer that you installed should be selected and ready to print.

If you encounter any problems during installation, or if your printer does not work correctly after you install it, contact the WordPerfect Customer Support department for further assistance. The phone number is listed in your LetterPerfect manual.

Selecting a Printer

You may have more than one printer that you use—perhaps you have one for printing rough drafts of your documents and one for the final proposals or papers. LetterPerfect lets you install a list of printers at the Select Printer screen. When you connect a different printer to your computer, you must select the appropriate printer driver for that printer.

The following exercise will show you how to select a different printer driver when you have two or more printers installed for LetterPerfect.

1. Press Print (SHIFT-F7), or choose Print from the File pull-down menu, to display the Print menu. Figure 7-2 shows how this menu may look on your screen.

2. Choose option **5**, Select Printer, and a list of installed printers is displayed. Your screen will look similar to Figure 7-3, although different printer names will appear. If a printer is already selected, then an asterisk appears next to the printer name.

```
Print

    1 - Full Document
    2 - Multiple Pages
    3 - View Document
    4 - Initialize Printer

Options

    5 - Select Printer         Diconix 150 Plus
    6 - Binding Offset         0"
    7 - Number of Copies       1
    8 - Graphics Quality       Medium
    9 - Text Quality           High




Selection: 0
```

FIGURE 7-2.   The LetterPerfect Print menu

```
Print: Select Printer

* Diconix 150 Plus
  Epson FX-85
  HP LaserJet IIP









1 Select; 2 Additional Printers; 3 Edit; 4 Copy; 5 Delete; 6 Help; 7 Update: 1
```

FIGURE 7-3.   Selecting a printer

3. Use the arrow keys to move the highlighted bar to the name of the printer you want to use, or click on the printer name with the mouse.

4. A menu at the bottom of the screen lets you select, add, delete, and edit the printer definitions on the list. Choose the first option, **1** Select, to select the highlighted printer.

After you make the selection, the Print menu is redisplayed. Now, you're ready to print. You do not need to select the printer each time you want to print a document. The printer selection is saved with the other program settings and will remain in effect until you change it again.

Editing Printer Settings

You can edit your printer definition and change the name that appears on the Select Printer screen. You can also change the computer port where your printer is connected and edit other printer settings.

From the Select Printer screen, highlight the name of the printer you want to edit, and choose option **3**, **E**dit, to display the menu shown in Figure 7-4. From this screen, you can select and define the following options:

NAME Option **1**, **N**ame, lets you type a different name for your printer. This does not change the DOS file name for the printer driver. Instead, it changes the name that appears on your Select Printer screen. The **N**ame option allows you to type a more descriptive name for your printer. If, for example, a group of people will be working on your copy of LetterPerfect, you may want to select this option and type something like "Terry's Printer" or "Resource Group Printer." When you finish typing the name, press ENTER to accept it.

PORT The printer port is where your printer connects to your computer through a special cable. Printer ports are labeled as LPTx or COMx, with x representing the number of the computer port. An LPT port is referred to as a *parallel port*, with the term "parallel" meaning one type of communication for printers. A COM port is known as a *serial port,* which is another type of communications port for printers.

Most printers support parallel communication, and it's likely that your printer is connected to LPT1. If it isn't, however, you can choose option **2**, **P**ort, and indicate which port your printer is using. For more information on printer ports, consult the manual that came with your computer equipment.

```
Select Printer: Edit

        Filename                  HPLASIIP.PRS

    1 - Name                      HP LaserJet IIP

    2 - Port                      LPT1:

    3 - Sheet Feeder              None

    4 - Cartridges and Fonts

    5 - Initial Base Font         Courier 10cpi

    6 - Path for Downloadable
        Fonts

    7 - Print to Hardware Port    No




Selection: 0
```

FIGURE 7-4.   Editing a printer definition

SHEET FEEDER   Some printers have built-in sheet feeders with *bins*, while other printers have optional sheet feeders that you can buy separately. If you have a sheet feeder attached to your printer, you can choose option **3**, Sheet Feeder, and select the one you're using. This feature is particularly important if you will be using the Paper Size/Type feature described in Chapter 2. The Sheet Feeder setting on this menu tells LetterPerfect where the different paper types may be found, so that it can feed them from the right bins when printing.

CARTRIDGES AND FONTS   If you have a laser printer, you can choose this feature to tell LetterPerfect which font cartridges you have plugged into your printer, if any. This feature is also available for some dot-matrix printers that allow font cards to be inserted into the printer. In most cases, you must purchase separate font cartridges or soft font diskettes to make use of the Cartridges and Fonts feature.

Unfortunately, LetterPerfect does not include the printer files that allow you to select the downloadable soft fonts for your laser printers. If you have soft fonts installed on your hard disk, you can contact the WordPerfect Orders Department and purchase the correct printer drivers. Once you have the diskettes, install the new printer drivers as described at the beginning of this chapter.

note
WordPerfect 5.1 printer files are fully compatible with LetterPerfect. If you already have your printer installed for WordPerfect—with soft fonts selected—you can copy your *.PRS and *.ALL files to your LetterPerfect program directory. For more information, see "Using WordPerfect's Printer Drivers," later in this chapter.

When you choose the Cartridges and Fonts option from the Select Printer Edit menu, the screen shown in Figure 7-5 appears. Move the highlighted bar to one of the font types—usually either Cartridges or Soft Fonts—and press ENTER to display your choices for that type. Then, you can move the highlighted bar to each font that you have and type an asterisk (*) to indicate that the font is installed for your printer. When you're finished marking fonts, press Exit (F7) until you return to the Select Printer Edit screen.

```
Select Printer: Cartridges and Fonts

Font Category                                    Quantity           Available
Built-In
Cartridges                                          1                  1
Soft Fonts                                        350 K              350 K




NOTE: Most fonts listed under the Font Category (with the exception of Built-In)
are optional and must be purchased separately from your dealer or manufacturer.
If you have fonts not listed, they may be supported on an additional printer
diskette.  For more information call WP at (801) 225-5000.

If soft fonts are marked '*', you must run the Initialize Printer option in LP
each time you turn your printer on.  Doing so deletes all soft fonts in printer
memory and downloads those marked with '*'.

If soft fonts are not located in the same directory as your printer files, you
must specify a Path for Downloadable Fonts in the Select Printer: Edit menu.

1 Select; 2 Change Quantity; N Name search: 1
```

FIGURE 7-5. Selecting cartridges and soft fonts

INITIAL BASE FONT The Initial Base Font option determines what the standard font will be, whenever the printer is selected. Choose option **5**, Initial Base Font, and a list of available fonts appears. Move the highlighted cursor to one of the fonts, and choose option **1**, Select, to choose a standard printer font. When you are finished, the Select Printer Edit menu reappears. Now, whenever you select this printer, the font that you specified will be used to print the text, unless you change fonts from within the document.

PATH FOR DOWNLOADABLE FONTS If you order the soft font printer drivers from WordPerfect Corporation, or use printer drivers from WordPerfect 5.1, then you must tell LetterPerfect where it can find the soft font files that are stored on your hard disk. Choose this option, Path for Downloadable Fonts, type the path name where the soft font files are located, and press ENTER to accept it.

When you print a document, LetterPerfect will automatically swap fonts into your printer to print the document you've created. This is a nice feature because LetterPerfect takes care of downloading the fonts as needed; however, if you do not enter a path name for soft fonts, LetterPerfect will not be able to send them to the printer.

PRINT TO HARDWARE PORT This option is necessary when your printer is not working correctly with your computer. Normally, a print job is sent through the operating system of your computer and directed to the correct printer port. However, if your computer is not 100-percent compatible with IBM computers, this may not work correctly. If this is the case, you can choose option **7**, Print to Hardware Port, and choose "Yes" to send print jobs directly to the port where your printer is connected to the computer. When set to "Yes," this option can also increase printing speed for situations where memory is limited, such as in network installations.

Using WordPerfect's Printer Drivers

If you have already installed printer files for use with WordPerfect 5.1, you can copy the *.ALL files to your LetterPerfect directory. Then, from within LetterPerfect, you can choose Select printer from the Print menu, and choose option **2**, Additional Printers, to install WordPerfect printer drivers for use with LetterPerfect.

If you've already installed your printer and selected fonts within WordPerfect 5.1, simply copy your *.PRS file to your LetterPerfect directory. Then choose option **4**, List Printer Files, from the Additional Printers screen. The names of the *.PRS files in your LetterPerfect directory are displayed, and you can select the one you want to use. This allows you to take full advantage of WordPerfect's printer and soft font capabilities.

note Printer drivers from WordPerfect 5.0 or earlier versions are not compatible with LetterPerfect.

PREVIEWING A DOCUMENT

Most of the time, a document on your screen closely resembles the printed document. However, the normal editing screen does not accurately show text spacing, fonts, and graphics. You must use the View Document feature to see the document as it will look when printed. Then, if you need to make corrections to the format or text, you can do so before you actually print the document.

1. Press Print (SHIFT-F7), or select **P**rint from the **F**ile pull-down menu to display the Print menu.

2. Choose option **3**, **V**iew Document, and LetterPerfect shows a preview of your document. The View Document screen uses a graphics display to show your document as it will appear when printed. This includes different fonts sizes and any graphics you've incorporated into your text.

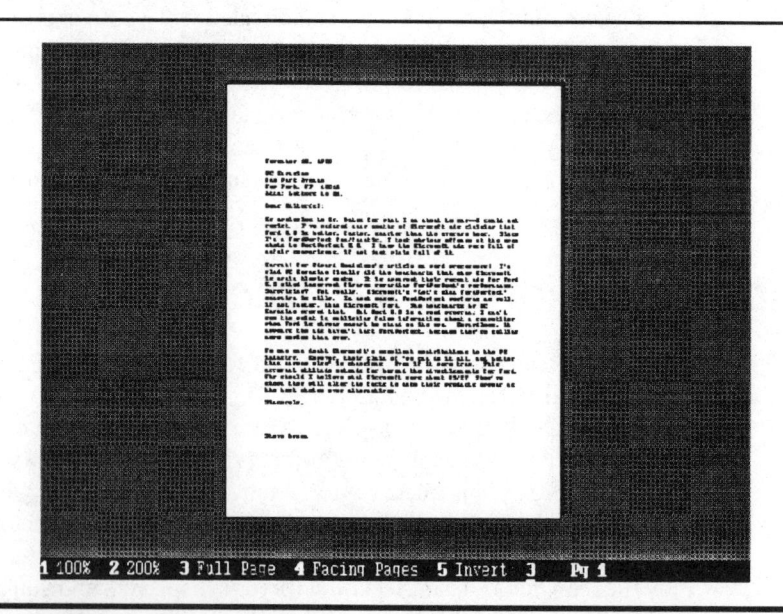

FIGURE 7-6.   Previewing a document

Figure 7-6 shows how the View Document screen may appear. If you've changed print margins or selected a different paper size, these changes are also reflected in the View Document screen.

The menu at the bottom of the screen lists options for viewing the pages. Choose **1**, 100%, to see your document in the actual size; the second option, 200%, displays your text at double the actual size. When you select 200%, you can use the cursor movement keys to view different parts of the text.

Choose option **3**, Full Page, to view an entire page on the screen; option **4**, Facing Pages, lets you view your text as if you were turning the pages of a book. Option **5**, Invert, switches the background and foreground colors of the display to show a reversed image; this helps improve the display for some laptop computers and monochrome monitors.

Press PGUP and PGDN to view each page, just as you would at the normal editing screen. When you are finished viewing your document, press Exit (F7) or click the right mouse button to return to your document.

PRINTING YOUR DOCUMENT

Nothing could be simpler than printing a document in LetterPerfect. You can print the entire document, print only certain pages, or print just a block of text.

Printing the Entire Document

The following steps show you how to print a document that is displayed on your screen.

1. Press Print (SHIFT-F7), or select **Print** from the File pull-down menu, to display the Print menu. The name of your printer should be displayed next to the Select Printer option on the menu.

2. Select option **1**, Full Document, from the Print menu. A copy of the current document is sent to the printer.

Printing is that simple. After you've selected the Full Document feature, your document is sent to the printer as a *print job,* and the Control Printer screen is displayed, similar to the screen shown in Figure 7-7. Messages at the top part of the screen report on the progress of the print job. When LetterPerfect has sent the entire

```
Print: Control Printer

Port:        LPT 1                          Page Number:  1
Status:      Printing                       Current Copy: 1 of 1
Message:     None
Paper:       Standard 8.5" x 11"
Location:    Continuous feed
Action:      None




1 Cancel Job; 2 Go (start printer); 3 Stop: 0
```

FIGURE 7-7.   The Printer Control screen

document to your printer, the Status indicator displays "no print jobs". Then, you can press Exit (F7) to return to the main editing screen.

Printing Multiple or Single Pages

Sometimes you'll need to make corrections to one or two pages in your document, and you don't want to reprint the entire document—just the edited pages. LetterPerfect provides an option that lets you select which pages you want to print.

To access this feature, press Print (SHIFT-F7) or select **Print** from the File pull-down menu. Choose option **2**, Multiple Pages. LetterPerfect prompts you with "Page(s) ". At this prompt, you can type the numbers of the pages you want to print. If you are printing nonconsecutive pages, type commas to separate the page numbers. If you are typing a range of pages, use a hyphen to indicate the range. For example, if you want to print pages 6, 17, and 23, you would type **6,17,23** at the "Page(s) :" prompt. If you want to print pages 11 through 27, you would type **11-27**. Type **e**, instead of a page number, to print only the even pages in the document; type **o** to print only the odd pages. After you type the page numbers or letter, press ENTER to accept your choice.

note: If you are familiar with WordPerfect, you'll notice that LetterPerfect does not have an option for printing a single page. But you can use the Multiple Pages option to perform the same task. At the "Page(s): " prompt, simply type the number of the page you want to print, and press ENTER.

What to Do When the Printer Doesn't Print

If your printer does not work correctly, make sure the printer cables are securely attached, and that the printer is "on-line" and ready to print. Next, make sure you have the correct printer driver selected.

Press Print (SHIFT-F7), and choose option **5**, Select Printer, to view the list of printer drivers. The currently selected printer is marked with an asterisk. If this is not the printer you are using, move the highlighted bar to the correct printer name, and choose option **1**, Select. Then, print the document from the screen. If the printer still does not work, contact WordPerfect Customer Support with the number listed in your LetterPerfect manual.

OPTIONS FOR PRINTING

LetterPerfect provides features that let you control how your documents are printed. Figure 7-8 shows the options on the Print menu. You can select a binding offset that adds extra space at the edge of the pages. A print option lets you print duplicate copies without reprinting your document several times. Other options let you specify the print quality of the text and graphics in your document.

Adding Space for Binding

If you're creating a long document or report, you may need to fasten the pages with staples, or punch holes for a binder. The Binding Offset feature on the Print menu allows you to specify how much space you need at the edge of each page for the binding of the document. LetterPerfect will adjust the placement of text on each page to allow for that space. It is assumed that you will be printing on both sides of the paper.

For example, assume you have a series of charts and diagrams to hand out to students in a class that you teach. You decide to print these documents and include

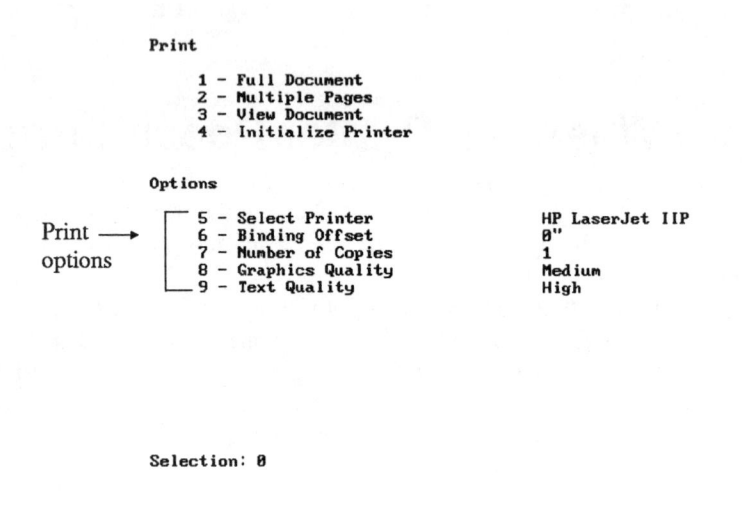

```
                    Print

                        1 - Full Document
                        2 - Multiple Pages
                        3 - View Document
                        4 - Initialize Printer

                    Options

Print ─→               5 - Select Printer           HP LaserJet IIP
                       6 - Binding Offset           0"
options                7 - Number of Copies         1
                       8 - Graphics Quality         Medium
                       9 - Text Quality             High




                    Selection: 0
```

FIGURE 7-8.   Selecting print options

the charts with the syllabus that is distributed to each student. Since the syllabus is bound with staples, you'll need about a quarter of an inch of extra space at the edge of each chart page. Select option **6**, **B**inding Offset, type **0.25**, and press ENTER.

When you print the document, the text on each page is moved over a quarter of an inch to allow space for binding. Odd pages will be shifted to the right; even pages will be shifted to the left. The Binding Offset is saved with your document, but the status line will not indicate the change in spacing; this adjustment occurs only when you send the document to the printer.

If you want to print the final document with binding space, but do not have a printer that can print on both sides of the pages, use the Multiple Pages option to print the odd pages first. Then, print the even pages. For example, press Print (SHIFT-F7), select option **6**, **B**inding Offset, and enter the measurement for binding space. Then, choose option **2**, **M**ultiple Pages. At the "Pages: " prompt, type **o** (for odd) and press ENTER. LetterPerfect will print only the odd pages in your document.

Then, reload the printed pages into your printer (make sure the correct side of the paper is facing up), and select **2**, **M**ultiple Pages, from the Print menu. This time, type **e** (for even) and press ENTER, to print only the even pages on the blank side of the pages you've already printed. The result is a document with text printed on both sides and binding space added to each of the pages.

Printing Several Copies

LetterPerfect can instruct your printer to create two or more copies of a document that you send to the printer. Press Print (SHIFT-F7), or select **Print** from the File pull-down menu. Then choose option **7, Number of Copies**. LetterPerfect prompts you to enter the number of copies. Type the number, then press ENTER. Now, when you send a document to the printer, LetterPerfect prints the number of copies that you specified.

When you are finished using this option, make sure to select it again, and enter **1** as the number of copies. If you forget this option is on, you may end up printing extra copies of a document when you need only one.

Selecting the Print Quality

You can print your documents in three different modes: Draft, Medium, and High quality. To select one, press Print (SHIFT-F7) or choose **Print** from the File pull-down menu. Select option **8, Graphics Quality**, or option **9, Text Quality** (explained shortly). A menu appears at the bottom of the screen with the different print qualities. Select one of the options: **1, Do Not Print; 2, Draft; 3, Medium;** or **4, High**. When you send your document to the printer, it will be printed with the text and graphics quality that you selected.

The Text Quality option works only when your printer can produce different fonts to match the print quality you select; laser printers, for example, do not have a draft mode for text, so your documents are always printed as high-quality text regardless of what you select from the menu.

Since graphics take longer to print than text, you can use the Graphics Quality option to help speed up the printing time for your documents. For example, assume you're in a rush to edit a printed copy of a proposal that includes several graphs and illustrations. If printed with high-quality graphics, your document could take several minutes to print, but you need a rough draft as soon as possible.

In this case, the document doesn't need to be perfect—at least, not yet. You can select the Draft quality for graphics because it prints faster than the other two types. When you're ready to submit your final proposal, the document should be printed with the High quality option.

SUMMARY

In this chapter, you learned about the printing features of LetterPerfect. You need to make sure that your printer is installed correctly, and is selected on the Print menu before you can view or print your documents.

The View Document screen lets you see your document as it will print—allowing you to make necessary changes before you actually print the text. You can select different view options to see your document at 100%, 200%, as a complete page, or facing pages.

LetterPerfect includes print options that let you select a space offset for binding and the number of desired copies. Different print qualities allow you to adjust the type of printing for your situation. Draft quality can be used when you need a quick copy of the document on the screen. Medium or High quality should be selected for final versions of your documents, charts, and illustrations.

chapter 8

MANAGING YOUR DOCUMENT FILES

Saving and Retrieving Files
Saving and Retrieving Other File Formats
Document Passwords
Automatic File Backup
Managing Your Documents with List Files
Summary

LetterPerfect includes several features that help you manage your document files. If you are familiar with WordPerfect, you already know how to perform many file management tasks, such as saving and retrieving files.

The List Files feature allows you to move, copy, or rename individual files or a group of files. You can even examine the contents of a file before you retrieve it into the document editing screen. You can also search for specific file names and remove unwanted document files.

SAVING AND RETRIEVING FILES

The topic of saving and retrieving files is discussed briefly at the beginning of this book, but there's more to these features than is covered in Chapter 1.

When you save or retrieve a file, you need to understand how LetterPerfect handles file names. You also need to know where LetterPerfect will look for document files if you don't specify a path when entering a name. The following sections discuss these topics.

File Names

Whenever you save or retrieve a document, you are asked to enter a file name, following the conventions of DOS. That is, you can type up to eight characters for the name, followed by a period and three additional characters (for example, BUSINESS.DOC). The characters after the period are called the *extension* of the file name. You can type any combination of text characters, and you don't need to use all three characters. These are all valid file names: OXFORD.LTR, TERRY.MO, MAY_90.J, and REPORT.89.

The extension is generally used to identify the type of document file. For example, you may want to type **.LTR** as the extension for each "letter" document file. Type **.DOC** for long document files, or **.MO** for "memo" document file names.

You don't have to use the file names and extensions given here; you decide which characters you want to use. However, a few names are reserved for DOS commands and program files, and should not be used to name a document file. These include: AUX, CLOCK$, COM, CON, LPT, LST, NUL, PRN, and the extensions .EXE, .COM, and .SYS. Refer to your own DOS manual for a complete list of reserved file names and extensions.

In addition, the following extensions are used to identify specific LetterPerfect program files: .PRS, .ALL, .SET, .DRS, .VRS, .FIL, .LEX, .SUP, .LCN, and .LRS. You can use most of these extensions to name your document files, but you may later confuse the document with a LetterPerfect program file—or worse, delete a program file that you thought was a document file.

Saving a File

When you create a document, the text and formatting information are stored in the memory of your computer. You can create and print a document without ever saving it to a disk file, but once you exit LetterPerfect, the file will be lost.

Obviously, it's important to save your document to a file on disk so that you can retrieve it later and, if necessary, make changes. Take the following steps to save the document on the screen to a file on disk.

Chapter 8　　　　　　　　　　　　　　Managing Your Document Files　　165

1. Press Save (F10) or choose **S**ave from the **F**ile pull-down menu.

2. LetterPerfect prompts you with "Document to be saved: ". Here you will enter a file name for the document on your screen. Type a name, eight characters or less, and press ENTER to accept the name.

After you accept the name, LetterPerfect saves the file to disk, and the file name appears at the left corner of the status line. LetterPerfect will store your document file in the default directory unless you type a path name before the file name.

Retrieving a File

There are two ways to retrieve a file. You can use the Retrieve feature to access a specific file, or you can retrieve from a list of files. The following information explains both methods of retrieving.

note　　LetterPerfect does not automatically clear an existing document from the screen before a new file is retrieved. Therefore, it is important to clear the screen (with F7, N, N) before you retrieve a file.

1. Press Retrieve (SHIFT-F10) or select **R**etrieve from the File pull-down menu.

2. LetterPerfect prompts you with "Document to be retrieved: ". Type the name of the document file that you want to retrieve and press ENTER. LetterPerfect retrieves a copy of the file into the document window.

After you've created several document files, it can be difficult to remember the file names. Sometimes you will try to retrieve a file, and then discover that it isn't found in the current directory. This can be frustrating when you're in a hurry to get something done. LetterPerfect can help you find the file you're looking for by displaying a list of all files from the current directory.

You can also display a list of files while using the Retrieve feature. For example, press Retrieve (SHIFT-F10). At the "Document to be retrieved: " prompt, press List Files (F5) and then press ENTER, instead of typing a file name. The List Files screen appears with an index of the current directory files. Move the highlighted cursor to the file you want, and then select option **1**, **R**etrieve, from the List Files menu. The document is retrieved into the document editing screen.

Directories and Path Names

When you start the LetterPerfect program, your computer is set to work with a *default directory*. The default directory is the first place your computer will look when it needs to get information from the disk drive. If you want to save a file to a place other than the default directory, you must change the default directory or precede the file name with a specific *path name*. The path name is like a zip code for a specific area on your disk drive. When saving or retrieving a document, you can type a path name before the file name to indicate where the file should be located.

For example, suppose you have a company memo on your screen. If you press Save (F10) and simply enter **company.mo** at the "Document to be Saved: " prompt, your file is saved to whatever directory is currently active or to the current default directory. If all your memo files should be saved on your C drive to a directory called "business", you would enter **c:\business\company.mo** as the file name. The path name "c:\business" specifies that you want the COMPANY.MO document saved to the business directory on the C drive.

Creating a Document Directory

LetterPerfect includes a feature that lets you indicate where document files should be saved so you don't need to type a path name every time you save a file. In the previous chapters, you've saved documents to the default LetterPerfect directory, but you should have a separate directory just for documents.

In the following exercise, you'll create a new directory for your document files, and you'll use a LetterPerfect setup option to specify where the directory is located.

note If you are running LetterPerfect on a double-floppy system, there's no need to create a new directory, and you can ignore steps 1 through 3 in the following exercise.

1. From the main document screen, press List Files (F5) or select **List Files** from the **File** pull-down menu. The current directory is displayed at the left corner of the status line.

2. Notice the message at the right edge of the screen, "Type = to change default Dir". Press **=** to indicate a new directory. Type **c:\ files** (or type the path name for the directory you want to create), and then press ENTER.

3. LetterPerfect prompts you with "Create c:\files? No (Yes)". Type **Y** for Yes, and LetterPerfect creates the directory.

4. Now you'll use a LetterPerfect setup feature to indicate that files will be saved in your document directory. Press Setup (SHIFT-F1) or select Setup from the File pull-down menu. The Setup menu appears as shown in Figure 8-1.

5. Choose option **4**, **L**ocation of Document Files. Type the path name where your document files should be stored, and press ENTER. For example, you've just created a directory called "files" on the C drive. So, you would enter **c:\ files** as the path name. If all your documents are stored on a diskette in the B drive, simply enter **b:** .

6. After you enter the path name, press Exit (F7) or click the right mouse button to return to the main editing screen.

Now, when you save or retrieve files without typing a path name, LetterPerfect looks in the directory you specified under the Location of Document Files option. LetterPerfect will continue to save and retrieve documents with this directory, until you change the specified path name.

```
Setup
        1 - Screen Colors                    Monochrome
        2 - Minutes Between Backup           10
        3 - Units of Measure                 Inches
        4 - Location of Document Files
        5 - Initial Codes
        6 - Alt Key Selects Menu Bar         Yes
        7 - Menu Bar Remains Visible         Yes
        8 - Function of F1                   Cancel
        9 - Format Retrieved Documents       No
            for Default Printer


Selection: 0
```

FIGURE 8-1. The LetterPerfect Setup menu

note: If you have a copy of LetterPerfect dated November 1990 or later, option **4** may also allow you to specify the location of printer drivers, backup files, and other program files.

SAVING AND RETRIEVING OTHER FILE FORMATS

You may need to share your LetterPerfect documents with other word processing programs. However, each software program creates files differently, and the program you want to share with LetterPerfect probably uses a different file format.

LetterPerfect can retrieve WordPerfect 5.1 files without requiring you to convert the files, and also includes features that let you save and retrieve other file formats. The following sections explain the file formats supported by LetterPerfect.

WordPerfect Files

If you are a WordPerfect 5.1 user, you'll appreciate LetterPerfect's file-sharing capabilities. Although many WordPerfect features are not supported by LetterPerfect, the two programs share the same general file format.

You can retrieve any WordPerfect 5.1 file directly into LetterPerfect and make editing changes. Then, you can save the file and retrieve it back into WordPerfect, without problems. You don't have to convert the file. LetterPerfect recognizes the WordPerfect file and automatically makes adjustments.

If you retrieve a WordPerfect 5.1 file with formatting codes that are not supported by LetterPerfect, the codes are temporarily converted or ignored and appear in French brackets in the Reveal Codes window (for example, {W/O On}, {Col Def}, and {Col On}). When you retrieve the file back into WordPerfect, the features are restored to your document. It couldn't be simpler.

However, if you have files from WordPerfect 5.0, you may encounter a few problems. The file format of WordPerfect 5.0 is slightly different than that of version 5.1 and LetterPerfect. You can retrieve a 5.0 file into LetterPerfect, but some of the formatting codes may not be recognized, and may appear as [Unknown] in the Reveal Codes window.

Also, remember that LetterPerfect saves documents to a file format that is compatible with WordPerfect 5.1. If you retrieve a 5.0 file and save it, it becomes a WordPerfect 5.1 file; depending on the format of your document, this may cause problems when you retrieve the file back into WordPerfect 5.0. If so, consider using LetterPerfect's Text Out feature (CTRL-F5), to convert the documents to a generic word processing format before retrieving them into WordPerfect, version 5.0 or earlier versions.

DOS Text Files

A DOS Text file contains no formatting codes, only text. Computer files, such as AUTOEXEC.BAT, CONFIG.SYS, and DOS batch files, are saved in this format. You can retrieve a DOS Text file directly into LetterPerfect, and the file is automatically converted. Then, edit the text and use LetterPerfect's Text Out feature to save the file back to the DOS Text format.

note
For more information about DOS batch files and the AUTOEXEC.BAT and CONFIG.SYS files, refer to your DOS manual, or see "DOS and LetterPerfect" in your LetterPerfect reference manual.

The DOS Text format is also useful for exchanging files with other word processing programs. Only WordPerfect 5.1 can accept LetterPerfect document files, but most word processing programs accept DOS Text files. You can use the Text Out feature to save a LetterPerfect document for other word processors.

To save the on-screen document as a DOS Text file, press Text Out (CTRL-F5) and choose option **1, DOS Text Out,** or select **DOS Text Out** from the File pull-down menu. LetterPerfect prompts you with "Document to be saved (DOS Text): ". Type a name for the converted file and press **ENTER**. Your document is saved as a DOS Text file.

The file on disk includes only text with carriage-return codes at the end of each line. Tabs and indents are converted to spaces; all other formatting codes are removed from the document. When you retrieve the DOS Text file into WordPerfect or LetterPerfect, a message, "DOS Text Conversion in Progess", appears briefly on the screen.

Generic Files

Generic files are similar to DOS Text files, except that tabs ([Tab]), soft return codes ([SRt]), and hard return codes ([HRt]) are kept in the document. All other formatting codes are removed from the converted file.

If you're having problems exchanging files with WordPerfect 5.0 or earlier versions of WordPerfect, you can save your documents in the Generic format, and this should correct the problems. Keep in mind, however, that this will also eliminate any other formatting codes.

To save the on-screen document to the Generic format, press Text Out (CTRL-F5) and choose option 3, Save Generic. If you prefer to use the pull-down menus, select Save Generic from the File pull-down menu. LetterPerfect prompts you with "Document to be saved (Generic WP): ". Type a name for the file and press ENTER. Your document is saved as a generic word processing document that can be retrieved into any version of WordPerfect, and some other word processing programs.

DOCUMENT PASSWORDS

In LetterPerfect, it's easy to retrieve and print the contents of document files. In fact, anyone can start your computer and examine the files on your diskette or hard drive. However, you may have documents, such as payroll records and personnel documents, that should be kept secret.

LetterPerfect includes a password feature that prevents anyone from retrieving, viewing, or printing the protected document, until the correct password is entered. In addition, any files associated with your document, such as backup and overflow files, are also locked.

note You *must* remember the passwords that you use. If you forget a password, there's absolutely no way to recover the information in the file, unless you've stored an unprotected copy of the document on another disk.

Adding a Document Password

Follow these steps to add password protection to the document displayed on your screen:

1. Press Text Out (CTRL-F5) and choose option 2, Password, from the Text Out menu; then, select option 1, Add/Change, from the Password menu. If you prefer to use the pull-down menus, select Add Password from the File pull-down menu.

2. A prompt appears at the bottom of the screen, "Enter Password: ". Type a word or phrase for the password and press ENTER. The password you type can include up to 23 characters, including spaces.

3. LetterPerfect prompts you to "Re-Enter Password: ". Type the password again and press ENTER. This is a safeguard against typing errors.

4. Now, you must save the document to protect the file on disk. Press Save (F10) or select Save from the File pull-down menu. At the "Document to be saved: " prompt, type a file name and press ENTER. If the document has already been saved, press ENTER to accept the current file name. When asked about replacing the existing file, type **Y** for Yes.

Your document is now protected. The next time you attempt to retrieve the document file, LetterPerfect will ask you to enter the password. Simply type the password, press ENTER, and the document will be retrieved.

If you want to change the password that you've assigned to your document, retrieve the file, and follow the steps outlined in this section for adding a password. When you enter a new password, it will replace the previous one. Then, remember to save the document again to save the new password.

Removing a Document Password

Sometimes, you may wish to store additional copies of your files that are not password-protected. Or, perhaps the information in a document file is no longer confidential and you don't need a password anymore. For these situations, you can remove the password from a document that is currently protected. Follow these steps to remove a password:

1. Press **Retrieve** (SHIFT-F10) or select **Retrieve** from the File pull-down menu. Type the name of the file that has the password you want to remove, and press ENTER.

2. LetterPerfect prompts you with "Enter Password *(filename)*: ". Type the password and press ENTER. Your document is retrieved.

3. Press **Text Out** (CTRL-F5) and choose option **2**, **P**assword, from the Text Out menu; then, select option **2**, **R**emove, from the Password menu. If you prefer to use the pull-down menus, select Remove Password from the File pull-down menu.

After you select this option, the password is removed from your document. Make sure you save the document again to replace the file on disk; if you don't save the document, the disk file will still be password-protected.

Additional Information

LetterPerfect's password feature will prevent anyone from accessing the information in your files, but it can't prevent anyone from moving, copying, or deleting the files. If you have files that should be kept under tight security, you should still keep copies locked away on diskettes.

AUTOMATIC FILE BACKUP

You will eventually encounter a computer failure, if you haven't already experienced one. Computers are powerful, but they're also vulnerable to power failures, disk drive errors, and static electricity. A problem can occur at any time, and often without warning.

With LetterPerfect's automatic backup feature, you can concentrate on your documents and worry less about equipment failure. This feature ensures that you won't lose your file, by making a backup copy of your document at regular timed intervals.

Remember, this file is created as a backup in case there is a power failure or computer error. The backup feature does not eliminate the need to save your documents and make regular backup copies; when you properly exit the program, LetterPerfect deletes its backup file. Follow these steps to turn on the automatic backup feature:

1. Press Setup (SHIFT-F1) or select Setup from the File pull-down menu. The Setup menu appears as shown in Figure 8-2.

2. Choose option 2, Minutes Between Backup. This determines the interval for timed backup. Type the number of minutes that you want to pass between each timed backup (the standard time is 10 minutes). Press ENTER to accept the number.

3. Press Exit (F7) or click the right mouse button to return to the document screen.

Each time the backup interval passes, the current document is saved to a backup file named LP{LP}.BK1. This file is stored in the directory where your LetterPerfect program files are located.

For example, if you entered 30 as the number of minutes between backups, LetterPerfect saves a backup copy of your document every thirty minutes. As you work with the program, this file is updated at regular intervals so you can recover the document in the event of a computer failure.

```
Setup
      1 - Screen Colors                    Monochrome
      2 - Minutes Between Backup           10
      3 - Units of Measure                 Inches
      4 - Location of Document Files       C:\FILES
      5 - Initial Codes
      6 - Alt Key Selects Menu Bar         Yes
      7 - Menu Bar Remains Visible         Yes
      8 - Function of F1                   Cancel
      9 - Format Retrieved Documents       No
          for Default Printer


Selection: 0
```

FIGURE 8-2. Selecting the automatic backup feature

The LP{LP}.BK1 backup file is deleted when you properly exit LetterPerfect, but if there is a computer problem that prevents you from exiting the program, the backup file remains on disk. Then, when you start the program again, LetterPerfect prompts you with "Are other copies of LP currently running? (Y/N)"; to continue, type **N** for No. Then, when LetterPerfect attempts the first timed backup, you are prompted with "Old backup file exists. 1 Rename; 2 Delete". Choose option **1** and enter a new file name; then, you can retrieve the file. Or, choose option **2** to delete the backup file.

When you want to turn off the backup feature, press Setup (SHIFT-F1), choose option **2, Minutes Between Backup,** and enter **0** as the backup interval.

MANAGING YOUR DOCUMENTS WITH LIST FILES

The List Files feature can help you manage your document files by displaying a list of all files on one directory. A menu provides options for manipulating the files.

From the List Files screen, you can retrieve a file, copy, move, and delete files, and even rename your documents. These operations can be performed on one file or on a group of files.

The List Files Screen

To display the List Files screen, press List Files (F5), or select **List Files** from the **File** pull-down menu. The current or default directory path appears on the status line, similar to the screen shown in Figure 8-3 (you may see a different directory name on your status line). Press ENTER to accept this directory, or type a different directory path name. After you press ENTER, the List Files screen is displayed as shown in Figure 8-4. (The list on your screen will show different file names.)

note You can also access the List Files screen while using the Retrieve feature. At the "Document to be retrieved: " prompt, press List Files (F5) and ENTER. The List Files screen will appear.

```
File Edit Search Layout Tools Font Graphics Help        (Press ALT for menu bar)
```



```
Dir C:\FILES\*.*                                    (Type = to change default Dir)
```

FIGURE 8-3. Displaying the current or default directory path

```
08-14-90  11:52a              Directory C:\FILES\*.*
Document size:        0   Free: 1,255,424 Used:    82,378    Files:      12
      .    Current    <Dir>          |    ..    Parent    <Dir>
      CALC112 .DOC   1,805  07-07-90 02:33p | COLEMAN .LTR   2,420  07-07-90 01:05p
      G_BROWN .ENV     694  04-16-89 01:28p | G_BROWN .LTR   7,164  08-08-90 01:51a
      LP{LP}  .BK1     326  08-14-90 11:51a | PARTY   .DOC   2,149  08-05-90 05:33a
      PHONLIST.MEM     805  07-07-90 02:54p | PSYCH101.DOC  49,330  01-14-90 10:15a
      Q&A     .DOC   6,135  08-11-90 02:57p | REPORT91.W51   3,023  08-05-90 10:11p
      RESUME  .DOC   2,854  07-18-90 09:25p | WEAVER1 .LTR   5,673  07-07-90 02:47p




1 Retrieve; 2 Delete; 3 Move/Rename; 4 Other Directory; 5 Copy; 6 Look;
N Name Search: 6
```

Reversed bar (annotation pointing to the file list area)

FIGURE 8-4. The List Files screen

At the top of the screen, today's date and the current time are displayed with the directory path name. The size of the current (on-screen) document is also shown in bytes. Also displayed is the amount of free space on your disk, the amount of used disk space, and the number of files in the directory. A menu at the bottom of the screen displays the options for the List Files screen.

A reversed bar near the top of the screen is used to highlight or select a file on the list. You can use the arrow keys to move the cursor and highlight the file you want to select, or click on the desired file name with the mouse. Once a file name is highlighted with the bar, you can select one of the file options from the List Files menu, such as Retrieve or Copy.

Viewing a Document in the List

The Look option, on the List Files menu, allows you to view a document file without actually retrieving it into the document editing screen. This is useful when you need to find a particular document, but aren't sure what the file is called. To

```
File: C:\FILES\RESUME.DOC                          Revised: 07-18-90 09:25p
                         WILLIAM J. RATHE

    92 Spencer Road                        Work: (415) 555-3481
    Berkeley, CA  94710                    Home: (415) 555-1284


    EDUCATION:         University of California, Berkeley
                         B.A. - Psychology, 1978

                       University of California, Los Angeles
                         M.A. - Theater/Motion Picture Arts, 1981

                       Ranglin' Bros. Clown College, Orlando, FL.
                         Graduated with Big Top Honors, 1983
                         Recipient, Golden Bozo Award

    EXPERIENCE:        PARTY SHACK CATERING, INC., Berkeley, CA
    1987 - Present

    Look: 1 Next Doc; 2 Prev Doc: 0
```

FIGURE 8-5. Looking at the contents of a document

view a document from the list, highlight the file and select option **6**, **Look**, from the List Files menu. Figure 8-5 shows a document in the List Files "look" screen. Select option **1**, Next Doc, from the menu at the bottom of the screen, to look at the next document file in the list. Select option **2**, **Prev Doc**, to look at the previous file. When you are finished viewing the document, press Exit (F7) to return to the List Files screen.

note Make sure the files you select are document files. You cannot view graphic or program files with LetterPerfect's Look feature.

Searching for a File Name

You'll soon have quite a collection of document files. In fact, the number may be large enough to fill the List Files screen, which can display up to 72 files. When the number of files exceeds the amount that can be displayed on the screen, you can move the highlighted cursor to scroll through the list. To scroll with a mouse, hold down the left mouse button and move the cursor down through the list.

When you have a large number of files, it may take a while to find the file you want. The Name Search feature can help you locate specific file names on the list.

First, select **F2**, Name Search, from the menu on the List Files screen. This enables the Name Search mode. (Notice that the List Files menu is not displayed when this mode is active.) Then, type the name of the file you want to find. As you type, LetterPerfect moves the highlighted cursor to match the name of the characters you are typing. Figure 8-6 shows an example of this. When enough characters match, the cursor moves to the file name. To disable Name Search, press ENTER or an arrow key, and the List Files menu returns.

Marking Document Files

Earlier in this chapter, you learned that you must move the reversed bar to a file before you can select an option from the List Files menu. When you select a List

```
08-14-90  11:56a              Directory C:\FILES\*.*
Document size:         0    Free: 1,255,424 Used:      82,378    Files:      12

      .   Current    <Dir>              ..    Parent     <Dir>
CALC112  .DOC    1,805  07-07-90 02:33p   COLEMAN  .LTR   2,420  07-07-90 01:05p
G_BROWN  .ENV      694  04-16-89 01:28p   G_BROWN  .LTR   7,164  08-08-90 01:51a
LP{LP}   .BK1      326  08-14-90 11:51a   PARTY    .DOC   2,149  08-05-90 05:33a
PHONLIST.MEM       805  07-07-90 02:54p   PSYCH101.DOC  49,330  01-14-90 10:15a
Q&A      .DOC    6,135  08-11-90 02:57p   REPORT91.V51   3,023  08-05-90 10:11p
RESUME   .DOC    2,854  07-18-90 09:25p   WEAVER1  .LTR   5,673  07-07-90 02:47p




report                              (Name Search; Enter or arrows to Exit)
```

FIGURE 8-6.   Using Name Search to find a file

Files option, it affects the highlighted file; however, you may want to copy, move, or delete a group of files on the list. You can do this by marking the files you want to affect, and then selecting the appropriate feature from the List Files menu.

For example, if you want to move all your correspondence files from the current directory to a floppy disk, you would mark the files you want to move, select Move from the menu, and then indicate the location where the marked files should be moved.

To mark a file, move the reversed bar to the file, and then type an asterisk (*). An asterisk appears next to the file name, to indicate that it is marked. You can continue marking additional files by highlighting each file and pressing the asterisk key. When all files that you want to affect are marked, select a file option from the menu. To mark all files in the list, press HOME-* or ALT-F5. To unmark all files, press HOME-* or ALT-F5 again.

Copying and Deleting Files

From the List Files screen, you can copy files to other directory locations and delete unwanted files. Copy a file by moving the reversed bar to the file on the list and selecting option **5**, **C**opy, from the List Files menu. LetterPerfect prompts you with "Copy this file to: ". Type the path name where you want the copy to be placed, and press ENTER. LetterPerfect makes a copy of the file and stores it in the directory path name that you specified. You can type a new file name, instead of a path name, to create a copy of the file in the current directory.

If you have any files marked in the list and you select option **5**, LetterPerfect asks you to verify that you want to copy all marked files.

To delete a file, highlight the file that you want to remove from your directory, and select option **2**, **D**elete, from the List Files menu. LetterPerfect asks you to verify that you want to delete the highlighted file. Type **Y** for Yes, and the file is removed from your disk.

If you want to delete several files, mark them before you select this feature. Be careful when you use the Delete feature; once you delete a file, you cannot restore it unless you have special data recovery software.

Moving and Renaming Files

An important part of file management includes moving files to other locations, and renaming your document files. LetterPerfect includes both of these features with one option on the List Files menu. To move or rename a file, follow these steps:

1. Display the List Files screen and move the reversed bar to the file that you want to move or rename.

2. Select option **3**, **M**ove/Rename, from the List Files menu.

3. LetterPerfect prompts you with "New Name: ". At this point, you can type a new file name or path name. Then, press ENTER to accept it.

If you enter a path name, LetterPerfect moves the file to that location. If you enter a file name, LetterPerfect renames the file. Enter a path name *and* a new file name, and LetterPerfect will rename the file and move it to the new location.

When files are marked, LetterPerfect assumes that you want to move the marked files to another location.

Changing the File Directory

When you are finished working with the files in one directory, you can change to a different directory to work with other files. To change the directory, follow these steps from the List Files screen:

1. Select option **4**, **O**ther Directory, from the List Files menu. A "New directory = " prompt appears at the bottom of the screen, followed by the current directory path name.

2. Type the path name of the directory you wish to view and press ENTER. For example, type **c:** and press ENTER to view the main directory of the C drive. If you have a diskette in drive B, type **b:** and press ENTER to view the files on that diskette.

3. The path name is displayed with a pattern for file names ("∗.∗"). Press ENTER to accept the pattern, and the files of the new directory are displayed on the List Files screen.

In this case, "∗.∗" is displayed after the path name, meaning that all files in the new directory will be displayed. The asterisks in the pattern act as *wildcard characters*. They represent any combination of characters that precedes or follows the period that separates the file name from the file extension.

You can press END to move the cursor to the end of the pattern, press BACKSPACE to delete the asterisk characters, and then type a new pattern. For example, if you want to view only the files with a .DOC extension in the new directory listing, replace the old pattern with ∗.**DOC**. Suppose you want to list only the following files: SURVEY88.RPT, SURVEY89.RPT, SURVEY90.RPT, and SURVEY91.RPT; you could enter **SURVEY∗.RPT** as the pattern. Only the files that match the pattern will be displayed on the List Files screen.

Creating a New Directory

Sometimes, you'll want to create a new directory. To do so, select option **4**, **Other Directory**, from the List Files menu. The "New directory = " prompt appears at the bottom of the screen, followed by the current directory path name. Type the path name of a directory that does not yet exist, and press ENTER. LetterPerfect recognizes that the path name you entered does not exist, and it asks whether you want to create it. Type **Y** for Yes, and LetterPerfect creates the directory for you.

The new directory is not automatically displayed because it doesn't contain any files yet. After you've copied or saved files to the new path name, you can select option **4**, Other Directory, again to view the contents of the directory.

SUMMARY

File management helps you organize and use your document files. The Save feature lets you save a document so you may use it at a later date. The Retrieve feature lets you bring a saved document into the LetterPerfect document screen.

When you save a document file, you can type a name up to eight characters, followed by a period and a three-character extension. Files are saved to and retrieved from the default directory, unless you specify a path name for document files. This is done from the Setup menu, with the Location of Document Files feature.

You also learned how to convert files to different formats that may be retrieved into other software programs. To protect your document from prying eyes, you can assign a password that prevents anyone from retrieving or viewing the document, without first entering the password. You learned how to use the timed backup feature to ensure that you won't lose your document in the event of a computer failure.

The List Files feature shows an index of the files on the current directory. Options on the List Files menu let you retrieve files, delete and copy, move and rename, and view the contents of a document file.

This chapter is the end of Part I, which concludes the basic program information about LetterPerfect. Part II shows you how to create useful applications with LetterPerfect, including office memos, outlines, business letters, printed envelopes, and documents for mass-mailings.

part II

PRACTICAL APPLICATIONS

Creating Memos and Outlines
Letters and Envelopes
Merging Letters and Mailing Labels

It's nice to learn all about the features of a new software program. But if you can't use the software to create what you *need,* then it isn't worth your time. The following chapters will help you create documents for practical situations. You can begin these projects immediately—easy instructions will guide you through each step for creating memos, outlines, business letters, printed envelopes, and labels. You'll even learn how to set up a mass-mailing system for bulk distribution of announcements, form letters, and other documents. Just follow the steps to get the documents shown in the illustrations.

It is assumed that you understand the information presented in Part I of this book. If you have not yet reviewed Chapters 1 through 8, you may wish to do so before continuing. The first eight chapters contain important information that will help you with the documents in the following exercises. Once you understand the basics of LetterPerfect, you're ready to create something useful.

The applications in the following chapters do not represent the limits of what you can create with LetterPerfect; rather, these examples show just a glimpse of what is possible and will help you get started with a few practical documents. The rest is up to you.

chapter 9

CREATING MEMOS AND OUTLINES

Creating a Business Memo
Automated Memos
Starting an Outline
Summary

In this chapter, you'll learn how to create two common documents for business and education—the office memo and the outline. Each will help you communicate more effectively with other people in your organization.

The memo application is presented in two forms: The first exercise shows how to create a standard business memo; the second exercise will help you create a special document that can automate the memo process when used with LetterPerfect's Merge feature.

You will learn how to use LetterPerfect's Outline feature to organize your thoughts, speeches, and written materials. The exercise in this chapter will show you how to create an outline for a travel brochure; this can be easily adapted for other applications.

CREATING A BUSINESS MEMO

The memorandum, or interoffice memo, is probably the most common form of business communication. There are several types of memos—some on preprinted forms, others on stationery or plain paper. The memo format you use depends on the requirements for your company or organization.

The following exercise will show you how to create a standard memorandum on blank paper, as shown in Figure 9-1. The exercise is divided into three sections; make sure you perform each section in the order presented here. You will begin by defining the memo format, either using the given measurements or substituting your own settings. Then, you will create the heading for the memo. This will include a title, *guide words* (such as DATE:, TO:, FROM:), and a horizontal line that separates the document heading from the message section of the memo. Finally, you will type your message, save it, and then print the memo document.

note This application is designed for people who occasionally need to send a memo. If you create memos on a daily basis, you may want to use the memo document described in the section, "Automated Memos."

Creating the Memo Format

The following steps will show you how to create the document format for an interoffice memo according to common guidelines for business communication. If you wish, you can alter the format to suit your own needs. Clear the screen (F7, N, N) before you begin.

1. From a clear screen, press Format (SHIFT-F8) or choose **F**ormat from the **L**ayout pull-down menu.

2. Choose option **5**, **T**abs, from the displayed Format menu. The Tab Set screen appears.

3. Press HOME, LEFT ARROW to move the cursor to the beginning of the tab ruler.

4. Press CTRL-END to clear the tab ruler.

5. Type **1"** and press ENTER. Then, type **r** to change the setting to a right-aligned tab. Type **1.5"** and press ENTER.

6. Press Exit (F7) twice, or click the right mouse button, to return to the document screen.

MEMORANDUM

DATE: November 10, 1991

TO: Terry Brown - Director, Conference Services

FROM: Julie Denver - Corporate Security

SUBJECT: Exhibit Hall Security

Because of the recent increase of equipment theft, our security officers will be posted at each entrance to the Exhibit Hall. They will monitor the building throughout the month, until the Fall conference is adjourned. In the future, this practice will be observed for each conference and exhibit.

We regret any inconvenience to you, but we feel this will improve the safety for our guests, as well as prevent the loss of company property. Please notify your department of the new security policy. We appreciate your cooperation in this matter.

JD

FIGURE 9-1. A standard business memo

note: You now have two tab stops defined for the document. A right-aligned tab is set at 1 inch from the left margin (the zero mark), and a left-aligned tab is set at 1.5 inches from the left margin.

Creating the Heading

Now you're ready to create the heading for the memo, which includes the title and guide words. You will use LetterPerfect's Line Draw feature to create the horizontal line that separates the memo heading from the message portion of your memo.

1. Press Center (CTRL-C or SHIFT-F6) or select Center from the Layout menu.

2. Press Bold (CTRL-B or F6) or select Bold from the Font pull-down menu.

3. Type **MEMORANDUM**. Press Bold (CTRL-B or F6) again, to turn off the bold attribute.

4. Press ENTER three times.

5. Press TAB. Type **DATE:** and press TAB again.

6. Press the Fast Key, CTRL-D, to insert the date, or choose Date Text from the Tools pull-down menu. Press ENTER twice.

7. Press TAB. Type **TO:** and press TAB again. Then, type the name of the person to receive the memo. If you wish, you can also type the job title (for example, Terry Brown—Director, Conference Services).

8. Press ENTER twice.

9. Press TAB. Type **FROM:** and press TAB again. Type your name and title or the name and title of the person sending the memo.

10. Press ENTER twice.

11. Press TAB and type **SUBJECT:**. Then, press TAB and type the subject of the memo. Press ENTER twice.

12. Press Line Draw (CTRL-F3), and a menu appears at the bottom of the screen with different options for drawing lines.

13. A single-line style is already selected, so press the RIGHT ARROW key to move the cursor across the screen. When the cursor stops and won't move any further to the right, you know you've reached the right margin. Press Exit (F7) to exit the Line Draw mode.

```
File Edit Search Layout Tools Font Graphics Help     (Press ALT for menu bar)
                            MEMORANDUM
        DATE:     November 10, 1991
          TO:     Terry Brown - Director, Conference Services
        FROM:     Julie Denver - Corporate Security
     SUBJECT:     Exhibit Hall Security




                                                  Pg 1 Ln 3.33" Pos 1"
```

FIGURE 9-2.   Creating the memo format

14. Press END to move the cursor beyond the line. Then, press ENTER three times.

Your memo document should now look similar to Figure 9-2. Don't mind the arrows at each end of the horizontal line; these appear on the screen as guides for the line drawing process, but won't print on your document.

Typing the Message and Printing the Memo

Follow these steps to type the message for your memo. Then, save and print the document.

1. Type the paragraphs for your memo. When you are finished, press ENTER twice to add extra space at the bottom of the memo.

2. Press Center (CTRL-C or SHIFT-F6) or select Center from the Layout menu.

3. Type your initials, or the initials of the person sending the memo.

4. Press Spell (CTRL-S or CTRL-F2) or select **Spell** from the **Tools** pull-down menu. Follow the prompts to spell-check your memo. When the Spell feature is finished, press the SPACEBAR to continue.

5. Press Save (F10) or select **Save** from the **File** pull-down menu.

6. At the "Document to be saved: " prompt, type a name for the file and press ENTER.

7. Press Print (SHIFT-F7) or select **Print** from the **File** pull-down menu. Select option **3**, **View Document**, to view the document, or choose option **1**, **Full Document**, to send a copy of the memo to your printer.

Your memo is finished. Remember, this exercise shows only one format for an interoffice memo. You may wish to alter the format for your own situation. For example, you may want to add additional guide words for DEPARTMENT:, TELEPHONE EXTENSION:, or JOB TITLE:. Although no font changes were selected for this document, you may want to take advantage of your printer's fonts to create a larger MEMORANDUM title or to emphasize text with bold, italics, and underlining. Before you continue, make sure you clear the screen (F7, N, N).

AUTOMATED MEMOS

LetterPerfect includes features that let you combine or *merge* text with a predefined document format. If you need to send several memos each day, you may want to create a document format file, or *primary file,* for your memo format. The primary file contains the memo format that you've defined, with special codes that indicate where text should be inserted. When used with LetterPerfect's Merge feature, this file will save you a great deal of time, and will ensure that the format is consistent for each memo.

The steps in this section will show you how to create an automated memo. The exercise is divided into three segments; make sure you perform each segment in the order presented here. You will begin by defining the primary file for the memo; this file will be the model that LetterPerfect uses to create the actual memos. You can create the format shown in the exercise, or substitute your own format settings.

Then you will type the text that should appear on each memo that you create. This includes the title, guide words, such as DATE:, TO:, and FROM:, and a horizontal line that separates the document heading from the message section of the memo.

You will also use a merge code, called {INPUT}, to specify where information should be merged into the memo format. For example, the recipient's name and the memo subject will be different for each memo that you create; therefore, when you create the primary file, you will insert {INPUT} codes after the guide words for TO: and SUBJECT:.

Finally, you will save the memo primary file, clear the screen, and use LetterPerfect's Merge feature to create a memo with the layout saved in the primary file. During the merge, the {INPUT} codes in the primary file will prompt you to enter information from the keyboard. When the merge is finished, you can type the message, and then print your memo.

The automated memo is fast and easy, and guarantees that your format will be the same every time you create a memo. If this seems a little complicated, don't worry. After you go through the exercise, you'll see that it's really quite simple.

Creating the Memo Format

The following information will show you how to create the format for a standard business memo. This is the first step to creating a primary file that will become the model for all your memos. Before you begin, make sure you clear the screen (F7, N, N).

1. Press Format (SHIFT-F8) or choose **Format** from the Layout pull-down menu.

2. Choose option **5**, **T**abs, from the displayed Format menu. The tab definition screen appears.

3. Press HOME, LEFT ARROW to move the cursor to the beginning of the tab definition ruler.

4. Press CTRL-END to clear the tab ruler.

5. Type **1"** and press ENTER. Then type **r** to change the setting to a right-aligned tab. Type **1.5"** and press ENTER.

6. Press Exit (F7) twice, or click the right mouse button to return to the document screen.

Creating the Heading with Merge Commands

Now you will type the text that should appear on each memo that you create. This includes the memo title, the guide words, and the horizontal division line. For the text that will be different with each memo, you will insert the {INPUT} merge code. You will also insert a merge code called {DATE}; this code automatically inserts the current date into your document, similar to the Date Text code feature discussed in Chapter 3.

1. Press Center (CTRL-C or SHIFT-F6) or select Center from the Layout menu.

2. Press Bold (CTRL-B or F6) or select Bold from the Fonts pull-down menu. Type **MEMORANDUM**. Press Bold again to turn off the bold attribute.

3. Press ENTER three times.

4. Press TAB. Type **DATE:** and press TAB again. Press Merge Codes (SHIFT-F9) or select Merge Codes from the Tools pull-down menu. The Merge Codes window appears on the screen, as shown in Figure 9-3.

5. The reversed bar should be already on the {DATE} code in the list. Press ENTER to insert this command into your document. Press ENTER twice to add line space for the next memo guide word (TO:).

6. Press TAB. Type **TO:** and press TAB again. Press Merge Codes (SHIFT-F9) or select Merge Codes from the Tools pull-down menu. Use the arrow keys to highlight the "{INPUT}message~" code on the list. Press ENTER to select the command.

```
File Edit Search Layout Tools Font Graphics Help       (Press ALT for menu bar)
                          MEMORANDUM
                                    ┌─────────────────────────────────┐
                                    │ {DATE}                          │
                                    │ {END FIELD}                     │
           DATE:                    │ {END RECORD}                    │
                                    │ {FIELD}field~                   │
                                    │ {FIELD NAMES}name1~...nameN~~   │
                                    │ {INPUT}message~                 │
                                    │ {NEST PRIMARY}filename~         │
                                    │ {NEXT RECORD}                   │
                                    │ {PAGE OFF}                      │
                                    │ {PAGE ON}              Reversed │
                                    │ {PRINT}                  bar    │
                                    │ {QUIT}                          │
                                    │ {STOP}                          │
                                    └─────────────────────────────────┘



                                  (Name Search; Arrows; Enter to Select)
```

FIGURE 9-3. Selecting a merge code for the primary file

7. A message at the bottom of the screen prompts you to enter an input message. Type **(Type recipient's name. Press F9 to continue.)** and press ENTER. The {INPUT} merge code is inserted into your document with the message that you just typed. Press ENTER twice.

note: The input message will be displayed at the bottom of the screen when you use the Merge feature. You can type anything for the message—just make sure the message is less than 48 characters in length. If an input message is longer than 48 characters, it may be hidden by the status line when it is displayed.

8. Press TAB. Type **FROM:** and press TAB again. Type your name or the name of the person who will be sending the memos. Press ENTER twice.

9. Press TAB. Type **SUBJECT:** and press TAB again. Press Merge Codes (SHIFT-F9). The reversed bar should already highlight the "{INPUT}message~" code, since this was the last command you selected. Press ENTER to select the code again.

10. At the "Enter message: " prompt, type **(Type the subject. Press F9 to continue.)** and press ENTER three times.

11. Now you're ready to create the horizontal division line. Press Line Draw (CTRL-F3), and a menu appears at the bottom of the screen with different options for drawing lines.

12. A single-line style is already selected, so press the RIGHT ARROW key to move the cursor across the screen. When the cursor stops and won't move any further to the right, you know you've reached the right margin. Press Exit (F7) to exit the Line Draw mode.

13. Press END to move the cursor beyond the line. Then, press ENTER three times.

Your memo primary file is now finished, and should look similar to Figure 9-4. The {DATE} code that you selected will insert the current date into the memo, whenever this file is used with the Merge feature. The {INPUT} code will suspend the merge, and allow you to type text from the keyboard. The rest of the format is identical to the standard memo that you created earlier in this chapter.

Saving the Document and Clearing the Screen

Take the following steps to save your primary file and clear the document screen.

1. Press Exit (F7) or select Exit from the File pull-down menu. When prompted with "Save document? Yes (No)", type **Y** for Yes.

```
File Edit Search Layout Tools Font Graphics Help      (Press ALT for menu bar)
                            MEMORANDUM
         DATE:      {DATE}
           TO:      {INPUT}(Type recipient's name.  Press F9 to continue.)~
         FROM:      Julie Denver
      SUBJECT:      {INPUT}(Type the subject.  Press F9 to continue.)~




                                                        Pg 1 Ln 3.33" Pos 1"
```

FIGURE 9-4. The finished memo primary file

2. At the "Document to be saved: " prompt, type a name for the primary file (for example, MEMO.PF) and press ENTER.

3. When prompted with "Exit LP? No (Yes)", type N for No. The LetterPerfect screen is cleared.

The memo primary file is now saved on your disk. Remember, this file contains only the format for a memo. You will use LetterPerfect's Merge feature to create an actual memo with the format saved in the file.

Using Merge to Create the Memo

Now that your primary file is complete and the screen is clear, you're ready to use LetterPerfect's Merge feature. Each time you need to create a memo, you can follow these steps:

1. Press Merge (CTRL-F9) or choose **Merge** from the **Tools** pull-down menu.

2. A message at the bottom of the screen, "Primary file: ", prompts you to enter the name of the file that contains the format you want to use (for example, MEMO.PF). Type the name of your memo primary file and press ENTER.

3. You are now prompted to enter the name of a secondary file. This application does not require a secondary file, so just press ENTER to continue. (You'll learn more about primary and secondary files in Chapter 11, "Merging Letters and Mailing Labels.")

4. The merge begins and the cursor stops after the TO: label. The input message you typed appears at the bottom of the screen, and prompts you with "(Type recipient's name. Press F9 to continue.)". Type the name of the person who should receive the memo, and press F9.

note: Make sure you press F9, and *not* ENTER. Pressing ENTER will only insert a hard-return code ([HRt]) into your text.

5. Now, the cursor stops after the SUBJECT: label. You are prompted with "(Type the subject. Press F9 to continue.)". Type a description of the subject for the memo. Then, press F9 to continue.

6. The cursor stops at the bottom of the memo format. Type the paragraph(s) for the memo. Then, save and print the document. When you are finished, clear the screen.

Keep in mind that the Merge feature "borrows" the format of the memo primary file to create the finished memo; your original memo primary file is still intact. Also, remember to press F9, instead of ENTER, to continue the merge after it has stopped for input. Pressing ENTER is the intuitive keystroke to continue, but, during a merge, ENTER inserts a hard-return command. This is the reason why you typed "Press F9 to continue" in your input message; it helps to remind you which key you should press.

Congratulations! You now have an automated memo system. With it, you can quickly create a memo by pressing Merge (CTRL-F9) and entering the name of your memo primary file (remember to press ENTER at the "Secondary file: " prompt, without typing a file name). LetterPerfect will stop and allow you to type the recipient's name, the subject matter, and the memo message—the rest is automatically created for you. In Chapter 11, you'll use the Merge feature again to create a system for form letters and mass-mailing documents.

CREATING AN OUTLINE

LetterPerfect's Outline feature can help you organize your thoughts for term papers, notes, speeches, or corporate meetings. An outline may be divided into several numbered levels, with different topics for lectures or printed materials. Figure 9-5 shows the numbered outline that you will create in this section.

Select LetterPerfect's Outline feature, and you enable a special *Outline mode*. When this mode is active, pressing ENTER moves the text cursor to the next line and automatically sets up the next numbered entry for the outline. Then, all you have to do is type the text for that entry. Press ENTER again, and the number for the next entry is inserted. You can have up to eight different levels of numbering in a single outline.

Starting an Outline

In the following exercise, you will create an outline about skiing in the Rocky Mountains. This will help organize the structure of a booklet that will be published for the Department of Tourism. Clear the screen before you begin.

1. With the text cursor at the top of a clear screen, type **ROCKY MOUNTAIN SKIING: A VISITORS' GUIDE** and press ENTER. Now you're ready to select the Outline feature.

2. Press Date/Outline (SHIFT-F5) and choose option **3**, **Outline On**. If you prefer to use the pull-down menus, choose **Outline On** from the **T**ools menu. This inserts an invisible [Outline On] code into your text. "Outline" appears on the status line, to show that the Outline mode is active.

3. Press ENTER to insert the first entry of the outline. You will notice the Roman numeral I. in your text.

4. Press Indent (F4) to indent the cursor, and type **Introduction to Downhill Skiing**.

5. Now, you want to create a heading beneath Roman numeral I. Press ENTER to move to the next line. LetterPerfect automatically inserts the Roman numeral for the next entry.

6. Press ENTER again to move the entire entry to the next line. Press TAB to indent the entry and change it to item A.

note: When you press TAB, the current level is indented to create a sublevel in the outline. You can do this for up to eight sublevels—just keep pressing the TAB key. If you change your mind, you can press SHIFT-TAB to move the entry back to the previous level.

7. Press Indent (F4) to indent the text cursor, and type **Skiing: A Brief History**.

ROCKY MOUNTAIN SKIING: A VISITORS' GUIDE

I. Introduction to Downhill Skiing

   A. Skiing: A Brief History

   1. Cross-Country Treks

   2. The Sporting Thing to Do

   3. The Ultimate Thrill-Ride

   B. Can Anyone Ski?

   C. It's Fun... After You Know How

II. Getting the Gear

   A. Weighing the Costs

   B. Buying the Right Equipment

   C. The Bare Accessories

III. Planning the Ski Vacation

   A. Accommodations

   B. When to Go

   C. Ski Packages

IV. The World's Greatest Snow?

   A. The Colorado Resorts

   B. Utah's Perfect Powder

FIGURE 9-5. The outline format

8. Press ENTER twice to move to the next entry; LetterPerfect automatically inserts the next item (B.) for the current level.

note
You may notice that LetterPerfect keeps the cursor at the same level as the previous outline entry. You can press SHIFT-TAB or TAB to change the current outline number to the previous or next level.

9. Press TAB to change this entry to a sublevel (1.), under item A. Press Indent (F4) and type **Cross-Country Treks**.

10. Press ENTER twice to insert the next entry. Press Indent (F4), and type **The Sporting Thing to Do**.

11. Press ENTER twice to move to the next entry. Press Indent (F4) and type **The Ultimate Thrill-Ride**.

12. Press ENTER twice to insert the next entry, number 4. Press SHIFT-TAB to move this entry back to the previous level, and change it to item B.

13. Press Indent (F4) and type **Can Anyone Ski?**. Press ENTER twice to insert the next entry.

14. Press Indent (F4) to indent the text cursor, then type **It's Fun . . . After You Know How** and press ENTER three times to insert the next entry.

15. Press SHIFT-TAB to move to the previous level, and change the D. to Roman numeral II.

16. Press Indent (F4) and type **Getting the Gear**. Press ENTER twice and then press TAB, to create an entry beneath Roman numeral II.

17. Press Indent (F4) and type **Weighing the Costs**. Press ENTER twice for the next entry. Press Indent (F4) and type **Buying the Right Equipment**.

So far, your outline should appear as shown in Figure 9-6. You can continue with the outline until it looks like the document in Figure 9-5. Remember, press ENTER to begin a new entry; press TAB or SHIFT-TAB to change the number for the next or previous level. Press Indent (F4) or type spaces to indent the text from the outline numbers.

When you are finished with the outline, press Date/Outline (SHIFT-F5) and choose option **4**, Outline Off. If you prefer to use the pull-down menus, choose Outline Off from the **T**ools menu. An [Outline Off] code is inserted into the text, and the Outline message disappears from the status line.

Whenever the text cursor is moved between the [Outline On] and [Outline Off] codes, the Outline mode becomes active, as indicated by the "Outline" message on

```
File Edit Search Layout Tools Font Graphics Help      (Press ALT for menu bar)
 I.  Introduction to Downhill Skiing
     A. Skiing: A Brief History
           1. Cross-Country Treks
           2. The Sporting Thing to Do
           3. The Ultimate Thrill-Ride
     B. Can Anyone Ski?
     C. It's Fun... After You Know How

II.  Getting the Gear
     A. Weighing the Costs
     B. Buying the Right Equipment
Outline                                                Pg 1 Ln 5" Pos 4.4"
```

FIGURE 9-6. Creating the outline

the status line. When you see this message, remember that pressing ENTER inserts a new entry for the outline. If you don't want a new outline entry, press BACKSPACE to delete the number.

At this point, you'll probably want to save the document to a file on disk. This application is just one example of what you can do. You can easily adapt this exercise to create an outline for other applications; simply change the text for the different entries.

Reorganizing Your Outline

You can use LetterPerfect's Move feature (CTRL-M or CTRL-F4) to block and move sections of your text. This will help you reorganize the outline material. Follow these steps to move a section of your outline to a different location:

1. Move the text cursor to the first line of the entry you want to move. For example, move the cursor to the line "Skiing: A Brief History", in the outline that you created earlier.

```
File Edit Search Layout Tools Font [Graphics] Help     (Press ALT for menu bar)
ROCKY MOUNTAIN SKIING: A VISITORS' GUIDE


I.   Introduction to Downhill Skiing
          A. Skiing: A Brief History
                    1. Cross-Country Treks
                    2. The Sporting Thing to Do
                    3. The Ultimate Thrill-Ride
          B. Can Anyone Ski?
          C. It's Fun... After You Know How


II.  Getting the Gear
Outline   Block on                                      Pg 1 Ln 3.33" Pos 1"
```

FIGURE 9-7.   Blocking and moving an outline section

2. Press HOME, LEFT ARROW to move the text cursor to the beginning of the line.

3. Press Block (ALT-F4 or F12). Then, move the cursor below the last line that you want to include in the block move. Figure 9-7 shows how your block might look on the screen. Notice that the block starts at the entry for "Skiing: A Brief History," and ends with the cursor below the last item for that entry.

4. Press Move (CTRL-M or CTRL-F4, 1). The blocked text is removed from its current location.

5. Move the cursor to the location where you want to move the block. In this example, move the cursor to the line below the entry that reads, "Can Anyone Ski?". Then, press ENTER and the text is retrieved at the new location.

That's all you need to do. After you move a section of your outline to a new location, LetterPerfect automatically renumbers all entries to reflect the new order.

SUMMARY

Interoffice memos and outlines are two important documents for business communication. You've learned how to create the layout for a memo in LetterPerfect. You've also learned how to create a primary file for a memo format. When the primary file, explained in this chapter, is used with LetterPerfect's Merge feature, you are prompted to enter the recipient's name and the subject, and LetterPerfect automatically creates the memo format for you.

LetterPerfect's Outline feature can help you organize your thoughts by inserting numbers for a document outline. You can create an outline with up to eight different levels, with each level numbered independently. You can also use the Move feature to reorganize your outlines.

In the next chapter, you'll learn more about documents for business communication. You'll create the document layouts for two letters—a personal letter and a business letter—as well as the layout for printing envelopes.

chapter 10

LETTERS AND ENVELOPES

Creating a Personal Letter
Creating a Business Letter
Formatting for Envelopes
Summary

This chapter shows you how to create letters for personal and business correspondence. The first exercise presents the layout for a personal letter; the second shows how to create a standard business letter on preprinted letterhead. Finally, you'll learn how to create the layout for printing on envelopes.

CREATING A PERSONAL LETTER

The letter shown in Figure 10-1 is formatted in a *modified block style*. This is an appropriate format for a personal or business letter printed on blank stationery. If you need to create a letter for preprinted letterhead, use the format in the next exercise, "Creating a Business Letter."

Carolyn Janson
41 Los Flores Blvd.
Westlake, CA 91361

September 6, 1991

John W. Riskin
Soordon, Riskin, & Walsh
218 Avenue of the Americas
Los Angeles, CA 90052

Dear Mr. Riskin,

    It was a pleasure to speak with you on the phone. I am enclosing a copy of my proposal, <u>Executive Publishing</u>, for your consideration. I am also sending course materials which I created for the Battelle & Lewis Company. These are examples of my writing abilities, but I prefer a relaxed style for my own projects. If you would like other writing samples, please let me know.

    <u>Executive Publishing</u> will be successful because it addresses the practical needs of the business user. As I've traveled to various corporations, I have discussed this project with several people. The response has been favorable, and I feel the project would appeal to a wide range of users. My primary focus will be on the publishing needs of technical developers; however, I am willing to make some adjustments to meet the needs of the current market. I look forward to your reply.

                                            Sincerely,

                                            Carolyn Janson

FIGURE 10-1. The personal letter

For the personal letter, you don't need to worry about setting margins. The standard one-inch margins are just right for this format.

note — This exercise presents only one version of a personal letter; there are several formats that are acceptable. If you find that this example doesn't suit your needs, use the information in Chapters 2 through 4 to create your own format.

1. Press Format (SHIFT-F8) or select Format from the Layout pull-down menu.

2. Choose option **9**, Center Page (top to bottom), and type **Y** for Yes.

3. Choose option **5**, **T**abs, to display the tab ruler.

4. Press HOME, LEFT ARROW to move the cursor to the beginning of the line. Then, press CTRL-END to clear the tab ruler.

5. Type **0.5"** and press ENTER. Then, type **3.5"** and press ENTER. This sets two tabs, one at 0.5 inches from the left margin of the page and one at 3.5 inches from the left margin.

6. Press Exit (F7) twice to return to the main document screen.

7. Now you're ready to begin typing the text of your letter. Press TAB twice and type your name. Press ENTER to move the text cursor to the next line.

8. Press TAB twice and type your street address. Press ENTER to move to the next line, press TAB twice, and type your city, state, and ZIP code.

9. Press ENTER twice to add space for the date. Then, press TAB twice.

10. Press Date/Outline (SHIFT-F5) and choose option **1**, Date Text, or select Date Text from the Tools pull-down menu. LetterPerfect inserts the date for you.

11. Press ENTER twice to add space for the recipient's name and address.

12. Type the name of the person who should receive the letter. Press ENTER to move to the next line.

13. Type the recipient's street address, and press ENTER.

14. Type the recipient's city, state, and ZIP code. Press ENTER twice to make room for the salutation.

15. Type the salutation (for example, Dear Mr. Gibson), and press ENTER twice.

16. Now you're ready to type the main body of your letter. If you wish, you can press TAB before typing to indent the first line. When you finish typing each paragraph, press ENTER twice to end it.

17. After you've typed all the paragraphs of your letter, you can type the closing. Press TAB twice and type the closing that you prefer (Sincerely, Best Wishes, and so on).

18. Press ENTER four times to add room for the signature.

19. Press TAB twice and type your name. Then, press ENTER. If you wish, press TAB twice again and type your title.

20. If your letter includes only a few short paragraphs, press ENTER four or five times to add extra space at the bottom of the text. This will help to balance the effect of the Center Page command that you selected earlier.

Your personal letter is complete. You can use the View Document feature (CTRL-P or SHIFT-F7, 3) to see how the printed letter will look; when you are finished viewing the letter, press Exit (F7) to return to the document screen.

You may want to use the Speller (CTRL-S or CTRL-F2) to check the spelling of your letter before you print it. Then, press Save (F10) or choose Save from the File pull-down menu. When prompted with "Document to be saved: ", type a file name and press ENTER. To print the letter, press Print (SHIFT-F7) and select option **1, Full Document**. After you have saved and printed the document, make sure you clear the screen (F7, N, N).

CREATING A BUSINESS LETTER

The following exercise shows you how to create a letter for preprinted letterhead, using the *block style* format shown in Figure 10-2. This format provides more space at the top margin, to allow for the address information on the letterhead. All text is aligned at the left margin, so there's no need to set any special tabs.

note: This exercise presents only one version of a business letter, but there are several formats that are acceptable. If you find that this example doesn't suit your needs, use the information in Chapters 2 through 4 to create your own format.

1. Press Format (SHIFT-F8) or select **Format** from the Layout pull-down menu.

2. Choose option **3, Top/Bottom Margins**. Type **2.5"** and press ENTER, for the top margin. For the bottom margin, just press ENTER to accept the one-inch measurement.

3. Press Exit (F7) to return to the main document screen.

4. Press Date/Outline (SHIFT-F5) and choose option **1, Date Text**, or select **Date Text** from the Tools pull-down menu. LetterPerfect inserts the date for you.

CASTLETON
CORPORATE TRAINING
41 Los Flores Boulevard • Westlake, California 91361

September 6, 1991

John W. Riskin
Soordon, Riskin, & Walsh
218 Avenue of the Americas
Los Angeles, CA 90052

Dear Mr. Riskin,

    It was a pleasure to speak with you on the phone. I am enclosing a copy of my proposal, <u>Executive Publishing</u>, for your consideration. I am also sending course materials which I created for the Battelle & Lewis Company. These are examples of my writing abilities, but I prefer a relaxed style for my own projects. If you would like other writing samples, please let me know.

    <u>Executive Publishing</u> will be successful because it addresses the practical needs of the business user. As I've traveled to various corporations, I have discussed this project with several people. The response has been favorable, and I feel the project would appeal to a wide range of users. My primary focus will be on the publishing needs of technical developers; however, I am willing to make some adjustments to meet the needs of the current market. I look forward to your reply.

Sincerely,

Carolyn Janson
Director
Castleton Corporate Training

FIGURE 10-2. The business letter

5. Press ENTER twice to add space for the recipient's name and address.

6. Type the name of the recipient. Press ENTER to move to the next line.

7. Type the recipient's street address, and press ENTER.

8. Type the recipient's city, state, and ZIP code. Press ENTER twice to make room for the salutation.

9. Type the salutation (for example, Dear Mr. Gibson), and press ENTER twice.

10. Now you're ready to type the paragraphs for your letter. If you wish, you can press TAB to indent the first line. When you finish typing each paragraph, press ENTER twice to end the paragraph.

11. After you've typed all the paragraphs of your letter, type the closing that you prefer (Sincerely, Best Wishes, and so on).

12. Press ENTER four times to add room for the signature.

13. Type your name. Then, press ENTER. If you wish, press TAB and type your title.

The business letter is finished. Press CTRL-P to see a preview of the printed document. Notice that there is more space at the top; this allows room for your printed letterhead. When you are finished viewing the letter, press Exit (F7) to return to the document screen.

You may want to use the Speller (CTRL-S or CTRL-F2) to check the spelling of your letter. Then, press Save (F10) or choose Save from the File pull-down menu. When prompted with "Document to be saved: ", type a file name and press ENTER. When you are ready to print, insert your letterhead into the printer; press Print (SHIFT-F7) and select option **1, F**ull Document. After you have saved and printed the document, make sure you clear the screen.

FORMATTING FOR ENVELOPES

Gone are the days of handwritten envelopes! You can create a more professional image by printing address information directly on the envelopes you send. LetterPerfect makes it easy. The following exercise will show you how to set up a document layout for printing on a standard 9.5" x 4" envelope, as shown in Figure 10-3.

Unfortunately, some printers cannot handle certain paper sizes, including envelopes. Consult your printer manual for more information about the sizes of envelopes, if any, that you can print on.

Creating the Standard Envelope Layout

The standard envelope is 9.5 inches wide and 4 inches tall, and is appropriate for sending both personal letters and business correspondence. The following exercise shows how to create a layout for printing on this type of envelope. You will set new margins and tabs and select the paper size (9.5" x 4") for the envelope format. Then, you will type the information that should appear on the envelope.

1. Press Format (SHIFT-F8) or select Format from the Layout pull-down menu. The Format menu is displayed.

2. Choose option **3**, Top/Bottom Margins. Type **0.35"** and press ENTER, for the top margin. For the bottom margin, type **0.65"** and press ENTER.

3. The Format menu is still displayed. Choose option **4,** Left/Right Margins. Enter **0.5"** for both the left and right margins.

4. Now, you need to select the envelope paper size. From the Format menu, select option **8,** Paper Size/Type. Figure 10-4 shows the menu that appears.

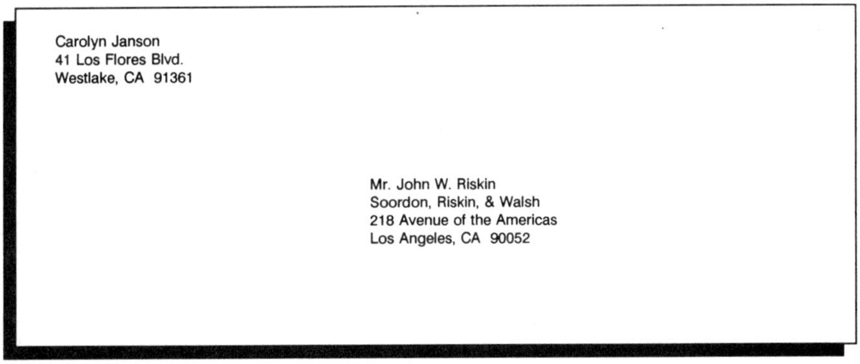

```
Carolyn Janson
41 Los Flores Blvd.
Westlake, CA  91361




                                    Mr. John W. Riskin
                                    Soordon, Riskin, & Walsh
                                    218 Avenue of the Americas
                                    Los Angeles, CA  90052
```

FIGURE 10-3. The standard envelope

5. Use the arrow keys to move the reversed bar to the 9.5" x 4" paper size, labeled "Envelope—Wide". From the menu at the bottom of the screen, choose option **1**, Select. The size is selected and you are returned to the Format menu.

6. Choose option **5**, **T**abs, from the Format menu to display the Tab Set screen. Press HOME, LEFT ARROW to move the cursor to the beginning of the line. Press CTRL-END to clear the tab ruler.

7. Type **3.5"** and press ENTER, to set a tab 3.5 inches from the left margin. Then, press Exit (F7) twice, to return to the main document screen. You've finished creating the layout and you're ready to type the text.

8. Type your name, or the name of the person sending the letter. Then, press ENTER to move to the next line.

9. Type the street address and press ENTER. Then, type the city, state, and ZIP code.

```
Format: Paper Size/Type

Paper type and Orientation    Paper Size         Location      Font Type    Labels

1 X 1 Labels - Wide           4" x 1"            Continuous    Portrait     1 x 1
3 X 10 Labels                 8.5" x 11"         Continuous    Portrait     3 x 10
A4 Envelopes - Wide           8.58" x 4.33"      Manual        Landscape
A4 Labels                     8.27" x 11.69"     Continuous    Portrait     2 x 7
A4 Standard                   8.27" x 11.69"     Continuous    Portrait
A4 Standard - Wide            11.69" x 8.27"     Continuous    Landscape
Envelope - Wide               9.5" x 4"          Manual        Landscape
Half Sheet                    5.5" x 8.5"        Manual        Portrait
Half Sheet - Wide             8.5" x 5.5"        Manual        Landscape
Standard                      8.22" x 12"        Continuous    Portrait
Standard                      8.5" x 11"         Continuous    Portrait
Standard                      8.5" x 14"         Continuous    Portrait
Standard - Wide               11" x 8.5"         Continuous    Landscape
Standard - Wide               14" x 8.5"         Continuous    Landscape
[ALL OTHERS]                  Width ≤ 8.5"       Bin 1


1 Select; 2 Edit; N Name Search: 1
```

FIGURE 10-4. The Paper Size/Type menu

10. Press ENTER about eight times to add space below the return address. Refer to the "Ln" label on the status line; your cursor should be about two inches from the top edge of the envelope.

11. Press TAB to move the text cursor to the tab stop you defined earlier. Type the recipient's name and press ENTER.

12. Press TAB and type the recipient's street address. Press ENTER to move to the next line.

13. Press TAB once more, and type the city, state, and ZIP code.

Now you're finished with your envelope. If you wish, you can view the envelope as it will appear when printed. Press CTRL-P to display the View Document screen. Your screen will look similar to Figure 10-5. When you are finished viewing the envelope, press Exit (F7) or click the right mouse button to return to the document screen.

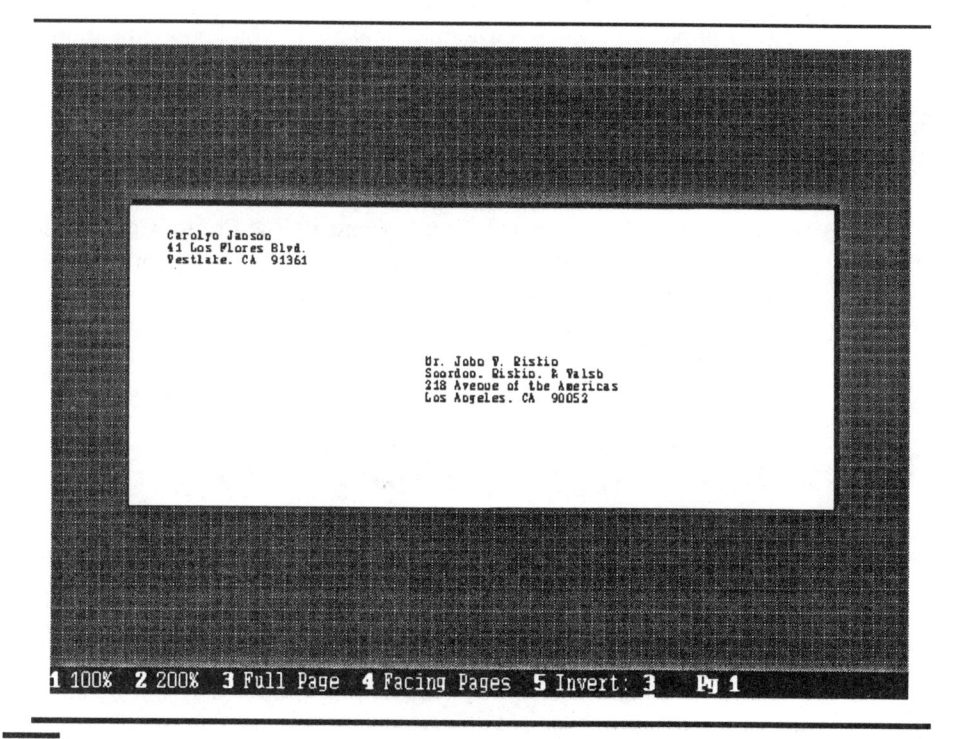

FIGURE 10-5. Viewing the envelope

Including Your Company Logo on the Envelope

LetterPerfect's graphics features allow you to include a graphic image with your address information. This means you can include your company logo, or another image, as part of the document you've created for envelopes—assuming you have a graphics file of the artwork. This can be a drawing file that you've created in another program—DrawPerfect, for example—or the file copy of an image that you have captured with a PC scanner. For detailed information about including graphics in your documents, refer to Chapter 6, "Using the Graphics Features."

Printing the Envelope

If your printer can accept envelopes, make sure you know how to insert them into the printer; generally, you must feed the long edge of the envelope into the paper path for dot-matrix printers, and laser printers require the short edge first. Figure 10-6 shows examples of each method.

To print the envelope document displayed on your screen, load an envelope into your printer, and press Print (SHIFT-F7), or select **Print** from the **File** pull-down menu. Then, choose option **1**, **Full Document**. The Printer Control screen appears, as shown in Figure 10-7, and displays a message that prompts you to insert the envelope into your printer. Depending on how your printer is set up, you may be prompted to type **G** (for **Go**) to continue with the printing process. Then Letter-Perfect prints the envelope.

Troubleshooting Tips for Printing on Envelopes

Creating the envelope layout is easy; however, you may encounter problems when printing the envelope. The mechanism that moves paper through your printer is designed for an 8.5-inch paper width; when you try to print on something with a smaller width—such as an envelope—your printer may not be able to move the paper through properly.

Fortunately, many printers are now designed to accept various paper sizes, including envelopes, but problems can still occur. The text may not be positioned

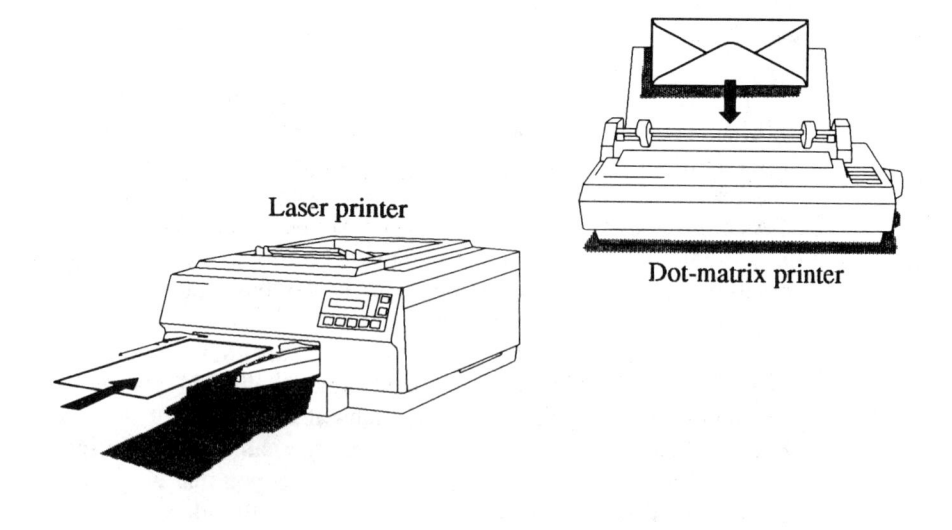

FIGURE 10-6. Feeding envelopes into printers

```
Print: Control Printer


Port:       LPT 1                        Page Number:  1
Status:     Printing                     Current Copy: 1 of 1
Message:    None
Paper:      Envelope 4" x 9.5"
Location:   Manual feed
Action:     Insert paper
            Press "G" to continue
```

```
1 Cancel Job; 2 Go (start printer); 3 Stop: 0
```

FIGURE 10-7. Printing the envelope

correctly on the page or perhaps your printer may not select paper from the correct sheet feeder bin. If you have problems like these, there are a few things you can do to fix the situation.

First, make sure you have the correct printer selected at the Print menu (SHIFT-F7, S). Then, print the envelope. If the text is not positioned correctly on the printed envelope, you may need to adjust your margin settings. If the printer selection and layout seem to be correct, you will probably need to edit the paper size definition.

As explained in Chapter 2, the paper size definition determines the dimensions of the printed page. If the printed text is not positioned correctly, or if your printer is pulling paper from the wrong sheet feeder bin, you can edit the paper size definition to correct these problems.

To edit a paper size definition, press Format (SHIFT-F8) and choose option **8,** Paper Size/Type. Move the highlighted cursor to the 9.5" x 4" envelope definition and choose option **2,** Edit, from the menu at the bottom of the screen. The menu shown in Figure 10-8 appears. Notice that the name of your printer driver file is displayed at the top of the screen. This reminds you that all paper definitions are saved to the driver file of the printer that is currently selected.

Option **1,** Location, lets you specify how this paper type will be fed into the printer: manually (by hand), continuously (tractor-fed printer paper or a single laser printer tray), or from a sheet feeder bin. The standard setting is Manual, meaning that LetterPerfect will stop at the Printer Control screen and prompt you to

```
Format: Edit Paper Definition

        Filename              HPLASIIP.PRS
    1 - Location              Manual

    2 - Prompt to Load        Yes

    3 - Text Adjustment - Top   0"
                        Side    0"




    Selection: 0
```

FIGURE 10-8.   Editing the envelope paper definition

insert the envelope. If you have a special sheet feeder bin for envelopes, select the sheet feeder option and type the bin number. Also, make sure you've selected the correct sheet feeder for your printer; for more information, see Chapter 7.

Option **2**, **P**rompt to Load, lets you decide whether you want LetterPerfect to wait for you to insert the paper type before it sends the document to the printer.

Option **3**, **T**ext Adjustment, is provided for laser printers, and it lets you adjust where LetterPerfect begins printing on the envelope. If you have a dot-matrix printer, this option has little effect; instead, it's best to adjust how you insert the paper into the printer.

The Text Adjustment setting is independent of the margins you've defined; it simply lets you compensate for spacing that your printer might add at the top and left edges of the printed page. Select this option, and you can choose the direction of the printing adjustment: up, down, right, or left. Enter the measurement for the adjustment, and LetterPerfect takes care of the rest. When you're finished editing the paper definition, press Exit (F7) until you return to the document editing screen.

Remember, LetterPerfect makes these adjustments when the document is printed; you won't notice a difference from the editing screen. Also, remember that the paper definition you've edited is saved with the driver file of the current selected printer. If you select a different printer, you'll need to edit the paper definitions for that printer as well.

SUMMARY

In this chapter, you've learned how to create two types of letters, one for blank sheets of paper and one for preprinted letterhead. You have also learned how to create a layout for printing envelopes.

These are only a few examples of the formats you can create. You can easily change the documents presented here to suit your own needs. For more information about editing a document format, refer to Chapter 4.

Chapter 11

MERGING LETTERS AND MAILING LABELS

Creating an Address List
Creating a Primary File for Letters
Merging the Files
Creating Mailing Labels
Creating a Primary File for Labels
Summary

In Chapter 2, you learned to create your own document layout. You learned how to change margins, define tab settings, and select different paper sizes. There are several options for formatting; sometimes it is difficult to keep track of them, especially if you need to create documents for a large group of people. Fortunately, LetterPerfect includes a feature that makes it easy to create multiple documents that share a common layout.

LetterPerfect's Merge feature lets you assemble documents by combining information from two or more sources. In other words, you can take the document layout from one file, merge it with address information from another file, and create a unique document.

For example, assume you need to send a form letter to a large group of people. (You've probably received a few of these letters yourself.) The layout and the body of each letter will be the same except that each letter will be personalized with the

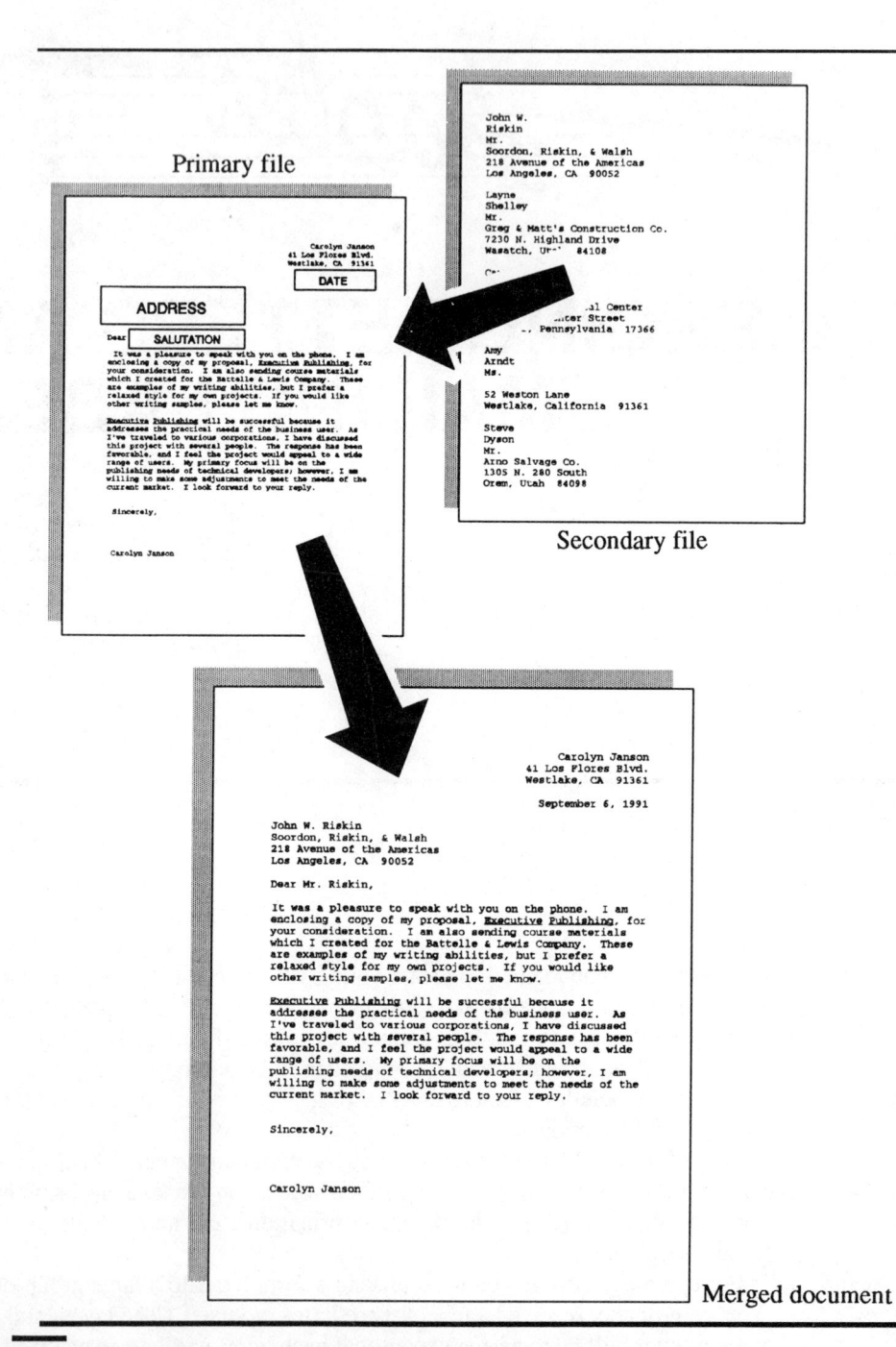

FIGURE 11-1. The Merge feature creates form letters

individual recipient's name and address. Figure 11-1 shows how the Merge feature can create these letters. A form letter, called a *primary file,* is combined or merged with a list of addresses, called the *secondary file.* Actually, the secondary file can contain anything that you want to merge with your document layout, but in this chapter, the secondary file will contain address information. When the merge is completed, you have a *merged document*—in this case a personalized letter for each name on your list.

Anything that would appear in a normal document can be included when you merge documents together. LetterPerfect also allows you to merge information into your document layout by typing text from the keyboard. Chapter 9 explains how to do this, under the heading "Automated Memos."

CREATING AN ADDRESS LIST

The address list, known as the secondary file, is an important file when you use the Merge features of LetterPerfect. This file contains all the information that should be unique with each letter, label, or document that you will create.

As shown in Figure 11-2, the address list will be divided into *records* and *fields.* This helps LetterPerfect to organize the information for the merge. A record contains *all* the information for one person in your address list; a field contains a *single* piece of information in the record.

For example, you will have one record for each person in your address file. Each record will be divided into five fields. The first field will contain the person's first name, the second field will contain their last name. Field 3 will contain the title to be used in the salutation, Field 4 will list the company name, and Field 5 will include the address information. All records in the file will follow the same format and have the same number of fields—regardless of whether or not you have the information for all the fields for each person. As you type the information for the address list, you will insert merge codes to indicate where the records and fields are divided.

The following exercise will show you how to create a secondary file for an address list. Before you begin, you must clear the screen (F7, N, N).

Assigning Names to the Fields

First, you will insert a special code that assigns names to the fields. These aren't the names of people in your address list; these are just labels that you assign, so that you'll know the type of information that each field contains.

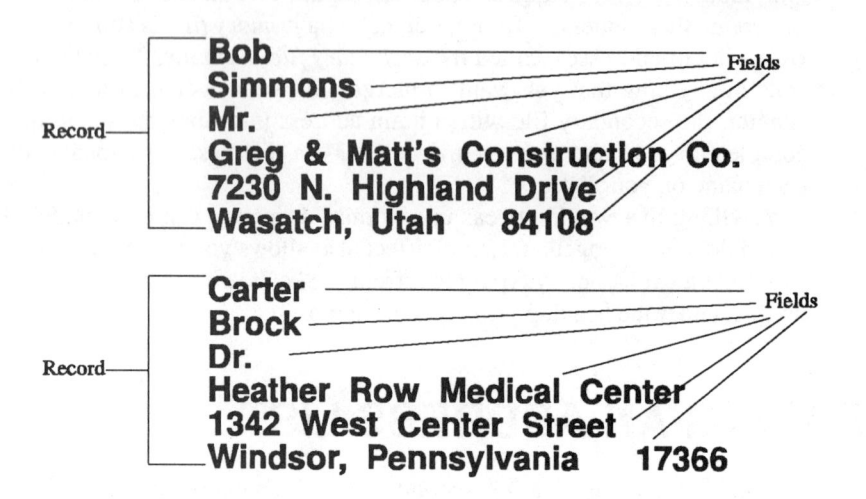

```
                    Bob ─────────────────── Fields
                    Simmons ──────────────╱╱
                    Mr. ─────────────────╱╱╱
        Record ─┤   Greg & Matt's Construction Co.
                    7230 N. Highland Drive
                    Wasatch, Utah    84108

                    Carter ──────────────── Fields
                    Brock ────────────────╱
                    Dr. ─────────────────╱╱
        Record ─┤   Heather Row Medical Center
                    1342 West Center Street
                    Windsor, Pennsylvania    17366
```

FIGURE 11-2. The address list is divided into records and fields

1. From a clear screen, press **Merge Codes** (SHIFT-F9) or select **Merge Codes** from the **Tools** pull-down menu. Figure 11-3 shows the list of merge codes that will appear on your screen.

2. Press DOWN ARROW until the {FIELD NAMES} code is highlighted. Press ENTER and you are prompted with "Enter Field 1: ". Type **First Name** as the label for Field 1. Press ENTER to continue.

3. You are prompted with "Enter Field 2: ". Type **Last Name** and press ENTER. The prompt is displayed for Field 3; type **Title** and press ENTER. At the "Enter Field 4: " prompt, type **Company Name** and press ENTER.

4. Type **Address** as the label for Field 5, and press ENTER. Finally, you are prompted to enter the name for Field 6. The records for your address file will have only five fields, so press ENTER without typing a label. The {FIELD NAMES} code is inserted into your document, and appears as shown in Figure 11-4.

You will refer to these field names when you create your form letter file, and this will help LetterPerfect to know where the information should be inserted into the document layout. Keep this information on the screen, and continue to the next exercise.

```
File Edit Search Layout Tools Font Graphics Help     (Press ALT for menu bar)

                        {DATE}
                        {END FIELD}
                        {END RECORD}
                        {FIELD}field~
                        {FIELD NAMES}name1~...nameN~~
                        {INPUT}message~
                        {NEST PRIMARY}filename~
                        {NEXT RECORD}
                        {PAGE OFF}
                        {PAGE ON}
                        {PRINT}
                        {QUIT}
                        {STOP}


                        (Name Search; Arrows; Enter to Select)
```

FIGURE 11-3. Selecting merge codes

```
File Edit Search Layout Tools Font Graphics Help     (Press ALT for menu bar)
{FIELD NAMES}First Name~Last Name~Title~Company Name~Address~~{END RECORD}
================================================================================
-









Field: First Name                                      Pg 2 Ln 1" Pos 1"
```

FIGURE 11-4. Assigning names to the fields

Creating the Records

Now you're ready to create the records. You may want to get your address book, so that you have a list of names to type. When you type the information for each person, you'll enter the first and last names into separate fields; when you create the form letter, this will allow you to insert the last name alone, as part of the salutation.

Before you continue, make sure the text cursor is at the bottom of the document, as shown in Figure 11-4. If you aren't sure whether it is, just press HOME, HOME, DOWN ARROW. You'll notice the "Field: First Name" message on the status line. This message tells you that the text cursor is now located in the First Name field of the current record, and you can type the information for this field.

1. Type the first name of a person you want to include in the address list. This is the first field of the record.

2. Press F9 to insert an {END FIELD} code at the end of the First Name field. This also inserts an invisible hard return code (HRt), which moves the text cursor to the next line. Figure 11-5 shows how your screen might look.

```
File Edit Search Layout Tools Font Graphics Help      (Press ALT for menu bar)
{FIELD NAMES}First Name~Last Name~Title~Company Name~Address~~{END RECORD}
================================================================================
Bob{END FIELD}
_




















Field: Last Name                                            Pg 2 Ln 1.17" Pos 1"
```

FIGURE 11-5.   Inserting an {END FIELD} code

3. Type the person's last name. Then, press F9 to insert an {END FIELD} code at the end of the Last Name field. This is the second field of the record.

4. Type the title (Mr., Ms., Mrs., and so on) that should appear before this person's name in the salutation of the letter. Then press F9 to insert the {END FIELD} code. This is the Title field, the third field of the record. If you aren't sure what the title should be, press F9, without typing anything, to insert just the {END FIELD} code. This indicates that a field exists, but without any text.

5. Type the company name where this person works, and then press F9. If you do not know the company name, press F9 without typing anything. This is the fourth field.

6. Type the street address where this person is located, and then press ENTER to move to the next line. Type the city, state, and ZIP code. Then, press F9 to end the field.

note

You did not press F9 at the end of the street address line because you want to keep the entire address in one field. The information in a field can include several lines if necessary. The {END FIELD} code is the only thing that separates one field from the next.

7. You've created five fields; now you're ready to end the record. Press Merge Codes (SHIFT-F9) or select Merge Codes from the **T**ools pull-down menu.

8. Press UP ARROW until the {END RECORD} code is highlighted. Press ENTER to insert the code into the document. This also inserts a hard page break ([HPg]) that appears as a double dotted-line on your screen.

You've finished the first record; Figure 11-6 shows how your screen might appear. Now, you can create the other records. Repeat these steps (1 through 8) for each person that you want to include in your address list. When you are finished, your screen will look similar to Figure 11-7.

remember

If you don't have the information for one of the fields, just press F9 to insert the {END FIELD} code. This is very important! You may not have the company name or title of someone on your list, but each record *must* have the same number of fields—even if some of the fields are left blank.

As you move the cursor through the address list, the "Field: " message on the status line shows the assigned name of the current field. Use this message as a guide to help you edit the record information.

Make sure you save the file and clear the screen before continuing. To do so, press Exit (F7) and type **Y** at the "Save document? Yes (No)" prompt. When prompted with "Document to be saved: ", type **address.sf** and press ENTER. The *.sf*

```
File Edit Search Layout Tools Font Graphics Help      (Press ALT for menu bar)
{FIELD NAMES}First Name~Last Name~Title~Company Name~Address~~{END RECORD}
================================================================================
Bob{END FIELD}
Simmons{END FIELD}
Mr.{END FIELD}
Greg & Matt's Construction Co.{END FIELD}
7230 N. Highland Drive
Wasatch, Utah  84108{END FIELD}
{END RECORD}
================================================================================
_




                                                                          
Field: First Name                                          Pg 3 Ln 1" Pos 1"
```

FIGURE 11-6.   Completing the first record

```
File Edit Search Layout Tools Font Graphics Help      (Press ALT for menu bar)
Greg & Matt's Construction Co.{END FIELD}
7230 N. Highland Drive
Wasatch, Utah  84108{END FIELD}
{END RECORD}
================================================================================
Carter{END FIELD}
Brock{END FIELD}
Dr.{END FIELD}
Heather Row Medical Center{END FIELD}
1342 West Center Street
Windsor, Pennsylvania  17366{END FIELD}
{END RECORD}
================================================================================
Amy{END FIELD}
Arndt{END FIELD}
Ms.{END FIELD}
{END FIELD}
52 Weston Lane
Westlake, California  91361{END FIELD}
{END RECORD}
================================================================================
Field: First Name                                          Pg 5 Ln 1" Pos 1"
```

FIGURE 11-7.   The finished address file

extension is not necessary, but it helps to identify this file as a *Secondary F*ile for a merge application. Then, you are prompted with "Exit LP? No (**Yes**)"; type **N** to continue working.

A secondary file can contain any information that should be merged with the document format of the primary file. In this example, you've created a secondary file for an address list. But you aren't limited to just name and address information—anything that would appear in a normal document can be included in the secondary file. Perhaps you want to include a paragraph of information that is specific to each person on your list. Simply add another field to each record, and type the paragraph into that field.

If you wish, you can organize the field information any way you want; you can have one field with both the first and last names, or divide the address information into several fields.

In the next section, you'll create the form letter for your address list. When you create the primary file for the form letter, you will include special merge codes—with the names that you've assigned—to indicate where the fields from your address list should be inserted into the completed letters.

CREATING A PRIMARY FILE FOR LETTERS

Now that you have an address file, or secondary file, you can create the primary file. Remember, the primary file contains the layout and text that should appear on each letter that you will create later; LetterPerfect uses this file as a model for the actual letters.

The layout for the primary file in this exercise is similar to the personal letter that you created in Chapter 10. Unlike the personal letter, you will insert the formatting commands as document initial codes (described in Chapter 4), rather than as formatting codes in the text. This will ensure that the formatting codes are correctly applied to each letter.

You will also insert special merge codes that indicate where information from the address file should be placed when the two documents are merged together. Follow these steps to create the primary file for your form letter:

1. From a clear screen, press Format (SHIFT-F8) or select **Format** from the **Layout** pull-down menu.

2. Choose option **I**, Document Initial Codes/Base Font. Another menu appears; select option **1**, Initial Codes, to display the Document Initial Codes screen. This is where you will place the formatting codes for the document.

3. Press Format (SHIFT-F8) or select Format from the Layout pull-down menu. Choose option **9**, **C**enter Page (top to bottom), and type **Y** for Yes.

4. Choose option **5**, **T**abs, to display the tab ruler. Press HOME, LEFT ARROW to move the cursor to the beginning of the line. Then press CTRL-END to clear the tab ruler.

5. Type **0.5"** and press ENTER. Then type **3.5"** and press ENTER. This sets two tabs—one at 0.5 inches from the left margin of the page and another at 3.5 inches. The first tab is for paragraph indents, if you choose to insert them. The second tab is set for the address block of the letter format.

6. Press Exit (F7) four times to exit the Format menu and the Document Initial Codes screen and return to the main editing screen.

7. Press the TAB key twice and type your name. Press ENTER to move the text cursor to the next line.

8. Press TAB twice and type your street address. Press ENTER to move to the next line, press TAB twice, and type your city, state, and ZIP code.

9. Press ENTER twice to add space for the date. Then press the TAB key twice.

10. Press Merge Codes (SHIFT-F9) or select Merge Codes from the Tools pull-down menu. Use the arrow keys to highlight the {DATE} code at the top of the Merge Codes list. Press ENTER to insert the code into the text. When you merge this document, the {DATE} code places the current date at this location.

11. Press ENTER twice to add space for the recipient's name and address.

12. Now you're ready to place the merge codes that will tell LetterPerfect what to insert from the address file. Press Merge Codes (SHIFT-F9) or choose Merge Codes from the **T**ools pull-down menu.

13. Press DOWN ARROW to highlight the {FIELD} code in the list. Press ENTER to select the code, and LetterPerfect prompts you with "Enter Field: ". Type **First Name** and press ENTER to indicate that you want the contents of the First Name field inserted at this point.

14. Press the SPACEBAR once to add a text space. Then, press Merge Codes (SHIFT-F9) and press ENTER to select the {FIELD} code again. At the "Enter Field: " prompt, type **Last Name** and press ENTER. Press ENTER again to move to the next line. Your screen should look similar to Figure 11-8.

15. Press Merge Codes (SHIFT-F9) or select Merge Codes from the **T**ools pull-down menu. Press ENTER to select the {FIELD} code. Type **Company Name** and press ENTER. Press ENTER again to move to the next line.

Chapter 11   Merging Letters and Mailing Labels   225

16. Press Merge Codes (SHIFT-F9) or select Merge Codes from the Tools pull-down menu. Press ENTER to select the {FIELD} code. Type **Address** and press ENTER. Press ENTER twice more to make room for the salutation.

17. Type **Dear** (or a different salutation) and press the SPACEBAR once. Now, press Merge Codes (SHIFT-F9) and press ENTER to select the {FIELD} code once more. Type **Title** and press ENTER. Press the SPACEBAR again, press Merge Codes (SHIFT-F9) and ENTER. Type **Last Name** as the next field and press ENTER. Type a comma (,) or colon (:) and press ENTER twice.

18. Figure 11-9 shows how your screen may look. Now, type the text for your form letter; press ENTER twice to end each paragraph.

19. After you've typed all the paragraphs for your letter, you can type the closing. Press TAB twice and type the closing that you prefer (for example, "Sincerely" or "Best regards," and so on).

20. Press ENTER four times to add room for your signature.

21. Press TAB and type your name. Then, press ENTER. If you wish, press TAB again and type your title.

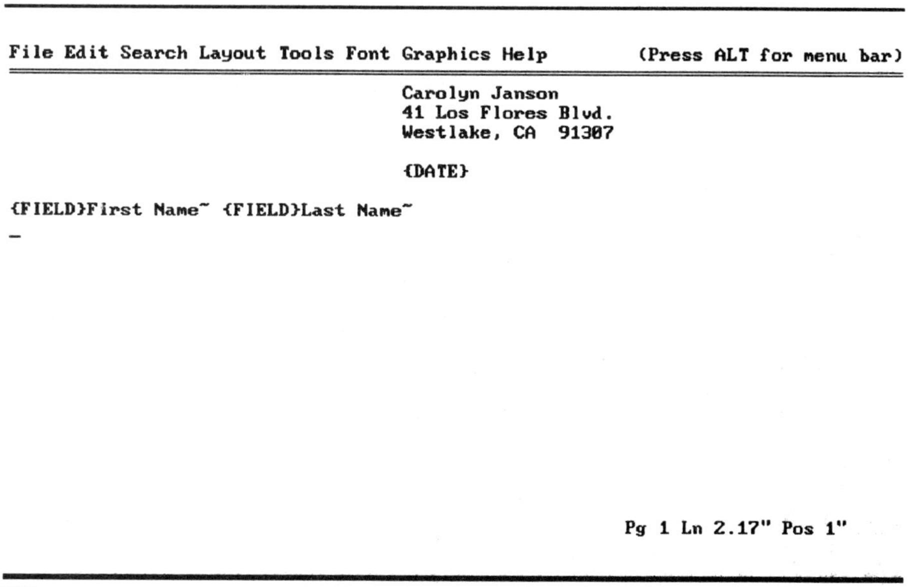

```
File Edit Search Layout Tools Font Graphics Help    (Press ALT for menu bar)
                        Carolyn Janson
                        41 Los Flores Blvd.
                        Westlake, CA  91307
                            {DATE}
{FIELD}First Name~ {FIELD}Last Name~
_
```

Pg 1 Ln 2.17" Pos 1"

FIGURE 11-8.   Creating the form letter file

```
┌─────────────────────────────────────────────────────────────┐
│ File Edit Search Layout Tools Font Graphics Help    (Press ALT for menu bar) │
│                         Carolyn Janson                       │
│                         41 Los Flores Blvd.                  │
│                         Westlake, CA  91307                  │
│                                                              │
│                              {DATE}                          │
│                                                              │
│ {FIELD}First Name~ {FIELD}Last Name~                         │
│ {FIELD}Company Name~                                         │
│ {FIELD}Address~                                              │
│                                                              │
│ Dear {FIELD}Title~ {FIELD}Last Name~:                        │
│                                                              │
│ _                                                            │
│                                                              │
│                                                              │
│                                                              │
│                                           Pg 1 Ln 3" Pos 1"  │
└─────────────────────────────────────────────────────────────┘
```

FIGURE 11-9.   Inserting codes for the salutation

22. If your letter contains only a few brief paragraphs, press ENTER four or five times to add extra space at the bottom of the text. This will help to balance the text on the page.

Your form letter is complete. If you wish, change the format of the letter to suit your own needs. You may want to use the Speller (CTRL-S or CTRL-F2) to check the spelling of the text before you save it.

Press Save (F10) or choose Save from the File pull-down menu. When prompted with "Document to be saved: ", type **letter.pf** and press ENTER. The *.pf* extension is not necessary, but it helps to identify the file as a merge *Primary File*. After you have saved the document, make sure you clear the screen (F7, N, N).

MERGING THE FILES

Now you're ready to merge the address list with your form letter. When you perform the merge, LetterPerfect copies information from the primary and secondary files to create the finished letters; the information in the original files is not altered. Follow these steps to merge the two files to create letters for mass-mailing:

1. Press Merge (CTRL-F9) or select Merge from the Tools pull-down menu. LetterPerfect prompts you with "Primary file: ".

2. Type **letter.pf** as the name for the primary file, and press ENTER. LetterPerfect prompts you with "Secondary file: ".

3. Type **address.sf** as the name of the secondary file. Press ENTER to continue.

You've just started the merge. If you have a long list of names in your address file, you may see a "Merging" message on the status line, while LetterPerfect creates a letter for each person in the address file. When the merge is finished, you will have a document with each page containing a personalized letter separated by a hard page break.

Press HOME, HOME, UP ARROW to move to the top of the document. Then press PGDN to display each letter. At this point, you can press Print (SHIFT-F7) and choose option 1, Full Document, to print all the letters. Or, you can print just one of the letters by selecting Multiple Pages from the Print menu, typing the page number, and pressing ENTER. After you finish printing the letters, clear the screen. You do not need to save the merged document because it only takes a few minutes to merge the files together.

CREATING MAILING LABELS

LetterPerfect includes features that let you create mailing labels just like the expensive word processors—and it's easy! All you need to do is set your margins and select the correct Labels paper size from the Format menu. Then, type the address information for each label. LetterPerfect does the rest. Once you've printed the labels, you can peel them from the backing sheet and stick them on mailing envelopes.

When working with labels, you will select a special paper size/type definition that helps LetterPerfect distinguish between the logical "page"—the actual label—and the physical page, that is, the paper to which the labels are attached. Figure 11-10 shows examples of the logical page versus the physical page.

The following sections will help you create two types of labels: continuous and sheet labels. Continuous labels are the type printed by dot-matrix printers or any printer that has a tractor-feed mechanism for moving paper through the printer.

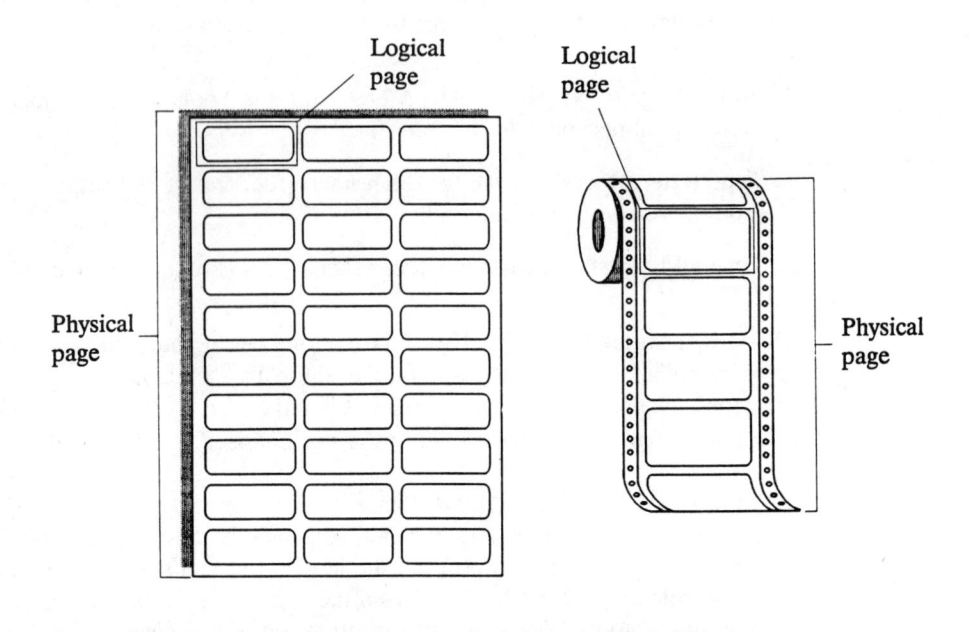

FIGURE 11-10. The logical "page" versus the physical page

Sheet labels are the standard type for laser printers or other printers that feed paper from a tray or sheet-feeder bin.

Creating Continuous Labels

Figure 11-11 shows an example of continuous labels; the term *continuous* refers to the long strip of paper to which the labels are attached. Since this is a continuous form, LetterPerfect doesn't care where the paper begins or ends; instead, Letter-Perfect considers each label on the paper as a separate page, and is concerned only about where each label begins and ends.

This type of label is commonly printed on dot-matrix printers; if you have a laser printer, refer to the next section, "Creating Sheet Labels." The following steps explain how to create continuous labels. Before you perform the steps, make sure the printer that will print the labels is selected (SHIFT-F7, S).

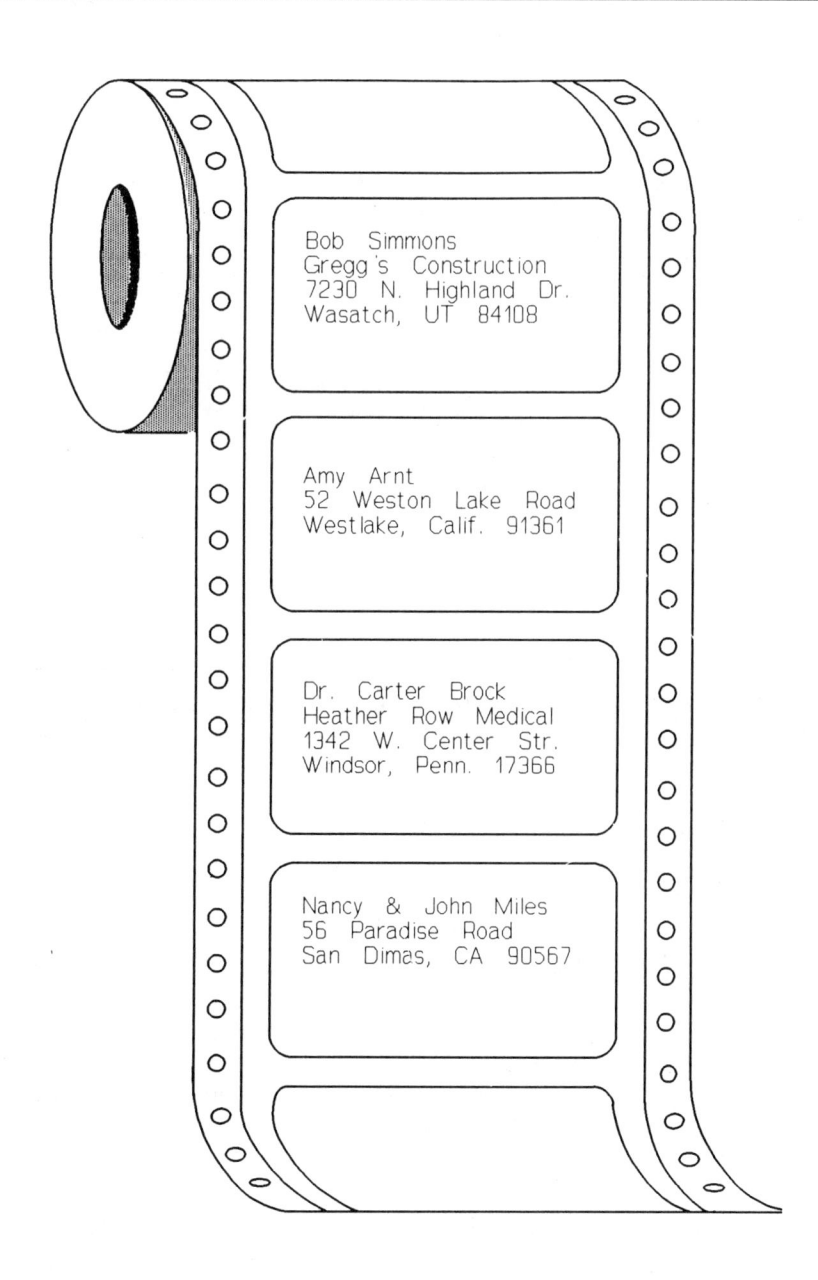

FIGURE 11-11. Continuous labels

```
Format: Paper Size/Type

Paper type and Orientation    Paper Size         Location     Font Type   Labels
1 X 1 Labels - Wide           4" x 1"            Continuous   Portrait    1 x 1
3 X 10 Labels                 8.5" x 11"         Continuous   Portrait    3 x 10
A3 Standard                   11.69" x 16.54     Continuous   Portrait
A4 Envelope - Wide            8.58" x 4.33"      Manual       Portrait
A4 Labels                     8.27" x 11.69"     Continuous   Portrait    2 x 7
A4 Standard                   8.27" x 11.69"     Continuous   Portrait
A4 Standard - Wide            11.69" x 8.27"     Continuous   Portrait
Envelope - Wide               9.5" x 4"          Manual       Portrait
Half Sheet                    5.5" x 8.5"        Continuous   Portrait
Standard                      8.22" x 12"        Continuous   Portrait
Standard                      8.5" x 11"         Continuous   Portrait
Standard                      8.5" x 14"         Continuous   Portrait
Standard - Wide               11" x 8.5"         Continuous   Portrait
[ALL OTHERS]                  Width ≤ 13.5"      Manual


1 Select; 2 Edit; N Name Search: 1
```

FIGURE 11-12. Selecting the "1 x 1 labels" definition

1. Press Format (SHIFT-F8) or select **Format** from the **Layout** pull-down menu.

2. Choose option **8**, Paper Size/Type, from the Format menu. Figure 11-12 shows examples of the paper sizes that you can select.

3. Use the arrow keys to highlight the "1 x 1 labels-wide" paper definition, and choose option **1**, Select, to select the paper size. The Format menu reappears.

4. Choose option **3**, Top/Bottom **M**argins, and enter **0.2"** as the top margin and **0"** as the bottom margin. Choose option **4**, Left/Right Margins, and enter **0.75"** as the left margin and **0"** as the right margin.

5. Press Exit (F7) to return to the main editing screen.

6. Type the name and address information for one of the labels. Then press CTRL-ENTER to begin the next label. Continue typing address information, and press CTRL-ENTER at the end of each one, to start a new "page." When you are finished, press HOME, HOME, UP ARROW to move the cursor back to the top of the document.

7. Press Save (F10) and enter **label-c.doc** (or a different file name) to save the document to a file on disk.

Your label file is finished. You may want to view the labels (SHIFT-F7, option **3**, View Document), to see how they will print. Figure 11-13 shows how one label appears at the View Document screen. Press Exit (F7) or click the right mouse button to return to the document screen. Then, load the label paper into your printer and print the document (SHIFT-F7, option **1**).

You'll probably need to adjust the position of the labels in the printer. Plan on printing a few before the text is positioned correctly on the labels. If the text lines are too long to fit onto a single label, move the cursor to the beginning of your document and select a smaller font (CTRL-F8, option **4**). If a smaller font is not available, try to reduce your margins to increase the printable area on the labels.

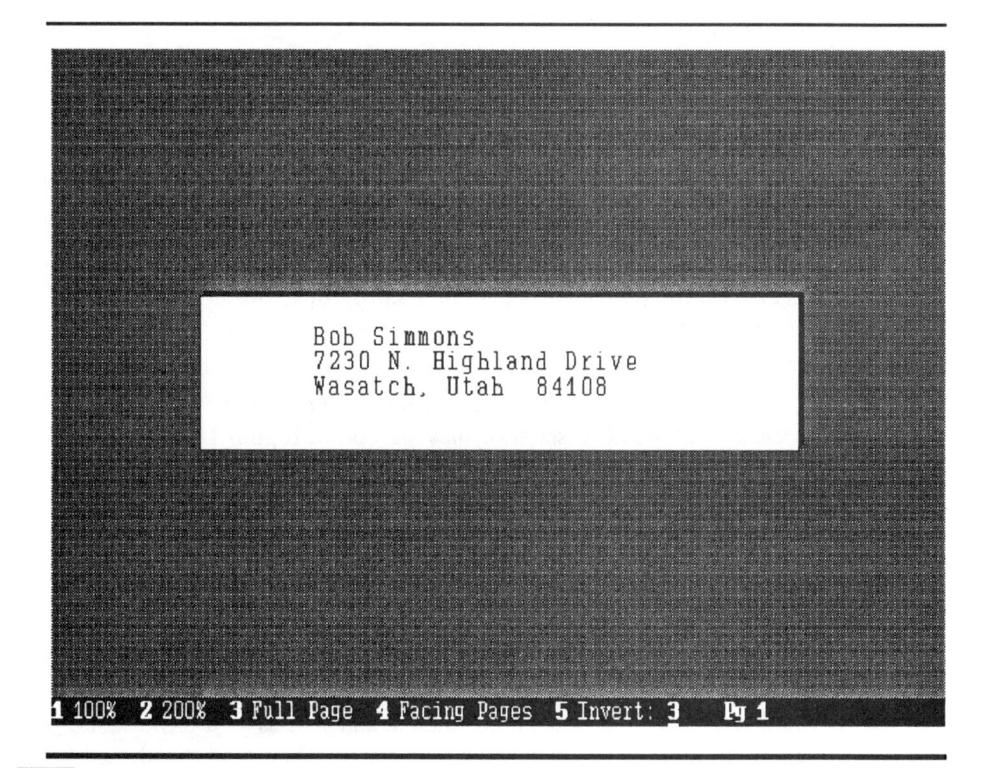

FIGURE 11-13. Viewing one of the labels

Creating Sheet Labels

Figure 11-14 shows an example of a *label sheet* where the labels are arranged in two or more columns for printing. If you own a laser printer, you must use these sheets for printing labels. Dot-matrix printers can also print on these sheets, but the text alignment is not as accurate as with laser printers. LetterPerfect includes a special paper size/type definition that allows you to print on sheets of labels, such as those described here.

1. Press Format (SHIFT-F8) or select Format from the Layout pull-down menu.

2. Choose option **8**, Paper Size/Type, from the Format menu.

3. Highlight the "3 x 10 Labels" paper definition, and choose option **1**, Select, to select the paper size shown in Figure 11-15. After you select the labels definition, the Format menu reappears.

4. Press Exit (F7) or click the right mouse button to return to the document screen.

5. Type the name and address information for one of the labels. Then, press CTRL-ENTER to begin the next label. Continue typing address information, and press CTRL-ENTER at the end of each one to start a new "page." When you are finished, press HOME, HOME, UP ARROW to move the cursor back to the top of the document.

6. Press Save (F10) and enter **label-s.doc** (or a different file name) to save the document to a file on disk.

Your sheet label file is finished. You may want to view the labels (SHIFT-F7, option **3**, View Document) to see how they will print. Figure 11-16 shows how the labels may appear at the View Document screen. Working from left to right, LetterPerfect places the addresses on the labels, with each page in the document representing one label on the sheet. Press Exit (F7) or click the right mouse button to return to the document screen.

You may need to select a smaller font (CTRL-F8, 4) if the text lines are too long to fit on the labels. If a smaller font is not available, try to reduce your margins to increase the printable area on the labels. It is a good idea to print the document on regular paper before you load the actual labels into your printer. This will show you whether you need to make adjustments, and will save you the cost of label sheets, which are much more expensive than paper. Then load the sheet labels into your printer and print the document (SHIFT-F7, option **1**).

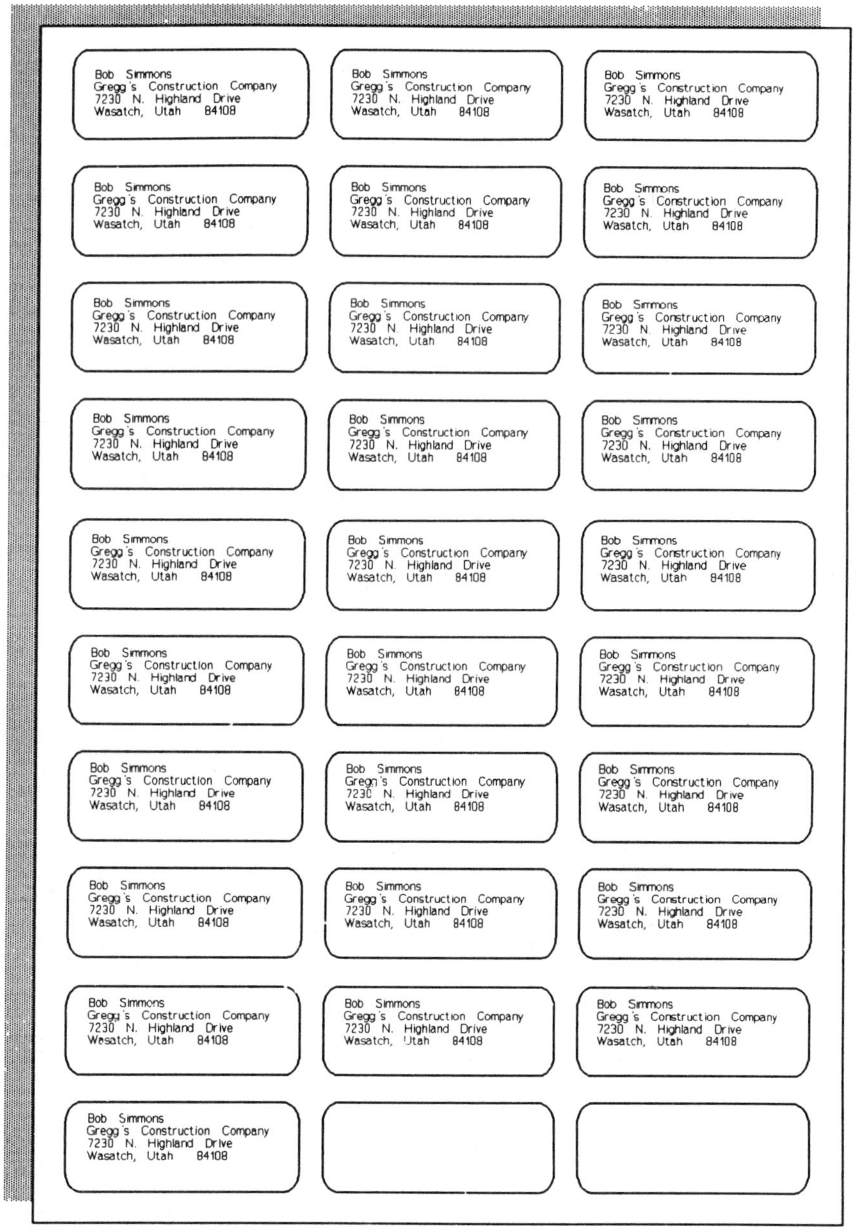

FIGURE 11-14. Sheet labels

```
Format: Paper Size/Type

Paper type and Orientation    Paper Size        Location     Font Type    Labels

1 X 1 Labels - Wide           4" x 1"           Continuous   Portrait     1 x 1
3 X 10 Labels                 8.5" x 11"        Continuous   Portrait     3 x 10
A3 Standard                   11.69" x 16.54    Continuous   Portrait
A4 Envelope - Wide            8.58" x 4.33"     Manual       Portrait
A4 Labels                     8.27" x 11.69"    Continuous   Portrait     2 x 7
A4 Standard                   8.27" x 11.69"    Continuous   Portrait
A4 Standard - Wide            11.69" x 8.27"    Continuous   Portrait
Envelope - Wide               9.5" x 4"         Manual       Portrait
Half Sheet                    5.5" x 8.5"       Continuous   Portrait
Standard                      8.22" x 12"       Continuous   Portrait
Standard                      8.5" x 11"        Continuous   Portrait
Standard                      8.5" x 14"        Continuous   Portrait
Standard - Wide               11" x 8.5"        Continuous   Portrait
[ALL OTHERS]                  Width ≤ 13.5"     Manual


1 Select; 2 Edit; N Name Search: 1
```

FIGURE 11-15. Selecting the "3 x 10 labels" definition

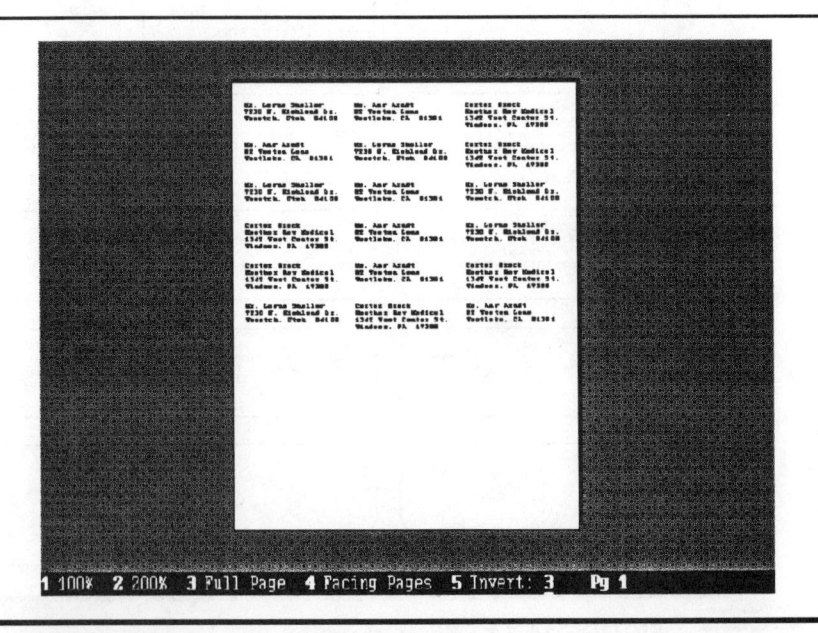

FIGURE 11-16. Viewing the sheet labels

Chapter 11　　　　　　　　　　　　　　　Merging Letters and Mailing Labels　235

CREATING A PRIMARY FILE FOR LABELS

At the beginning of this chapter, you learned how to create letters for a mass-mailing. You can apply the same principles to create a primary file for mailing labels. This file will contain the format for labels, with merge codes that specify where information from your address list (secondary file) should be placed on each label. When you merge this primary file with your address file, you'll have a mailing label for each person on your list.

Remember that the formatting codes for a primary file must be stored as document initial codes. Therefore, you will begin the following exercise by inserting a paper size/type definition at the Document Initial Codes screen. Then, you will create the format and place merge codes that indicate where information from the address file should be inserted. When you are finished, you will save the file and use the Merge feature to create the actual mailing labels. As always, clear the screen before you begin.

1. Press Format (SHIFT-F8) or select Format from the Layout pull-down menu.

2. Choose option **I**, Document Initial Codes/Base Font. Another menu appears; select option **1**, Initial Codes, to display the Document Initial Codes screen.

3. Press Format (SHIFT-F8) or select Format from the Layout pull-down menu. Choose option **8**, Paper Size/Type from the Format menu.

4. Highlight the paper definition that you want to use for labels (1 x 1 or 3 x 10), and choose option **1**, Select, to select the paper size. The Format menu reappears.

note ▸ If you choose the 1 x 1 labels definition, you may need to change your margins before you select the paper size from the Format menu. Simply choose option **3**, Top/Bottom Margins, or option **4**, Left/Right Margins, and enter the desired measurements.

5. Press Exit (F7) three times to exit the Document Initial Codes screen and return to the main editing screen.

6. Press Merge Codes (SHIFT-F9) or select Merge Codes from the Tools pull-down menu. Move the cursor to highlight the {FIELD} code, and then press ENTER. At the "Enter Field: " prompt, type **First Name** and press ENTER.

7. Press the SPACEBAR to add a text space. Then press Merge Codes (SHIFT-F9) or select Merge Codes from the Tools pull-down menu. Press ENTER to select the {FIELD} code again. At the "Enter Field: " prompt, type **Last Name** and press ENTER twice to accept the code and move to the next line.

8. Press Merge Codes (SHIFT-F9) or select Merge Codes from the Tools pull-down menu. Press ENTER to select the {FIELD} code. Type **Address** and press ENTER.

The labels primary file is completed. When you merge this document with your address file, LetterPerfect will create a separate label for each person on the list. The paper size/type code that you inserted at the Document Initial Codes screen ensures that the labels are formatted correctly.

Press Save (F10) or select Save from the File pull-down menu. At the "Document to be saved: " prompt, type **labels.pf** and press ENTER. Then clear the screen; you're ready to create the labels.

Press Merge (CTRL-F9) or choose Merge from the Tools pull-down menu. At the "Primary file: " prompt, type **labels.pf** and press ENTER. Then enter **address.sf** at the "Secondary file: " prompt. When the merge is finished, you'll have a separate label for each person in the list. Select option 3, View Document, from the Print menu, and you can view the labels before you print.

You do not need to save the file on your screen—unless you want to—because both the primary and secondary files are already saved, and it takes only a few minutes to merge them together.

Now you know how to create form letters and labels for mass-mailing. The Merge feature will save you a great deal of time because you don't have to create a document layout each time you want to print. If you keep your address file current, you won't have to worry about anything else. LetterPerfect takes care of the rest.

SUMMARY

The Merge feature in LetterPerfect lets you assemble documents by combining information from two or more sources. To create a mass-mailing system, you need to create a primary file, which contains the layout and text for the form letter you want to send. You also need to create a secondary file; this file contains the information that you want to merge with the form letter, including the names and addresses of the people who should receive the letter. When you merge these files together, LetterPerfect copies information from the primary and secondary files to create a personalized letter for each name in the address list.

LetterPerfect also includes features that allow you to print on continuous or sheet labels. Special paper size/type definitions can be selected from the Format menu to help LetterPerfect distinguish between the logical page (the label) and the physical page, which is the paper onto which the label is attached. You can use LetterPerfect's Merge feature to create a primary file for labels; this file can be merged with the address secondary file to create labels for mass-mailing.

The merge features are flexible and provide endless possibilities for you to explore. Consult your LetterPerfect manual for more information about the merge codes and other merge applications.

This chapter concludes Part II of this book. You've learned a great deal about LetterPerfect. The applications in this book present only a few examples of the documents you can create—don't let the simplicity of LetterPerfect fool you. It's a powerful program, and you'll discover many new uses for the features discussed here. Now, you'll need to apply this information to your own word processing needs.

part III

APPENDIXES

Installing the LetterPerfect Program
Using the Shell Program
Information for WordPerfect Users
LetterPerfect Macros

The following appendixes contain important information about the LetterPerfect program, but all of this information may not be necessary for every user. Appendix A explains how to install the LetterPerfect program and defines different program options. Appendix B shows you how to use the Shell program that is included with LetterPerfect, and Appendix C presents information that will be helpful for WordPerfect users. Appendix D explains how to use the LetterPerfect Macro features, and includes practical examples that you can apply to your own working environment.

appendix A

INSTALLING THE LETTERPERFECT PROGRAM

Hardware Requirements
Installation with a Hard Disk System
Installation with a Floppy-Drive System
Your Registration Number
Installing an Updated Version of LetterPerfect
Defining Program Options

The LetterPerfect package includes diskettes for the program files, utility files, and printer drivers. You must use the LetterPerfect installation program to install these files for use with your computer. The following information explains how to install LetterPerfect.

note — Before starting installation, you should have the command FILES=n in your CONFIG.SYS system file, where n represents the number 20 or greater. Refer to your DOS manual for information about creating this file and adding the command. If you do not have the FILES=20 command in your CONFIG.SYS file, the installation program will not be able to install a printer for you, and you will have to do it manually, as described in Chapter 7.

After you have installed the program, refer to Chapter 1, "Getting Started with LetterPerfect," for information on starting and using the LetterPerfect program.

HARDWARE REQUIREMENTS

Your computer must have at least 330K of free computer memory (512K total) in order to run LetterPerfect. You can run LetterPerfect on a floppy-drive system or from a hard disk. If you plan to install and use the Shell program included with your LetterPerfect software, you should have a hard disk drive.

INSTALLATION WITH A HARD DISK SYSTEM

You will need about 2MB of free disk space to install the entire program on a hard disk, although the actual required disk space depends on the type of printer you are using, and whether you decide to install the LetterPerfect supplemental files. The minimal installation of LetterPerfect requires approximately 900K of hard disk space.

The following steps explain how to install LetterPerfect for a hard disk system. Exit to the DOS prompt, and have your LetterPerfect Program diskettes nearby. You will be prompted to insert the correct diskettes as necessary.

1. Insert the Install/Program 1 diskette into drive A. At the DOS prompt, type **a:install** and press ENTER. Figure A-1 shows the opening screen of the LetterPerfect installation program.

2. You are prompted about whether you want to continue with the program. Type **Y** for Yes, and another prompt asks whether you see colored boxes on your screen, indicating that you have a color monitor. If so, type **Y** for Yes; otherwise, type **N**.

3. You are asked whether you are installing to a hard disk. Type **Y** again to continue. The main Installation menu appears, as shown in Figure A-2. Choose option **1**, Install.

4. You are prompted to enter the drive from which you are installing the program. Type **a:** and press ENTER. Then you are asked to specify the hard disk directory

Appendix A — Installing the LetterPerfect Program

```
         ┌─────────────────────────┐
         │    LetterPerfect        │
         │    Installation         │
         │        1.0              │
         └─────────────────────────┘

              (C) Copyright 1990
              All Rights Reserved
            WordPerfect Corporation
                Orem, Utah  USA
    ┌──────────────────────────────────────────────────┐
    │   Welcome to the LetterPerfect 1.0 Installation Program. │
    │ The files on the disks in the LetterPerfect Package are in │
    │ compressed format.  You must use this installation program │
    │ to use these files.                                        │
    │         Do you want to Continue? Yes (No)                  │
    └──────────────────────────────────────────────────┘
```

FIGURE A-1.   Starting the LetterPerfect installation program

```
Installation

    1 - Install      First time installation of LetterPerfect.

    2 - Network      First time installation of LetterPerfect on a Network.

    3 - Printer      Install a Printer (.ALL) File.  Use this
                     option to install more printers after
                     you have already installed LetterPerfect.

    4 - Update       Update previously installed LetterPerfect 1.0 software.

    5 - Copy Disks   Install every file from an installation diskette to a
                     location you specify.  (Useful for installing all the
                     Printer (.ALL) Files.)

    6 - Exit         Exit Install program.




Selection: 1
```

FIGURE A-2.   The main installation screen

where the program should be installed. Press ENTER to accept the C:\LP10 directory, or type a different directory and press ENTER.

> *note* The LetterPerfect program files will be copied from the original diskette in drive A to a hard disk directory called C:\LP10, or to the directory you specified. If this directory does not already exist, the installation program can create it for you.

5. LetterPerfect prompts you with "Do you want to install the Supplemental Files? Yes (No)". These include the file conversion programs, the LetterPerfect graphic images, the Shell program, and other useful files. Type **Y** for Yes.

6. While the installation program copies the files, you may be prompted to insert the Install/Utilities 2 diskette; if so, replace Install/Utilities 1 with Install/Utilities 2 and press ENTER to continue.

7. After the supplemental files are copied, you are prompted to insert the Program 1 diskette. Replace the Install/Utilities diskette with the Program 1 diskette and press ENTER. LetterPerfect copies the program files. During this procedure, you may be asked to insert the Program 2 diskette. If so, replace Program 1 with Program 2 and press ENTER to continue.

8. After the program files are copied, the installation program checks to see that your computer is correctly configured for LetterPerfect. As mentioned earlier, your CONFIG.SYS file should have the command FILES=n, where n is a number greater than 20. If the FILES=20 command is not found in your CONFIG.SYS file, the installation program will prompt you to add it. Type **Y** for Yes. Then be prepared to reboot your computer. The instructions on your screen will tell you what to do.

> *note* Since you started your computer without the FILES=20 command, your computer is not configured to start LetterPerfect, and the installation program cannot continue to set up your printer. Therefore, you'll have to reboot your computer and install the printer manually, as described in Chapter 7.

9. The installation program will also check that the new LetterPerfect directory is indicated in the PATH command of your AUTOEXEC.BAT file. If the settings are not correct for the AUTOEXEC.BAT file, the installation program will tell you so, and ask if you want to add the LetterPerfect directory to the path. Type **Y** for Yes as prompted, and the installation program will automatically update your AUTOEXEC.BAT file.

10. Next, you are asked what you want the function of the F1 key to be. This determines whether the F1 function key will perform the Cancel feature or select

Appendix A		Installing the LetterPerfect Program		245

Help, while in LetterPerfect. Select option **1**, Cancel, or option **2**, Help, to indicate your choice.

11. The installation program will prompt you about installing a printer; type **Y** for Yes. When prompted to do so, replace the Program diskette with the Printer 1 diskette, and press ENTER to continue. An alphabetical list of printers appears on your screen, as shown in Figure A-3.

12. Press PGDN or PGUP until the name of your printer appears on the list. Type **Y** for Yes. (If you don't find your printer, press F3 for help.) Type the number next to your printer's name, and press ENTER. A message appears asking you to verify your selection. The installation program copies the appropriate files to your LetterPerfect directory.

13. Then you are prompted with "Do you want to install another printer?". Type **Y** or **N** to indicate your choice.

```
 1 *Acer LP-76
 2 *AEG Olympia Compact RO        Printers marked with '*' are
 3 *AEG Olympia ESW 2000          not included with shipping
 4 *AEG Olympia Laserstar 6       disks.  Select printer for
 5 *AEG Olympia Laserstar 6e      more information.
 6  AEG Olympia NP 136-24
 7 *AEG Olympia NP 136-24 (Additional)   If you do not see your printer
 8  AEG Olympia NP 136 SE         listed, press F3 for Help.
 9  AEG Olympia NP 30
10  AEG Olympia NP 80-24
11 *AEG Olympia NP 80-24 (Additional)
12  AEG Olympia NP 80 SE
13  AEG Olympia NPC 136-24
14 *AEG Olympia NPC 136-24 (Additional)
15 *AEG Olympia Startype
16 *AGFA Compugraphic 9400PS
17  Alphacom Alphapro 101
18  Alps Allegro 24
19 *Alps Allegro 24 (Additional)
20 *Alps Allegro 500
21  Alps ALQ200 (18 pin)
22  Alps ALQ200 (24 pin)

N Name Search; PgDn More Printers; PgUp Previous Screen; F3 Help; F7 Exit;
Selection: 0
```

FIGURE A-3.   Selecting a printer

14. At this point, you may be prompted to enter your registration number. Type the number printed on your LetterPerfect license card and press ENTER. Refer to the section "Your Registration Number" in this appendix for more information.

The LetterPerfect program is now installed on your computer, and the installation program sets up your printer. A message at the top of the screen displays the status of the printer installation. When it is finished, your screen may look similar to this:

```
Installation Complete.

When you want to run LetterPerfect, change to the LetterPerfect directory,
type LP, and press Enter.


C:\>
```

You can now start LetterPerfect as outlined in Chapter 1, "Getting Started with LetterPerfect."

INSTALLATION WITH A FLOPPY-DRIVE SYSTEM

If you do not have a hard drive, you will need a set of blank formatted diskettes to install the LetterPerfect program from the master program diskette. If your computer has 5.25-inch disk drives, you will need seven blank diskettes; for computers with 3.5-inch disk drives, you'll need four blank diskettes. During the installation procedure, you'll also need your DOS boot diskette, so keep it nearby. The following steps will show you how to install the LetterPerfect program for a single- or double-floppy system.

note — Since there are several diskette types (360K, 720K, 1.2MB, and 1.44MB) and two possible floppy drive configurations for computers (single- or double-floppy drives), the actual installation procedure may be different than described here, depending on your situation. The following steps present a general procedure for floppy-drive installation, but pay close attention to the instructions displayed by the LetterPerfect installation program. They are your best guide for installing LetterPerfect on floppy diskettes.

1. Insert the Install/Utilities 1 diskette into Drive A. Type **a:install** and press ENTER.

2. The opening screen of the installation program appears and asks whether you want to continue. Type **Y** for Yes. Another prompt asks whether you can see colored

boxes on the screen. If you can, you have a color monitor and should type **Y** to continue; otherwise, type **N** for No. You are then asked whether you are installing on a hard disk. Type **N** for No.

3. You will be prompted to insert your DOS boot diskette, and the installation program checks to see that your computer is correctly configured for LetterPerfect. As mentioned earlier, your CONFIG.SYS file should have the command FILES=n, where n is a number greater than 20. If you've already placed this command in your CONFIG.SYS file, press ENTER to continue.

note If the FILES=20 command is not found in your CONFIG.SYS file, the installation program will prompt you to add it. Type **Y** for Yes. Then, be prepared to reboot your computer. The instructions on your screen will tell you what to do. Since you started your computer without the FILES=20 command, your computer is not configured to start LetterPerfect, and the installation program cannot continue. Therefore, you'll have to reboot your computer and then run the installation program again.

4. The Floppy Disk Drive Installation screen appears, and a message asks you the size of the diskettes you are using. Type **1** to indicate 3.5-inch diskettes, or **2** for 5.25-inch diskettes.

5. The next prompt asks you how many disk drives your computer has. Type **1** to indicate a single-floppy system or **2** for a double-floppy system.

6. The installation program asks you to indicate the capacity of the diskettes you are using. Make a selection from the menu to indicate the storage capacity of the blank diskettes.

7. After you select the disk capacity, the installation program asks you to verify the disk information that you've entered. Figure A-4 shows how your screen may appear. Type **Y** if the information is correct. If you type **N**, the installation program will ask you the questions again, so you can make the correct selections.

Depending on the choices you've made, the installation program may display an additional screen with two options for the installation: Normal or Minimum. If the screen appears, select option **1**, **Normal Installation**, to install the entire LetterPerfect program. Or, select option **2**, **Minimal**, to install just the LetterPerfect program files without the utility programs, graphics files, and learning files.

8. The main Installation screen now appears, as shown in Figure A-5. Select option **1**, **Install**, to install the LetterPerfect program for the first time. You are prompted

248 LetterPerfect Made Easy

```
Floppy Disk Drive Installation

Do you want to install to 3½" or 5¼" disk drive(s)?      5¼" Drive(s)

Do you have one or two 5¼" floppy drives?                2

What is the storage capacity of your floppy disk(s)?     Low




                       Is this correct? Yes (No)
```

FIGURE A-4. Setting up for installation with a floppy-drive system

```
Installation
          1 - Install     First time installation of LetterPerfect.

          2 - Network     First time installation of LetterPerfect on a Network.

          3 - Printer     Install a Printer (.ALL) File.  Use this
                          option to install more printers after
                          you have already installed LetterPerfect.

          4 - Update      Update previously installed LetterPerfect 1.0 software.

          5 - Copy Disks  Install every file from an installation diskette to a
                          location you specify.  (Useful for installing all the
                          Printer (.ALL) Files.)

          6 - Exit        Exit Install program.




          Selection: 1
```

FIGURE A-5. The main installation screen

Appendix A Installing the LetterPerfect Program 249

to enter the drive from which you are installing the program. Then you are asked to specify the drive where the program files should be installed.

9. Now the installation program will mark your blank diskettes. You are prompted to label one of the blank diskettes as "LetterPerfect 1", and to insert it into drive A. Write "LetterPerfect 1" on one of the blank diskettes and replace the DOS boot diskette with it. Press ENTER to continue.

10. The installation program will then ask you to label and insert the remaining blank diskettes. In each case, write the name on a blank diskette and replace the diskette in drive A with the diskette you just labeled. After you've inserted the diskette, press ENTER to continue. Repeat this procedure for each of the blank diskettes.

11. After each diskette is marked, you are prompted about whether you want to install the supplemental files. These include the file conversion programs, the graphics files, and the tutorial files. Type **Y** for Yes. You are asked to insert the diskette that you labeled "Utilities." After you do so, press ENTER to continue.

12. The installation program will install the program files and will prompt you to insert the appropriate diskettes as necessary. Pay close attention to the prompts that are displayed on the screen; they will tell you when to insert a master LetterPerfect diskette or one of the blank diskettes that you have created.

13. You are asked whether you want to install a printer definition. When prompted to do so, replace the diskette in Drive A with the Printer 1 diskette, and press ENTER to continue.

14. An alphabetical list of printers appears on your screen. Press PGDN or PGUP until the name of your printer appears on the screen. (If you can't find your printer on the list, press F3 for Help.) Type the number next to your printer's name, and press ENTER. A message appears asking you to verify your selection. Type **Y** for Yes.

15. Another message may ask "Do you want to install the printer (.ALL) file? Yes (No)". The ∗.ALL file contains information for your printer and printers similar to yours. Although this file is not necessary, you'll need it if you want to change some of the printer settings later. If you need to conserve disk space, type **N** for No. Otherwise, type **Y** for Yes.

16. The installation program copies the appropriate printer files to your diskette, then asks "Do you want to install another printer?". Type **Y** or **N** to indicate your choice.

17. After you've selected printers, the installation program will prompt you to insert the diskette that you labeled "LetterPerfect 2." Press ENTER to continue, and you will be prompted to enter your registration number. For more information about this, refer to the next section in this appendix, "Your Registration Number."

18. Since you are working with floppy diskettes, you'll be instructed to swap disks a few times before the installation is finished. The installation program starts Letter-Perfect and sets up your printer.

When the installation is finished, your screen will look similar to this:

```
Installation Complete.

When you want to run LetterPerfect, insert the LetterPerfect 1 diskette,
type LP, and press Enter.


A:\>
```

Now, you can start the LetterPerfect program as outlined in Chapter 1, "Getting Started with LetterPerfect."

YOUR REGISTRATION NUMBER

When you install LetterPerfect for the first time, you will be asked to enter your registration number. A unique number, assigned to your copy of LetterPerfect, it is printed on the registration card included with your LetterPerfect package.

When prompted to do so, type the number from your registration card, then press ENTER. Now, your registration number will be displayed at the top of the screen when you select the LetterPerfect Help feature. This is important because you may be asked for this number when you call WordPerfect's Customer Support department for assistance.

It's also a good idea to fill out the registration card and send it to WordPerfect Corporation. When you send the card, you will be notified when new versions of LetterPerfect are available.

INSTALLING AN UPDATED VERSION OF LETTERPERFECT

WordPerfect Corporation occasionally releases interim copies of LetterPerfect to fix software errors and problems with certain types of computer equipment, and also to introduce program enhancements. If you order an updated copy of LetterPerfect, simply run the installation program with the new diskettes and select the Update option from the Installation menu. You will be prompted to enter the drive directory where LetterPerfect is currently installed, and the drive that you are installing from.

Appendix A Installing the LetterPerfect Program   251

Then, the installation program displays a menu, asking which of the program files you want to install. Choose the desired menu options, and type **Y** for Yes or **N** for No at the appropriate prompts to indicate your preferences. You don't need to install the entire program—only the files that have changed. Then, the LetterPerfect program is updated to reflect your latest selections.

DEFINING PROGRAM OPTIONS

The LetterPerfect Setup menu provides features for screen colors, automatic file backup, initial document codes, and other program settings. These options let you "personalize" your copy of LetterPerfect. Since these features are selected from the Setup menu, they become permanent settings of the LetterPerfect program (saved in a file called LP{LP}.SET). You can change the settings as often as you like, or set them once and forget about them.

In previous chapters, you have learned about some of the program options, such as automatic file backup, units of measure, and menu display. The following sections present a brief overview of the program options you can define, and the keystrokes necessary to make your selections.

Once you've installed and started the LetterPerfect program, you can choose from the options on the Setup menu; press Setup (SHIFT-F1), or select Setup from the File pull-down menu, to display the menu shown in Figure A-6.

note — If you have an updated version of LetterPerfect, the following screens may contain additional options, or may look different than the menus shown in the figures.

Define Screen Colors

From the Setup menu, choose option **1**, Screen Colors, to display the menu shown in Figure A-7. Select the option that represents the display you want for your monitor. For example, choose option **2**, **B**lue on White, for blue text on a white background, or choose option **3**, LCD Display "Colors", for a monochrome LCD monitor that requires a CGA driver.

After you choose an option, the Setup menu reappears, and the monitor display is adjusted according to your selection. You may want to experiment with the different screen color options to see what looks best.

```
Setup
        1 - Screen Colors                      White on Blue
        2 - Minutes Between Backup             10
        3 - Units of Measure                   Inches
        4 - Location of Files
              Document Files
              Speller/Thesaurus Files
              Printer Files                    C:\LP10
        5 - Initial Codes
        6 - Alt Key Selects Menu Bar           Yes
        7 - Menu Bar Remains Visible           Yes
        8 - Function of F1                     Cancel
        9 - Format Retrieved Documents         No
              for Default Printer

Selection: 0
```

FIGURE A-6. The LetterPerfect Setup menu

```
Screen Colors
        1 - White on Blue (Default)
        2 - Blue on White
        3 - LCD Display "Colors"
        4 - LCD Display "Colors" - No Intensity
        5 - Plasma Display "Colors"
        6 - Monochrome
        Note: Options 3, 4, 5 and 6 may also be useful on color screens.




Selection: 0
```

FIGURE A-7. Options for screen colors

Automatic File Backup

Choose option **2, Minutes Between Backup**, and enter the number of minutes for the timed backup interval. This enables LetterPerfect's automatic file backup feature. For more information, see the section "Automatic File Backup" in Chapter 8.

Selecting the Unit of Measurement

LetterPerfect normally measures all margins, tabs, and other document settings in terms of inches. However, you may prefer to use a different unit of measurement. Choose option **3, Units of Measure**, from the Setup menu. The following menu appears at the bottom of the screen:

```
1 Inches; 2 Centimeters; 3 Points; 4 1200ths of an inch; 5 WP 4.2 units: 0
```

You can choose an option to select Inches, Centimeters, Points (a typesetting measurement), 1200ths of an inch (LetterPerfect's internal measurement), or WP 4.2 units, which mimic the line/column system of WordPerfect 4.2. Once you've made a selection, all formatting menus (such as Margins, Tabs, Paper Sizes) use the selected measurement to display the format settings.

If you wish, you can also change the measurement while you are entering a format setting. LetterPerfect will accept special letters after an entry to convert a setting to a specific measurement. For example, suppose you change the Units of Measure to centimeters, but later find that you want to enter margin settings in inches. No problem. Select the appropriate margin feature, type the measurement for the margin, followed by an **i** or **"** (for example, **0.75i** or **0.75"**). The i or " character tells LetterPerfect that you want to enter this setting in terms of inches, rather than the default unit of measure defined on the Setup menu. When you press ENTER to accept the measurement, LetterPerfect converts the number to the centimeter equivalent. The other valid characters are: c (centimeters), p (typesetting points), w (WordPerfect units, 1200ths of an inch), and u (WordPerfect 4.2 units).

Location of Document Program Files

Choose option **4, Location of Files**, to specify where the document and program files should be stored. This feature is discussed in Chapter 8, in the section "Creating a Document Directory."

If you have a version of LetterPerfect dated November 1990 or later, this feature may include additional options for specifying the location of the Speller and Thesaurus files and the printer files.

Defining Initial Codes

Choose option **5**, Initial Codes, to define a standard format for each document that you will create in LetterPerfect. This option is explained in detail in Chapter 4.

Menu Options and the F1 Key

Two options on the Setup menu determine how the menu bar is displayed for the pull-down menus. Choose option **6**, **A**lt Key Selects Menu Bar, and type **Y** for Yes. Then, you can press ALT to activate the pull-down menu at the main document screen. This is the standard method of selecting the menu bar. If you answer "No" instead, then you must press ALT-= (hold down the ALT key and type the equal sign) to activate the menu bar.

Option **7**, Menu Bar Remains Visible, determines whether the menu bar is always displayed as you use the program. If you want to see the menu bar only when it is active, choose "No" for this option.

When you installed the LetterPerfect program, you were asked to select a function for the F1 key, and define the key as either Help or Cancel. You can choose option **8**, **F**unction of F1, from the Setup menu to redefine the function of the F1 key. Select option **1**, **H**elp, or option **2**, Cancel, and the F1 key will perform that function after you exit the Setup menu.

note — In the LetterPerfect program, ESC will always perform the Cancel function and F3 will always access the Help feature, regardless of the function you assign to the F1 key.

Automatic Document Formatting

When you create a document, LetterPerfect formats the text for the printer that is currently selected. This guarantees that your document will look its best when it's sent to the printer. However, if you select a different printer, LetterPerfect will have to reformat your document to match the current printer. This usually happens automatically when you retrieve your documents, but there may be some situations where you do not want LetterPerfect to do this.

In this case, you can choose option **9**, **F**ormat Retrieved Documents for Default Printer, and type **N** for No. Then LetterPerfect will simply retrieve documents without reformatting for the printer that is currently selected.

When you are finished selecting the program options, press Exit (F7), or click the right mouse button, to return to the main LetterPerfect screen.

appendix B

USING THE SHELL PROGRAM

Starting the Shell Program
Using the Shell Program
Using the Clipboard
Additional Information

LetterPerfect is shipped with the WordPerfect *Shell program.* This is a memory-management program that allows you to start your programs from an on-screen menu that you define. The Shell program also makes it possible to keep several programs open and exchange information between them.

STARTING THE SHELL PROGRAM

When you install the LetterPerfect program to a hard disk, the files for the Shell program are also installed in your LetterPerfect directory. There are two ways to start the Shell program: You can start the Shell program from the DOS prompt, or you can add commands to your computer's AUTOEXEC.BAT file to start the Shell each time you turn on your computer.

To start from the DOS prompt, change to the directory where the Shell program files were installed. For example, if you followed the standard installation procedure, the Shell program files were copied to the C:\LP10 directory. You would type **cd\lp10** and press ENTER to change to that directory. Then, type **shell** and press ENTER to start the Shell program. The Shell menu appears on your screen. If you are installing the Shell for the first time, the Shell menu is set up for you, as shown in Figure B-1. If you have updated from a previous copy of the Shell program, you'll see your usual menu.

If you want to automatically start the Shell program each time you turn on your computer, use a text editor or word processor to type the following command lines at the end of your AUTOEXEC.BAT file:

cd\lp10
shell

If you've copied the Shell program files to a directory other than \LP10, type the appropriate path name instead. Save the edited AUTOEXEC.BAT as an ASCII file, and reboot your computer. The Shell program is automatically started.

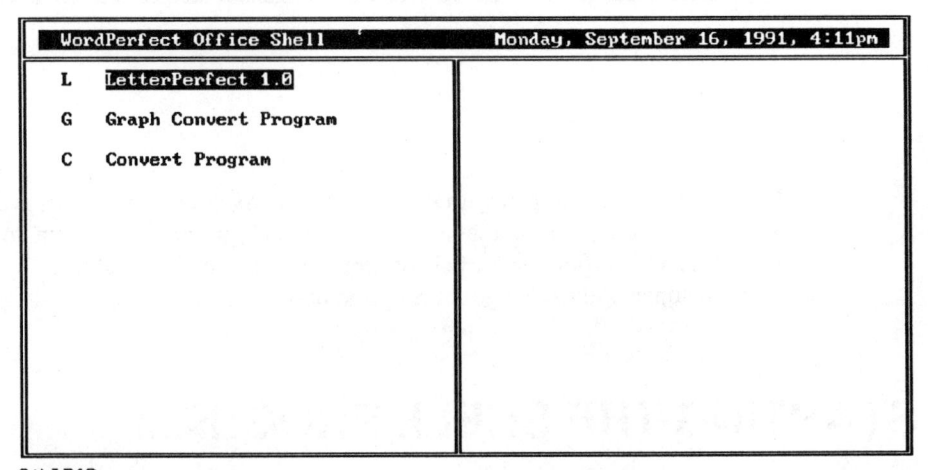

```
┌─────────────────────────────────────────────────────────────────┐
│ WordPerfect Office Shell           Monday, September 16, 1991, 4:11pm
│                                                                 │
│   L   LetterPerfect 1.0                                         │
│   G   Graph Convert Program                                     │
│   C   Convert Program                                           │
│                                                                 │
└─────────────────────────────────────────────────────────────────┘
C:\LP10
1 Go to DOS; 2 Clipboard; 3 Other Dir; 4 Setup; 5 Mem Map; 6 Log:    (F7 = Exit)
```

FIGURE B-1. The Shell menu

For more information about the AUTOEXEC.BAT file, consult the DOS manual that came with your computer system.

USING THE SHELL PROGRAM

Once you have the Shell program installed and running on your computer, you can start programs from the menu and quickly switch to other programs.

Starting Programs from the Shell Menu

To start a program from the Shell menu, simply type the highlighted letter of the program entry. For example, assume you want to start LetterPerfect, and the letter next to the "LetterPerfect" listing is *L*. Type l to start the program, and the Shell program remains active in the background while you are using LetterPerfect.

When you start LetterPerfect from the Shell menu, you can display the Shell menu and switch to another program. From the LetterPerfect screen, press Shell (CTRL-F1) and then select the Go To Shell option from the menu that appears. The Shell menu is redisplayed, and you will notice an asterisk (*) next to the LetterPerfect listing; the asterisk means that the program is still active. At this point, you can start one of the other programs on the Shell menu, or return to LetterPerfect.

To return to the program, select the program letter again from the Shell menu. The number of programs you can keep open depends on the amount of computer memory that is available. If you do not have enough memory to keep a program open, the Shell program swaps the program information to your hard disk.

Using the Shell Hot-Keys

Hot-keys are special keystrokes that instruct the Shell program to perform specific tasks. Sometimes, these hot-keys invoke special macros. One Shell hot-key, ALT-SHIFT-*n*, allows you to quickly switch to other programs on the Shell menu. The *n* represents the letter of the program on the Shell menu to which you want to move.

For example, assume that WordPerfect is also listed on the Shell menu, assigned to the letter *w*. You can start the LetterPerfect program by selecting l from the Shell menu. Then, you can press ALT-SHIFT-W to bypass the Shell menu and move directly to the WordPerfect program. Press ALT-SHIFT-l to switch back to LetterPerfect.

USING THE CLIPBOARD

The Shell program also includes a *clipboard* that can be used to temporarily store blocked text. While you are in LetterPerfect, you can press Shell (CTRL-F1) to display the Clipboard menu.

For example, you can block some text, press Shell (CTRL-F1), and then select the Save option from the Clipboard menu to save the blocked text to the clipboard. You can then switch to another program through the Shell menu and retrieve the text into that program. To retrieve the text, press Shell (CTRL-F1). Then, select the **R**etrieve option from the Clipboard menu, and the saved text is "dumped" into the text screen.

ADDITIONAL INFORMATION

Included with your LetterPerfect package is a booklet that presents detailed information about the Shell program. Refer to this booklet for complete information about the use of the Shell program, special Shell macros, and defining the Shell menu.

appendix C

INFORMATION FOR WORDPERFECT USERS

Sharing Files with LetterPerfect
WordPerfect Codes in LetterPerfect Documents
Using the Speller
Sharing WordPerfect's Hyphenation Module
Printer Drivers
WordPerfect Characters

B ecause of LetterPerfect's close relationship to WordPerfect, it is assumed that many LetterPerfect users will be familiar with at least one version of WordPerfect. For this reason, the information in this appendix is provided to help WordPerfect users take advantage of LetterPerfect's similar features. This information is most useful for those who use LetterPerfect on a home computer or laptop computer, but also use a copy of WordPerfect on another computer.

SHARING FILES WITH LETTERPERFECT

WordPerfect 5.1 documents are fully compatible with LetterPerfect. This means you can retrieve any WordPerfect 5.1 file directly into LetterPerfect and make editing changes. LetterPerfect recognizes the WordPerfect file and automatically makes adjustments. After editing, you can save the file and retrieve it back into WordPerfect without converting it.

However, if you have files from WordPerfect 5.0 or an earlier version, you may encounter a few problems. The file format of WordPerfect 5.0 is slightly different than that of version 5.1 and LetterPerfect. You can retrieve a 5.0 file into LetterPerfect, but some of the formatting commands may not be recognized, and may appear as [Unknown] in the Reveal Codes window.

Also, remember that LetterPerfect saves documents to a file format that is compatible with WordPerfect 5.1. If you retrieve a WordPerfect file (from version 5.0 or an earlier version) and then save it, it becomes a WordPerfect 5.1 file. Depending on the format of your document, this will cause problems when you retrieve the file back into WordPerfect 5.0. If problems occur, consider using LetterPerfect's Text Out feature (CTRL-F5) to convert the documents to a generic word processing format before retrieving them back into WordPerfect.

WORDPERFECT CODES IN LETTERPERFECT DOCUMENTS

When you retrieve documents into LetterPerfect from WordPerfect, the formatting codes are carried over or converted so that you can edit the document in LetterPerfect. WordPerfect codes that are not supported by LetterPerfect are displayed in French brackets on the Reveal Codes window (for example, {Block Pro}, {Col Def}, {W/O On}). Many of these codes, such as {Style On} or {Style Off}, do not have equivalent features in LetterPerfect, but may still affect the format of your document. You can edit the text, but if one of the codes in French brackets is deleted, there is no way to replace the code in LetterPerfect.

Several WordPerfect codes can't be converted and so LetterPerfect ignores them. When you retrieve the file back into WordPerfect, the features that appeared in French brackets are restored to your document. In Chapter 4, in the "Editing Document Codes" section, you'll find more information about editing WordPerfect documents in LetterPerfect. For a complete list of the WordPerfect codes and features that are supported by LetterPerfect, see the appendix section of your LetterPerfect manual.

USING THE SPELLER

LetterPerfect's Speller dictionary contains over 80,000 words, while WordPerfect's Speller dictionary contains over 115,000. LetterPerfect's smaller dictionary makes it easier to install the entire LetterPerfect program on a floppy-drive system. This is important for users with limited computer equipment.

However, WordPerfect's Speller dictionary (version 5.1) is fully compatible with LetterPerfect. If you have a hard disk, you can copy your WordPerfect Speller file (WP{WP}US.LEX) to your LetterPerfect directory. This will provide over 35,000 more words for spell-checking your documents.

You can use the DOS COPY command to copy the files from your WordPerfect directory, or use WordPerfect's installation program to install the Speller files to your LetterPerfect directory. Also, any WordPerfect 5.1 foreign-language dictionaries may also be installed for use with LetterPerfect.

Likewise, you can copy or install WordPerfect 5.1's Thesaurus file (WP{WP}US.THS) to your LetterPerfect directory, and access more synonyms than are available with LetterPerfect's Thesaurus. For more information about using the Speller and Thesaurus features, refer to Chapter 5.

SHARING WORDPERFECT'S HYPHENATION MODULE

The hyphenation module is a separate disk file that provides WordPerfect with the information it needs to hyphenate text. As described in Chapter 3, you can copy WordPerfect's hyphenation module to your LetterPerfect directory, and LetterPerfect will automatically hyphenate the text in your documents. This file must be installed on the diskette or directory where the LetterPerfect program files are located.

For the U.S. release of WordPerfect, the hyphenation module is named WP{WP}US.HYC. If you own WordPerfect 5.1, the hyphenation module is already installed with your Speller files, and you can copy it to your LetterPerfect directory. Once the module is copied to your program diskette or directory, LetterPerfect will hyphenate your documents as they are retrieved or reformatted on the screen.

If you use the Language feature (ALT-F8) to change the language in your document, then LetterPerfect will look for a hyphenation module that matches the chosen language. For example, if you change the language to *IT* (for Italian), you'll need the WP{WP}*IT*.HYC hyphenation module, which is sold separately. If you do not have the hyphenation module that matches the selected language, LetterPerfect will not hyphenate the text for you. Refer to Chapter 3 for more information about hyphenation in your LetterPerfect documents.

PRINTER DRIVERS

As mentioned in Chapter 7, the LetterPerfect printer drivers do not include soft font information. If you own WordPerfect 5.1, you can copy your *.PRS files to your LetterPerfect directory or diskette. Then, start LetterPerfect, and press Print (SHIFT-F7). Choose option **5**, **S**elect Printer, to display the Select Printer screen. From the menu at the bottom of the screen, choose option **2**, **A**dditional Printers. This may display a list of printers on your screen; choose option **4**, **L**ist Printer Files, to display all the *.PRS files that are installed in your LetterPerfect directory.

Any printer files that you've copied from WordPerfect should be displayed in the list of printer files. Move the cursor to highlight the WordPerfect printer file that you want to use, and choose option **1**, **S**elect. Then, press Exit (F7) until you return to the document screen. This will create a new printer definition in LetterPerfect, with the WordPerfect *.PRS file.

note When you select a printer definition that was created from a WordPerfect printer file, the LetterPerfect paper size/type definitions (stored in a resource file called {LP}SPC.FRM) are ignored. Instead, you will have the paper sizes that were defined for the WordPerfect 5.1 printer file that you've selected. This may cause some formatting problems when you retrieve documents that were created when a standard LetterPerfect printer was selected.

WORDPERFECT CHARACTERS

If you have used WordPerfect's Compose feature, you know how to insert special characters and symbols into your WordPerfect documents. This feature also exists in LetterPerfect (where it is called the Characters feature), but there is a limit to the characters you can insert into your documents.

In WordPerfect, there are 12 character sets that contain foreign-language characters, mathematic symbols, and special typographic characters. WordPerfect's WP.DRS file contains the information that allows WordPerfect to display the characters on the View Document screen, and to print them in the document.

LetterPerfect's LP.DRS file contains the information to produce these characters for LetterPerfect documents. This file performs the same function as WordPerfect's WP.DRS file, except that it contains less information. Again, this file is smaller to allow LetterPerfect to be installed on a floppy-drive system.

You can use the Characters feature to insert any WordPerfect character into your LetterPerfect documents, but only those characters supported by the LP.DRS file can be displayed and printed. The LP.DRS file supports all characters in Word-

Perfect Character Set 0, characters 0-89 of WordPerfect Character Set 1, and all characters in WordPerfect Character Set 3.

WordPerfect's WP.DRS file is fully compatible with LetterPerfect. If you have LetterPerfect installed on a hard disk, you can copy the WP.DRS file from your WordPerfect directory to your LetterPerfect directory. The WP.DRS file must be copied to the directory where your LetterPerfect program files are located. This will enable LetterPerfect to display and print all characters for the entire WordPerfect character sets.

Refer to Chapter 3 for information about using the Characters feature in LetterPerfect. Also, refer to your WordPerfect Reference manual for complete information about inserting characters from the WordPerfect character sets.

appendix D

LETTERPERFECT MACROS

Creating and Using a Macro
Macro Names
Macro Options: Pause and Display
Macro Applications
Additional Information

Versions of LetterPerfect dated November 1990 or later include the ability to create program *macros*. Generally, a macro is a series of keystrokes or commands stored in a file on disk; you can quickly "retrieve" a macro to repeat a keystroke sequence or perform specific tasks. Macros are ideal for performing routine chores, such as typing the closing of a letter or setting up a document format—anything that should be performed exactly the same way each time you need to accomplish a given task.

To create a macro, you select a special feature that records your keystrokes as you type them. Then, you can tell LetterPerfect to "play back" the keystrokes you typed. Macros can save you a great deal of time by reducing a complex sequence of commands to a single keystroke that executes the macro where the commands are stored.

This appendix explains how to create and execute a LetterPerfect macro. You will also learn about the different ways to name your macros, and choose options for macro execution. The last section presents a few practical applications for the macro features.

note — Macros created for WordPerfect cannot be used with LetterPerfect because of feature and menu differences between the two programs; many LetterPerfect menu options have different numeric and mnemonic assignments than their WordPerfect counterparts. A WordPerfect macro that selects specific features would often select different features (or none at all) if executed in LetterPerfect. Therefore, any WordPerfect macros you wish to use with LetterPerfect must be re-created within the LetterPerfect program. Also, LetterPerfect does not support the macro editing capabilities of WordPerfect—only the Pause and Display commands are supported, as described later in this appendix.

CREATING AND USING A MACRO

Macros are created with a simple procedure: first, you select the Macro Definition feature and assign a name to the macro; next, you type the keystrokes that the macro should record; finally, you select the Macro Definition feature to end and save the macro.

note — Remember that the Macro feature can record only keystrokes; when you define a macro, use the keyboard—not the mouse—to select menu options.

The following steps will show you how to create a simple macro that inserts your name and address information. After you create the macro, you will execute it.

1. Press Macro Def (CTRL-F10) or select Macro **D**efine from the **T**ools pull-down menu.

2. LetterPerfect prompts you with "Define macro: ". This message asks you to type a name for the macro. Hold down the ALT key and type **A**. This will name the macro as ALT-A.

note — There are different ways to name your macros. Refer to the next section, "Macro Names," for more information.

3. Now you are prompted to enter a description for the macro. You can type up to 39 characters, including spaces, to describe what the macro will do. After you type the description, press ENTER to continue. (The description you typed will appear when you highlight the macro file name and choose the **L**ook option from List Files (F5).)

4. A "Macro Def" message flashes at the lower-left corner of the screen. While this message appears, you should type the keystrokes that you want the macro to perform. For this example, type your name and press ENTER. Then, type your street address and press ENTER. Finally, type your city, state, and ZIP code and press ENTER twice.

5. Press Macro Def (CTRL-F10) or select Macro Define from the Tools pull-down menu. This ends the macro and saves the recorded keystrokes to a file on disk.

6. Press Exit (F7) or select Exit from the File pull-down menu. Type **N** at the "Save document? Yes (No)" prompt. At the "Exit LP? No (Yes)" prompt, type **N** again. This will clear the screen.

7. Now you're ready to execute the macro. Simply press ALT-A and the macro repeats the keystrokes that you pressed during the macro definition. Press ALT-A a few times to insert copies of your address information into the current document.

You've just reduced many keystrokes to one ALT-A key combination. The macro was saved to a file called ALTA.LPM in your LetterPerfect directory; all LetterPerfect macro files will end with the .LPM extension. This is just one example of what you can store in a macro; practically anything you do in LetterPerfect can be stored in a macro file, and executed whenever you want.

LetterPerfect does not allow you to edit the macros after you've created them. If you own WordPerfect Office 3.0, you can retrieve LetterPerfect macros into the Editor program and edit them. Otherwise, you'll need to re-create the macros in LetterPerfect to change any keystrokes or correct mistakes made during the definition of the macro.

note If WordPerfect Office 3.0 is installed on your computer, you'll need to copy the LP.MRS file from your LetterPerfect directory to the directory where the Editor program is stored. Then, start the Editor program, press CTRL-F5, and select the "LP" Macro editor mode. This will enable you to retrieve and edit your LetterPerfect macros with the Editor program.

MACRO NAMES

You just learned how to create a macro, which included assigning a name. LetterPerfect provides different ways to name a macro, allowing you flexibility in organizing and retrieving your macros.

After you press Macro Def (CTRL-F10), LetterPerfect displays the "Define Macro: " prompt. This is where you name the macro. While the "Define Macro: "

prompt is displayed, you can choose one of three ways to name your macro: you can hold down the ALT key and type a letter (A - Z), you can type a macro name (eight characters or less) and press ENTER, or you can just press ENTER without typing anything (if you just press ENTER, you create a temporary macro, explained shortly). Then, type the keystrokes that the macro should record and press CTRL-F10 again to end the macro definition.

The name you assign to the macro determines how you can retrieve it. For example, pressing ALT-A will execute the ALTA.LPM macro that you created earlier. Simply hold down the ALT key and type the letter. This is the fastest way to execute a macro, but since there are only 26 letters in the alphabet, you're limited to 26 macros that can be named with this method. Use the ALT key to name those macros that you will use every day, and select letters that will help you remember what each macro does (for example, ALT-A for your Address).

If you type a macro name (eight characters or less) at the "Define Macro: " prompt, the macro is stored in a file called *name*.LPM, with *name* representing the macro name that you typed. You should use this method when you want to create a more descriptive name for the macro. For example, after you've created several macros, it might be difficult to remember that ALT-A will insert your address. Instead of typing ALT-A at the "Macro Def" prompt, you could type **address** and press ENTER to assign this name to the macro. After defining the macro, you can use the Macro key to execute it. First, press Macro (ALT-F10) or choose Macro Execute from the **T**ools pull-down menu. At the "Macro: " prompt, type the name that you assigned when you defined the macro (for example, Address), and press ENTER. Then, the macro is executed.

If you simply press ENTER at the "Define Macro: " prompt, without typing a macro name, you create a *temporary macro*. A temporary macro is stored in the LetterPerfect program directory in a file called LP{LP}.LPM; the keystrokes you recorded will be saved in this file until replaced by the next temporary macro that you create. You can execute this type of macro by pressing Macro (ALT-F10) and just pressing ENTER. A temporary macro is useful when you have a specific task that should be repeated, but only for the current editing session. This is not the type of macro you would need on a regular basis.

MACRO OPTIONS: PAUSE AND DISPLAY

While you are defining a macro, you can select two options that let you control the execution of the macro. Simply press Macro Commands (CTRL-PGUP) while the "Macro Def" mode is active, and a menu appears on the status line with the two options, Pause and Display.

Pause

Select option **1**, **P**ause, and you insert a command that tells the macro to pause during execution until the ENTER key is pressed. This can be useful when you need to temporarily stop the macro and type some text, move the cursor, or select an option from a menu. For example, assume you want to create a macro that changes the format of your document and pauses to let you enter measurements from the keyboard.

During the definition of the macro, you can select the appropriate format features and select the **P**ause command to temporarily stop the macro. Then press ENTER to continue the macro definition. When the macro is executed, it will pause at the format features you selected to allow you to type a measurement. When you press ENTER, macro execution continues. Later in this appendix, under the heading "Changing the Unit of Measure," you'll find an example of a macro that pauses to allow the user to make a selection from the keyboard.

Display

Choose option **2**, **D**isplay, to turn on or turn off the display of menus during macro execution. When you execute a macro, you won't normally see each keystroke or menu option performed on the screen. Since LetterPerfect wants to perform the macro as quickly as possible, each action is hidden and only the end result of the macro is shown. However, occasionally, you will want to see what the macro is doing; this is especially true if you've also selected the **P**ause command to stop the macro for input from the keyboard.

The macros you define can display the execution of the entire macro or only certain sections of the macro. You decide where the display will be turned on. During macro definition, press Macro Commands (CTRL-PGUP) and choose option **2**, **D**isplay. LetterPerfect will prompt you with "Display Execution? No (Yes)". Select **N** to turn off the macro display, or choose **Y** to turn it on. The standard setting is "No." The command you select is stored at that point in the macro and will control the display when the macro is executed.

MACRO APPLICATIONS

Now that you know the basic information about macros, you can create some macros of your own. The following information presents a few practical examples for the macro features. Remember, LetterPerfect's Macro feature can record any keystrokes you type—even the keystrokes that exit LetterPerfect. You'll need to experiment with these features to discover how macros can help you with your own applications. If things don't work perfectly the first time, don't get discouraged; it takes practice to master the art of macro definition.

Typing the Closing for a Letter

The following steps show how to create a macro that will insert the signature block for a letter.

1. Press Macro Def (CTRL-F10) or select Macro Define from the Tools pull-down menu.

2. LetterPerfect prompts you with "Define Macro: ". This message asks you to type a name for the macro. Hold down the ALT key and type C. This will name the macro as ALT-C, with *C* representing "Closing."

3. Now you are prompted to enter a description for the macro. After you type the description, press ENTER to continue.

4. A "Macro Def" message flashes at the lower-left corner of the screen. Type **Sincerely,** or whatever closing you prefer for your letters. Then press ENTER four times to add space for your signature. Finally, type your name and press ENTER. If you wish, type your title beneath your name.

5. Press Macro Def (CTRL-F10) or select Macro Define from the Tools pull-down menu. This ends the macro definition and saves the recorded keystrokes to your LetterPerfect directory in a file called ALTC.LPM.

6. Press Exit (F7) or select Exit from the File pull-down menu. Type **N** at the "Save document? Yes (No)" prompt. At the "Exit LP? No (Yes)" prompt, type **N** again. This will clear the screen.

7. Now you're ready to execute the macro. Simply press ALT-C and the macro inserts the closing for a letter.

You can use this macro to insert the signature block each time you create a letter. You may want to use different keystrokes during the macro definition, to set up your own format for the closing, if it differs from the one created here.

Appendix D   LetterPerfect Macros   273

Changing the Document Format

The following steps show how to create a macro that inserts margin changes for a document layout.

1. From a clear screen, press Macro Def (CTRL-F10) or select Macro **Define** from the **Tools** pull-down menu.

2. LetterPerfect prompt you with "Define Macro: ". Type **format** as the macro name, and press ENTER. This will create a macro file called FORMAT.LPM.

3. At the "Description: " prompt, type a description for the macro (up to 39 text characters). After you type the description, press ENTER to continue.

4. A "Macro Def" message flashes at the lower-left corner of the screen. First, you'll change the left and right margins. Press HOME, LEFT ARROW to move the text cursor to the beginning of the current line.

5. Press Format (SHIFT-F8), or choose Format from the Layout pull-down menu.

6. Select option **4**, Left/Right Margins, and the cursor moves to the place where you enter the measurement for the left margin.

7. Type the desired measurement for the left margin and press ENTER. The cursor moves to the right margin option. Type the measurement for the right margin and press ENTER.

8. Change any other settings that you wish, such as line spacing, top/bottom margins, or justification.

9. Press Exit (F7) to return to the main document editing screen.

10. Press Macro Def (CTRL-F10) or select Macro **Define** from the **Tools** pull-down menu. This ends the macro definition and saves the recorded keystrokes to a file on disk.

11. Press Exit (F7) or select Exit from the File pull-down menu. Type **N** at the "Save document? Yes (No)" prompt. At the "Exit LP? No (Yes)" prompt, type **N** to clear the screen.

12. Now you're ready to execute the macro. First, press Reveal Codes (ALT-F3 or F11) to display the Reveal Codes window. Then, press Macro (ALT-F10) or select Macro Execute from the **Tools** pull-down menu. Type **format** and press ENTER.

The macro repeats the keystrokes to set up the format, and the codes are displayed in the Reveal Codes window. If you wish, you can press other keystrokes during the macro definition if you want different format settings from the ones used here. It's important to note that macros don't actually store the format codes; they store the sequence of keystrokes that can insert the codes.

Changing the Unit of Measure

This is a simple macro that can quickly change a unit of measure to a different setting. During the macro definition, you will select the Pause option to allow the user to select the type of unit measurement.

1. Press Macro Def (CTRL-F10) or select Macro Define from the Tools pull-down menu.

2. At the "Define Macro: " prompt, hold down the ALT key and type U. This will name the macro as ALT-U, with *U* representing "Units of Measure."

3. Now you are prompted to enter a description for the macro. After you type the description, press ENTER to continue.

4. Press Setup (SHIFT-F1) or select Setup from the File pull-down menu. Then, choose option 3, Units of Measure. A menu appears at the bottom of the screen with the different measurement types.

5. This is where you want the macro to pause to allow for user input. Press Macro Commands (CTRL-PGUP), and choose option 1, Pause, from the menu that is displayed.

6. The macro is now temporarily suspended. Choose one of the options from the menu. It doesn't matter which measurement you choose because the macro is in a "paused" state; at this point, keystrokes are not recorded until you press the ENTER key. After you select a measurement, press ENTER to end the pause and continue with the macro definition.

7. Press Exit (F7) to exit the Setup menu and return to the document editing screen.

8. Press Macro Def (CTRL-F10) or select Macro Define from the Tools pull-down menu. This ends the macro definition and saves the recorded keystrokes to a file on disk.

Appendix D   LetterPerfect Macros   275

9. Before you test the macro, clear the screen. Press Exit (F7) or select Exit from the File pull-down menu. Type **N** at the "Save document? Yes (No)" prompt. At the "Exit LP? No (Yes)" prompt, type **N** to clear the screen.

10. Now you're ready to execute the macro. Simply press ALT-U and the macro displays the menu for Units of Measure and pauses so that you may make a selection.

11. Choose one of the measurement types. Your choice is displayed after the "Units of Measure" option on the menu. Press ENTER to continue the macro execution. The macro redisplays the document editing screen, and you will notice that the status line shows the new measurement type.

These are only a few examples of what you can do. Remember that while the "Macro Def" message is flashing on the screen, any keystroke you type—arrow keys, tabs, text characters, and function keys—is recorded, and will be "played back" when you execute the macro.

ADDITIONAL INFORMATION

A macro does much more than simply insert codes or text into your document; it actually repeats the tasks that you performed during the definition of the macro.

Before you create a macro, you should identify exactly what the macro should do for you. Then, perform the keystrokes in the document screen without actually creating a macro. After you know what keystrokes should be pressed, go ahead and define the macro. If your macros don't work correctly the first time, be patient. Macro definition is often an exercise in trial and error.

For more information about the macro features supported by LetterPerfect, consult your LetterPerfect manual.

The manuscript for this book was prepared and submitted to
Osborne/McGraw-Hill in electronic form. The acquisitions
editor for this project was Roger Stewart, the technical
reviewer was Julie Denver, and the project editor was
Madhu Prasher.

This book was designed by Judy Wohlfrom, using
Times Roman for text body and Helvetica for display.

Production services were provided by Sybil Ihrig of
VersaTech Associates, using Ventura Publisher from
Ventura Software, Inc., Corel DRAW! from Corel Systems,
Publisher's Paintbrush from ZSoft Corp., and HiJaak from
Inset Systems, Inc.

Cover art was created by Bay Graphics Design, Inc.
The color separation and cover supplier was Phoenix Color
Corporation. Screens were produced with InSet, from InSet
Systems, Inc. This book was printed and bound by R.R.
Donnelley & Sons Company, Crawfordsville, Indiana.

INDEX

A

Absolute option, 55
Absolute tabs, setting, 55
Accented characters, composing, 80
Additional Printers screen, 155
Address fields, assigning names to, 217-219, (illus., 219)
Address lists
    creating, 217-223
    with records and fields, (illus., 218)
Address record
    complete, (illus., 222)
    creating, 220-223
Addresses, as a secondary file, 217
Aligning text, 71-72. *See also* Text
.ALL extension, 148, 164
ALT key, 19
Arrow keys, moving cursor with, 15-16
ASCII file, AUTOEXEC.BAT as, 258
Attributes
    applying, 84
    applying to a block, 86-87
AUTOEXEC.BAT file, 169, 244, 257, 258
Automatic backup feature, 172-173, (illus., 173)
    turning off, 173
    turning on, (exercise, 172)
Automatic page numbering, 56
AUX, 164

B

B drive, changing to, 8
BACKSPACE, 12
Backup, automatic file, 172-173, 253
    turning off, 173
    turning on, (exercise, 172)
Backward Search command, 97
Binding, adding space for, 159-161
Binding Offset feature, 159
Bins, 152
Block
    defining with keyboard, 84-85
    deleting text, 89, (illus., 90)
Block feature, 71, 83-87
    copying in, 94
    removing block in, 12
    tips for using, 87
    using, 83-87
Block style, 204
Block text, 21, 198
Bold typeface, 70, 71, 86
Boot disk, 6, 7
Box
    creating a figure, 129-133
    numbering figure, 134
    sizing the figure, 133
    with Line Draw, (illus., 141)
Box settings, editing the figure, 134-135
Boxes
    finished, (illus., 142)
    inserting text into, (illus., 144)
Breaks, soft page, 60, (illus., 61)
Business letters, creating, (exercise, 204-206)

C

Cancel key (F1), 19, 20
CAPS LOCK key, 9, 12
Cartridges, laser, 153-154
Cartridges and Fonts feature, 153, 154
Center justification, 48
Centering text, 47, 71-72
Chapter titles, in headers and footers, 57
Characters, composing accented, 80
Click (mouse movement), 22

Clipboard, using, 260
Clocks, 164
Code pair, 70
Codes
    defining initial, 254
    formatting, 88, 97, (illus., 99)
    initial document, 105-109
    input, 188, 189, 190, 191
    inserted salutation, (illus., 226)
    inserting an END FIELD, (illus., 220)
    invisible, 36, 49
    replacing, 97-98
Codes, LetterPerfect, 101, (table, 102, 103)
Codes, WordPerfect, 101, (table, 104)
    converting, 104
Colors
    defining screen, 251-253
    options for screen, (illus., 252)
COM, 164
Communication, printer, 148
.CON extension, 164
CONFIG.SYS, 169, 241, 244, 247
Continuous labels, creating, 228-231, (exercise, 228-231)
Control Printer screen, 157, (illus., 158)
Conversion, margin measurement, 41
COPY command, 7
Copying files, 178
Copyright information, 8
Create option, 133
CTRL key, 19
Cursor, location of, 9
Cursor movement, 14-18
    alignment of, 18
    extended, 16-18
    keys, 32
    keystrokes, (table, 17)
    scrolling, 18
    with arrow keys, 15-16
    with mouse, 22

D

Data diskette, 7
Date Code
    feature, 72-75
    inserting, 73

Date Format
    changing the, 73-75
    editing, (illus., 74)
    numbers/characters for the, (table, 75)
Dates, inserting, 72-73, (exercise, 190)
Default directory, 166
Default layout, 36
DEL key, 12
Delete keys, using, 88-89, (table, 88)
Deleted text, restoring, 91-92, (illus., 92)
Deleting, with DEL, 12
Deleting files, 178
Dictionaries
    creating, 120
    foreign-language, 121-122
Dictionary file, supplemental, 120
DIR command, 7
Directories
    and path names, 166
    creating, (exercise, 166-167)
Directory
    creating a document, 166-168
    creating a file, 179-180
    creating a new, 180
    default, 166
Directory path, current and default, (illus., 174)
Directory prompt, 22
Display, character-based, 25
Display option, 271
Document codes, editing, 98-100
Document editing mode, 23
Document editing screen, 46
Document files, managing, 163-180
Document Initial Codes feature, 105-106, 108-109, (illus., 107)
    creating a format with, 106-109
    editing, (illus., 107)
Document layout
    creating a, 35-65
    editing, 109-111
Documents
    contents of, (illus., 176)
    creating, (exercise, 23-24)
    initial codes for, 105-109
    inserting into other, 29
    printing, 27, 147-162
    retrieving, 28-29
    saving, 24-25

DOS batch files, 169
DOS prompt, 7, 8, 258
DOS text files, 169
Double-click (mouse movement), 23
Double-floppy system, 166
DOWN ARROW, 15, 17, 18
Downloadable soft fonts, 68
Draft Quality option, 161
Dragging (mouse movement), 22
.DRS extension, 164

E

Editing, in typeover mode, 14
END FIELD code, 221
Endnotes
    creating, 76, (illus., 77)
    editing, 76-77
    inserting, 98
    placed in the document, 76-77
ENTER key, 14
Envelope layout
    creating, 207-210
    creating a standard, (exercise, 207-209)
Envelopes
    company logo on, 210
    editing paper definition for, (illus., 212)
    fed into printers, 210, (illus., 211)
    formatting for, 206-213
    letters and, 201-213
    printing, 210, (illus., 211)
    standard, (illus., 207)
    tips for printing, 210-213
    viewing, (illus., 209)
Errors, correcting spelling, 116-119
ESC key, 12
Exit feature, 27-28
Exit key, 23
Exiting, program, 33

F

F1 key, 254
Fast Keys, 18, 21, 29
    using to move and copy, 95
Field labels, 217
Field names, creating, (exercise, 218)

Fields
    defined, 217
    information, 217
    number of, 221
Figure box, (illus., 131)
    code, 132
    creating, 129-133, (exercise, 130-132)
    graphic files inserted into, (exercise, 129)
    sizing, 133
    within a flyer, (illus., 139)
Figure box settings, editing, 134-135
.FIL extension, 164
File backup, automatic, 172-173, 253
File directory, 179-180
    changing, (exercise, 179)
File format, 262
    compatibility with WordPerfect, 168
File names, 164
    extensions, 164
    locating, 177
    number of characters in, 164
    searching for, 176-177
File option, 22
Files
    accessing specific, 165
    copying, 148
    copying and deleting, 178
    displaying with Retrieve feature, 165
    DOS text, 169
    generic, 169-170
    list, 173-180
    location of, 166
    location of program, 253-254
    managing document, 163-180
    marking, 178
    marking all, 178
    marking document, 177-178
    merging, 226-227
    moving and renaming, 178-179
    primary, 188
    retrieving, 165
    retrieving from a list of, 165
    saving, 164-165
    saving and retrieving, 163-168
    unmarking all, 178
    WordPerfect, 168-169

Floppy disk, 6
    starting from single, 6-7
    starting from two, 7-8
Floppy drive configurations, 246
Floppy drive system, installation with, 246-250
Flush Right Margin feature, 72
Flyer, editing, (exercise, 109-114)
Font changes, 36
Font option, 19
Font selection, 154
    in Document Initial Codes feature, 109
Fonts, 68, 188
    base, 68
    cartridge, 153-154
    Document Initial Codes/Base, 223
    downloadable, 155
    selecting, 68-70
    selecting a base, (illus., 70)
    selecting a new, 68-69
Footers, 36
    adding, 57
    creating, 57-58
    page numbering with, 58-59
    turning off, 59
Footnote, 101
    code, 101
Foreign customer dictionaries, in WordPerfect, 121
Foreign-language dictionaries, 121-122
Form letter, as a primary file, 217
Form letter file, creating, (illus., 225)
Format
    changing the directory, 273-274
    commands, 60
    for business letters, 204
    for personal letters, 203
    menu, 36, (illus., 39)
Formatting
    automatic document, 254
    code, 36-37
    envelope, 206-213
Formatting codes
    in LetterPerfect, 262
    in WordPerfect, 262
Forms, predefined, 41
Forms resource file, 41, 45
Forward Search command, 97

Full Document option, 227
Full Justification option, 49
Function key help, 31-32
Function keys, 11-12
    additional, 12
    assignments, (table, 13)
    combinations, 12
    using, 19

G

Generic files, 169-170
    and formatting codes, 169
Go To, 18
Graphic images, (illus., 128, 132)
    adjusting, 135-136
    creating, (exercise, 135)
    editing, 134-136
    inserting, 128-134
Graphics, 210, (exercise, 136-140)
    features, 127-145
    flyer, (illus., 137, 139)
    shortcuts for inserting, 133-134
Graphics Definition menu, 133
Graphics Quality option, 161
Graphics screen, 26

H

Half page, moving cursor up or down by a, 18
Hanging indent, creating, 51-52
Hard disk, 6
    installing on a, 242-246
Hard page breaks, 60, (illus., 61)
Hard return, 40
    code, 14
Hardware requirements, 242
Headers, 36
    adding, 56-57
    creating, 57-58
    page numbering with, 58-59
    turning off, 59
Headlines, editing, (illus., 111)
Help, context-sensitive, 32
Help, on-line, 29-32
    Fast Key, 31

Help, *continued*
    function key, 31
    main screen, 30-31, (illus., 30)
    menu, 31
    template, 31, (illus., 31)
Help feature, 7, 9
Help key, to display function key diagram, 21
HOME key, 17, 20
Hot-keys, Shell, 259
Hyphen
    character, 78
    hard, 78
    invisible soft return, 78
    soft, 78
Hyphenation
    automatic, 79
    in WordPerfect, 263
    manual, 77-78
Hyphenation module, 77

I

IBM printers, 155
Indent, 194, 196
    features, 51
    with TAB key, 50-51
Indentation, left, 20
    removing, 20
Index, feature, 30, 31
Index cards, printing on, 45, 46
Initial Base Font option, 154-155
Initial Codes screen, copying document codes to, 109
Input message, maximum length of, 191
Insert mode, 14
Install program, 6, 241-255. *See also* Installation program
Install/Utilities disk, 149
Installation, (exercise, 243-246)
    disk space needed for, 242
    number of files in CONFIG.SYS, 241
    of LetterPerfect on floppy drive, 246-250, (illus. 248)
    of LetterPerfect on hard drive, 242-246
    of updated version of LetterPerfect, 250-251
    printer, 245
    registration number in, 250
    screen, (illus., 243, 248)

Installation program. *See also* Install program
    printer, 148
    starting the, (illus., 243)
Italics, 70, 71
    option, 19

J

Justification, 36, 47-49
    changing text, 47-49
    code, 106
    setting, 71

K

Keyboard, 10-14
    activating menu bar from, 20
    defining blocks with, 84-85
    enhanced, 31, (illus., 11)
    IBM PC/XT, 15, (illus., 11)
    modes, 9
Keypad, numeric, 9, 14

L

Labels
    and font size, 231
    and margins, 231
    and text lines, 231
    continuous, (illus., 229)
    continuous defined, 228
    creating a primary file for, 235-236
    creating continuous, 228-231
    creating mailing, 227-234
    creating sheet, 232-234
    positioned in printers, 231
    viewing, (illus., 231)
    viewing sheet, (illus., 234)
Labels, sheet, (illus., 233)
Labels definition
    selecting the, (illus., 230, 234)
Landscape orientation, 44, (illus., 45)
Laptop computer, running LetterPerfect on, 6
Laser printer, 153, 213
Layout pull-down menu, 20

.LCN extension, 164
Left indent (F4), 51
Legal landscape paper type, (illus., 44)
Letter, business, (illus., 205)
    creating, 204-206
Letter, personal, 201-204, (illus., 202)
    creating, 201-204
LetterPerfect program files, 164
Letters
    envelopes and, 201-213
    created with Merge feature, (illus., 216)
    merging, 215-237
    typing closing of, 272
.LEX extension, 164
Line Draw figures, (illus., 144), (exercise, 140-143)
Line spacing, 15, 47-49
    changing, 49
    single, 36
Lines and boxes, drawing, 140-144
List, viewing a document in, 175-176
List files, 166, 173-180
    defined, 163
    option, 22, 23
    screen, 174-175, (illus., 175)
    screen accessed with Retrieve feature, 174
Location of Document Files option, 167
Look feature
    and graphics files, 176
    and program files, 176
Look option, 175
LPT, 164
.LRS extension, 164
LST, 164

M

Macro applications, 271-272
Macro Definition feature, 268
Macro names, 269-270
Macro options, pause and delay, 270-271
Macros
    creating, 268-269
    in WordPerfect, 268
    LetterPerfect, 267-275
    shell, 259, 260
    temporary, 270

Macros, *continued*
    using, 268-269
Mailing labels
    creating, 227-235
    merging, 215-237
Margin alignment, left, 36
Margin Release keystrokes, 51
Margin Set code, 108-109
Margins, 186, 230
    choosing, 37-41, (illus., 38)
    defining bottom, 38-39
    defining left, 40
    defining right, 40
    defining top, 38-39
    for personal letters, 203
    overlapping, 46
    page, 36
    predefined, 15
    right, 72
    standard, 38
    top, 36
Measurement
    changing units of, 274-275
    selecting units of, 253
Measurements
    format, 40-41
    horizontal, 9
    vertical, 9
Memo formats, creating, 184-186, 189, (illus., 187), (exercise, 184, 189)
Memo headings
    creating, 186-187, (exercise, 186-187)
    with merge commands, 189-191
Memo messages, typing, 187-188
Memo primary file, finished, (illus., 192)
Memos, 183-199
    automated, 188-193
    created with Merge feature, 192-193
    creating, 192-193
    creating business, 184-186
    margins for, 186
    printing, 187-188, (exercise, 187-188)
    saving, 191-192, (exercise, 192)
    standard business, (illus., 185)
    typing, (exercise, 187-188)
Menu bar
    deactivating, 20

Menu bar, *continued*
    hiding the, 21
    pull-down, 9
Menu items, selecting, 22-23
Menu options, 254
Menus, 18-21
Menus, pull-down, 19-20
    deleting with, 91
    using in lieu of function keys, 12
    using with keyboard, 20
Merge codes, 218, 224
    selecting, (illus., 190, 219)
Merge commands, 189-191
Merge feature, 192-193, 236
    creating a memo with, (exercise, 193)
    defined, 215-217
Merge texts, 188
Merged documents, 217
Merging
    files, 226-227
    letters and mailing labels, 215-237
    message, 227
Messages
    displayed on status line, 9
    help, 32
Mnemonic letter, 19, 20
Modified block style, 201
Mouse, 20-23, 45, 84
    canceling with the, 23
    cursor movement with, 22
    defining a block with, 85-86
    using, 21-23
Mouse button, 56
Mouse driver, 21
Mouse pointer, 10, 22, 45, 85
MOUSE.COM, 21
Move, using Fast Keys to, 95
Move feature, 87
    deleting with, 90-91
Move key, deleting with, 90-91
Moving, outline, (exercise, 197-198)
Moving files, 178-179, (exercise, 178-179)
Multiple Pages option, 158-159, 227

N

Name option, 152

Name Search, 30, 177, (illus., 177)
    disabling, 177
Names
    assigned to fields, 217
    reserved, 164
NUL, 164
NUM LOCK key, 9, 14

O

Options, customizing, 10
Outline, (illus., 197)
    creating, 193-198, (exercise, 194-196)
    reorganizing, 197-198
Outline format, (illus., 195)
Outline mode, 194
    activated, 196
Outline section, blocking and moving an, (illus., 198)
Outlines and memos, creating, 183-199
Overflow files, 33

P

Page
    logical, 227, (illus., 228)
    physical, 227, (illus., 228)
Page breaks
    hard, 60
    soft, 60
Page numbering, 58-59
    screen, (illus., 57)
    with headers and footers, 58-59
Page numbers, 37
    adding, 56
Page orientation, 44
Pagination, document, 59-60
Paper, legal size, 43
Paper size, 36, 37, 41-43
    creating custom, 44-47, (illus., 46)
    definition, 212
    restrictions, 46-47
    selecting, 41-43, (illus., 42)
Paper Size feature, 41
Paper Size/Type menu, (illus., 208)
Paper Size/Type screen, 45, (illus., 43)
Paragraph indents, 49-52

Paragraph margins, indenting, 51
Parallel port, 152
Password, 170-172
    adding, 170-171
    changing, 171
    document, 170-172
    protection, (exercise, 170-171)
    removing, 171, (exercise, 171)
Path names
    defined, 166
    designating, 165
    directories and, 166
Pause option, 271
Personal letters, creating, (exercise, 201-204)
Pg label, 9
PGDN, 18
PGUP, 17
Point size, 69
Points, typesetting, 40
Port, hardware, 155
Portrait orientation, 44, (illus., 45)
Preview, document, 156-157, (illus., 156)
Preview Fast Key, 43
Preview screen, 25
Primary files
    creating, (exercise, 223-226, 235-236)
    creating for letters, 223-226
    defined, 217
    document initial codes and, 235
Print drivers. *See also* Printer drivers
    in WordPerfect, 264
Print job, 157
Print menu, 155, (illus., 28, 151)
Print options, (illus., 160)
Print quality, selecting, 161
Print screen, 26
Printer, 68
    dot-matrix, 44
    installing, 148-150, (illus., 149)
    laser, 153, 213
    manual feed, 212
    paper selection for, 212
    port, 152
    prompt to load, 213
    selecting, 150-152, (illus., 151, 245)
    sheet feeder bin for, 212, 213

Printer, *continued*
    Text Adjustment and, 213
    tractor-fed, 212
    types, 148, (listed, 149-150), (illus., 149)
Printer Control screen, 27
Printer drivers, 148, 150
    using WordPerfect, 155
Printer file, 47, 148
    WordPerfect, 154
Printer settings, editing, 152-155
Printer selection, 27
Printing
    document, 27
    entire document, 157
    envelopes, 210-213
    memos, 187-188
    multiple, 158-159
    options for, 159-161
    several copies, 161
    single pages, 158-159
PRN, 164
Program options, defining, 251
.PRS extension, 164
Pull-down menu. *See* menu

R

Records, 217
    creating, (exercise, 220-221)
Reformatting, page, 43
Registration number, 250
    entering, 7, 8
Renaming files, 178, (exercise, 178-179)
Replace feature, 96, 97
    care exercised with, 98
Replacement text, 98
Résumés, creating, (exercise, 60, 62, 64-65), (illus., 63)
Retrieve feature, 28-29, 165, 260
Retrieving files, 163-168
    clearing screen before, 165
    saving other file formats and, 168-170
Reveal Codes, 37, 98, 105, 132
    editing with, 98-100
    option, 36, 51, 54, 55
    WordPerfect, 104
Reveal Codes window, 100, 101, 108, 274, (illus., 100, 108)
    displaying when editing hanging indents, 52

Reverse video highlight, 100
Right margin, 72
Roman numerals, 56

S

Save feature, 94, 204
Saving
    and retrieving files, 163-168
    as a DOS text file, 169
    files, 164-165
    files on C drive, 166
    files on disks, 164-165
    in default directory, 165
    LetterPerfect to other word processors, 169
    memos, 191-192
    retrieving other file formats and, 168-170
    to generic format, 170
Screen, 9-10, (illus., 10)
    clearing, 27-28, 165, 191-192
Scrolling
    text, 18
    through a list, 176-177
Search criterion, 96
Search feature, 96-97
Secondary file, 223
    defined, 217, 223
Select Printer screen, 150
Serial port, 152
.SET extension, 164
Settings, default, 36
Setup feature, 21, 29, 167
Setup menu, 10, 251, (illus., 252)
    LetterPerfect, (illus., 167)
    redefining F1 key in, 19
Sheet feeder, 152-153
Sheet labels
    creating, 232-234, (exercise, 232)
    font sizes, 232
    margins, 232
    text lines, 232
Shell menu, 258, (illus., 258)
    starting programs from, 259
Shell program, 257-260
    starting, 9, 257-259
Soft font printer, 155

Soft fonts, 154, (illus., 154)
Soft page breaks, 60, (illus., 61)
Spacing, line, 36
Special characters, inserting, 79-80
Spell-check, 188. *See also* Speller
Spell-checking a page or block, 119
Speller, 116-119, 204, 262-263
    checking double words with, (illus., 118)
    dictionaries, 119-122
    displaying synonyms in, (illus., 125)
    installing, 116
    replacement words in, (illus., 118)
    screen, (illus., 117)
Spelling errors, correcting, 116-119
Standard printer font, 154
Starting LetterPerfect, 6
    from hard disk, 8-9
    from single floppy, 6-7
    from two floppy, 7-8
Status line, 9
Subscript, 70
.SUP extension, 164
Superscript, 70, 86
Suppress code, 59

T

Tab, 194
    indenting with, 50-51
    ruler, 53
Tab Set screen, 54
Tab settings, 15, 49-55
    defining, 52-54
    editing, 54-55, (illus., 55)
    predefined, 52
Tab stops, 100
Tables, 104
    creating, 112-114, (illus., 113)
    retrieving into LetterPerfect, (illus., 105)
    setting columns for, 51
    tabular, (illus., 54)
Tabs
    decimal-aligned, 52
    for personal letters, 203
    setting absolute, 55
Template, function key, 19, 29

Text
    aligned at the right margin, 72
    centered between margins, 48, 71-72, (illus., 48)
    centering, 47
    copying, 94-95
    deleting, 88-91
    deleting and restoring, 87-92
    editing, 111-112
    formatting, 35-37
    left-justified, 47, (illus., 48)
    moving, 92-94, (illus., 93)
    replace, 97-98
    restoring, 87-92
    right-justified, 48, (illus., 48)
    searching for, 96-97
    special features for, 67-81
    typing, 14-18
    scrolling, 18
    underlining, 86
Text attributes, 68-71
    selecting, 70-71, (exercise, 70-71)
Text cursor, 10
Text Out feature, 169
Text Out menu, 170
Text Quality option, 161
Thesaurus, 7, 8, 122-126, (illus., 123)
    finding the right word in, 122-123
    in WordPerfect, 263
    navigating through menus, 123-126
    window, (illus., 124)
Title screen, 8
Tools option, 20
Toshiba T1000 laptop computer, 6
Typefaces, 68. *See also* Fonts
Typeover mode, 14

U

Undelete feature, 87, 89, 91, 92
Underline, 70, 71
    text, 30
UP ARROW, 15, 17, 18
Uppercase text, typing, 12
Utilities/Images diskette, 7

V

View Document feature, 25-26, 69, 204
View Document option, 49, 56
View Document screen, 26, 43, 156-157, 162, (illus., 26)
.VRS extension, 164

W

Width measurement, page, 45
Wildcard characters, 179
Word, moving cursor to next, 17
WordPerfect, 6, 18, 250
    characters, 264-265
    codes in LetterPerfect, 262-263
    compatibility with LetterPerfect, 168
    compose feature, 264
    exchanging files with, 170
    file format, 262
    files, 168-169
    incompatibility with LetterPerfect, 168
    information to users, 261-265
    macros, 268
    print drivers, 264
    shared hyphenation module, 263
    sharing LetterPerfect files, 261-262
    speller dictionary, 263
    speller in LetterPerfect, 262-263
    units, 40
    using character sets, 80
    with foreign customer dictionaries, 121
WordPerfect Customer Support, 29, 150
    contacting, 32
Word wrap, 15, (illus., 16)